THE CHACO COAL SCANDAL

The People's Victory Over James Watt

By Jeff Radford

RHOMBUS PUBLISHING COMPANY

First Edition

ISBN 0-936455-01-2

Printed in the United States of America
Cover Design by Mary Schold Robert

Rhombus Publishing Company P.O. Box 806, Corrales NM 87048

DEDICATION

TO TIM MORGAN

**A Navajo tribal official,
who despaired that his peoples'
"No!" to coal strip mining
would ever be heard.**

ACKNOWLEDGMENT

Without the significant risks accepted by former co-workers within the Department of the Interior who collaborated in making this material available to the public, the documentation herein would have been far less complete. I, along with other members of the public, am indebted to them for their courage and effectiveness in the face of persecution for daring to live up to their sworn allegiance to the U.S. Constitution and to the public interest.

In addition to assistance from dedicated civil servants who must remain unnamed, important contributions to this work were made by Navajo Author John Redhouse, Planner Jonathan Teague and Coal Consultant Jim Cannon.

Much of the reporting herein on actual conversations involving attempts by unscrupulous governmental officials to subvert the laws of the land is derived from notes taken by the author as an eyewitness to the events described. When it became clear that political appointees under the direction of Interior Secretary James Watt were determined to violate federal laws and regulations, I began to record significant conversations in the hope that those subversive acts could be thwarted.

Official documents used in preparing this manuscript are already in the public domain. As the public affairs officer for the Albuquerque District Bureau of Land Management from 1979 to 1984, I did my utmost to assure that members of the public were as informed as possible about government actions and policies involving the public's property. Assuredly, James Watt and his ideological brethren would have preferred considerably less diligence on my part. But to have withheld from the public evidence of governmental corruption, fraud and deceit would have constituted complicity.

I am grateful to Paul Frye, Bob Uram, Dave Glowka and several people inside the Bureau of Land Management for their review of the manuscript. The support and understanding of my wife and son have been crucial to the fulfillment of this effort.

CONTENTS

FOREWORD

In a world where human, social concerns take precedence over corporate demands for higher profits, can a modern economy survive and thrive? Or do the rights and interests of individuals need to be cast aside for the betterment of the nation, as embodied by America's large corporations?

If a corporate proposal put before government is weighed against seriously adverse impacts to large numbers of people, to their livelihood and to their very culture, will government give its blessing to the venture anyway, in the name of "economic growth", and "national security"?

This book is written for the ever-suspicious, but determined citizens who never stop resisting what they consider destructive corporate and government-corporate ventures. This tells of a victory, or at least partial victory, of "the people" facing insensitive plans for strip mining the traditional homes of thousands of American Indians—corporate plans with which high federal officials colluded to disregard the public interest, public safety and welfare.

"The people" were victorious, in that they halted a federal giveaway of their mineral wealth on the nation's public lands, and they shut down a government-corporate program to plunder that wealth with reckless disregard for the environment and communities' livelihood.

These pages are windows into the real world in which politics and corporate greed combine in government offices to trample the rights and interests of the powerless. Your author is a former government official, a veteran of five years with the U.S. Department of the Interior during the controversial regime of James Watt.

As a public participation specialist in the Albuquerque District of the Bureau of Land Management, U.S. Department of the Interior, from 1979 to 1984, I watched and documented the unfolding of an oft-repeated drama in which big companies enlist the aid of the federal government to evict, dispossess and disenfranchise Indians on land bearing enormous mineral wealth. I saw high-ranking government officials blindly deny the existence of major, theory-shattering archeological ruins lying over that mineral wealth so that coal companies wouldn't suffer uneconomical delays and detours as they strip mined. I heard federal officials conspiring with private industry to undermine acts of Congress. I saw lower level civil servants pleading in vain for their superiors to obey the law.

Big corporations run over powerless individuals and seek to evade the law with a regularity that surprises no one these days. But in this case, *you* own the land where the coal is, *you* own the archeological sites, *you* own the semi-desert land where traditional Navajo Indians eke out a precarious living only a few feet above the coal seams. The coal, the traditional Navajo grazing lands, the stark, breathtaking wilderness areas, the eagle habitat, the remarkable Chacoan Anasazi archeological remains, the unique fossil beds, all belong to you, you and other Americans, since they are publicly-owned and federally-administered.

I believe in democracy. I believe in the right of local people to make, or at least participate meaningfully in, the major decisions affecting them. I believe in peoples' ability to make those decisions. I believe that the people closest to a decision, those to be impacted most, positively or negatively, should be the ones to make that decision, based on full and truthful information.

I believe that government officials, particularly civil servants, should uphold the laws of the land; should not deliberately collude with private interests to betray the public interest; and should be honest and open in informing the public about what they are doing.

My credo led me to resign as an Interior Department public affairs official during the waning days of the Reagan re-election campaign. Swirling in a coal lease scandal originating in Wyoming at the time, Interior was feverishly trying to cover up improprieties and illegalities initiated during Watt's tenure. At the same time, they were setting the stage for more of the same during a Reagan second term.

So this book salutes the tireless citizens . . . retired electrical engineers, nuclear physicists, professional environmentalists, Navajo sheep herders, Legal Aid attorneys, doctors, artists, tradesmen, teachers, archeologists and the thousands of other private citizens . . . who fought for their beliefs, their sense of fair play and the public interest, to thwart federal-corporate collusion for wanton strip mining in the West during the Reagan first term. And these pages are intended to tell the inside story of what happened and to scout the terrain ahead for the next battles.

I began working for the federal government without illusions. Watergate and the Nixon years were fresh in all Americans' minds back in 1979. But if you can't trust government, who can you trust? In a democracy, we answer that with the reply, "the people". And how do the people affect government? Through elections, of course, but also through "public participation", a method of governing in which officials deliberately and continually encourage citizens and interest groups to follow an agency's decisionmaking processes and to enunciate their concerns and demands regarding those impending decisions.

In the mid- and late 1970s, public participation was an all-pervasive requirement for federal agencies. Congress specifically demanded it in many laws, and federal bureaucrats dutifully incorporated the concept into their regulations. The idea was to make government more responsive to citizens, particularly local citizens and local conditions, rather than force Washington's policies and solutions across-the-board, with what might be disastrous results. It made a lot of sense.

Having experienced centralized planning in several foreign countries while working aboard as a newspaper reporter, I harbored doubts that central governments can effectively solve local problems. Even less likely is sound Washington-level decisionmaking when local conditions are atypical. And what if the local people and culture are themselves fundamentally atypical? What if a federal program will have a great effect on Indians living traditional lifestyles?

Federal proposals for leasing of publicly-owned coal reserves in the San Juan Basin of New Mexico seemed to me a classic example of the need for public participation.

My five years with the Bureau of Land Management produced results. While local people may yet be treated as so much over-burden to be scraped aside in getting at the coal beds, there is at least some real prospect that local conditions and individual Navajos residing over the coal will dictate the over-all pace and direction of federal actions there.

Still, the 1980s seem to be marked by a significant conservative trend, a blind patriotism and a willingness to forgive and forget the excesses of American industry. The emphasis is on unfettering industry, on turning business loose to bring America back to greatness, on letting "the marketplace" make crucial economic, social and political decisions.

Perhaps the American people are prepared to permit industry to plunder the public lands, to destroy the lives and lifestyles of Indian families, to irrevocably ruin the land's productive capacity. If so, at least let it be done with full understanding of the facts and processes by which the actions were approved.

And let there be no ignorance or misunderstandings about the intentions of government and corporate officials responsible for decisions which lay waste the land. Neither government officials nor members of the public at large have any grounds for assuming that, in general, corporate leaders will act to protect the public interest, or to fully obey the laws enacted to protect the public and its resources. Our history shows quite clearly that, left to its own objectives, unfettered, the mining industry will leave a devastated land and a sacrificed people.

Before federal laws were passed in the late 1970s to protect against such devastation, the coal mining industry had left nearly 400,000 acres of abandoned, unreclaimed strip mines; more than 10,000 miles of streams and rivers were polluted by coal mine drainage.

That was the marketplace decision.

CHAPTER ONE

HOW THE PUBLIC THWARTED JAMES WATT

Rarely has a high government official been so roundly disliked and opposed as James Watt. As Secretary of the Interior during the first three years of President Ronald Reagan's first term, Watt had an almost uncanny capacity for instilling fear of his meanness and zealotry. Repeatedly caricatured as the nation's Number One despoiler of the environment, Watt symbolized the pro-industry bigot who had no use for wildlife or trees outside of zoos, city parks, or spacious lawns.

Yet as head of the Department of the Interior, he was the caretaker of more than 500 million acres of the public's land.

Considered by many to have been one of the most right-wing of Reagan's first cabinet, Watt's ideological credentials were developed in the generally conservative West. After work as a Washington bureaucrat during the Nixon Administration, he returned to

Denver where he headed the conservative Mountain States Legal Foundation, founded and funded by arch-conservative business interests like the Adolph Coors family to aid ranchers and miners confronting the government's new environmental legislation in the 1970s.

Guided by Watt, the foundation fought environmental protection at every turn; helping the operators of the heavily polluting Four Corners Power Plant renege on a contract agreement to install sulphur dioxide scrubbers on its smokestacks, fighting to prevent the Department of the Interior from cracking down on ranchers' overgrazing on the public lands, and generally doing what it could to assure that federal environmental protection measures would not be put into effect if they caused discomfort for business interests.

Said former Nevada Governor Mike O'Callaghan just after Watt assumed control of Interior under Reagan: "Watt is long-known as a hired gun for business interests fighting to open up federal lands for their own use."

Watt had, in fact, been the Washington spokesman for the U.S. Chamber of Commerce from 1966 to 1968, representing business in congressional legislation on mining, public lands, energy, water and environmental pollution.

When Richard Nixon moved into the White House in January 1969, Watt went to the Department of the Interior as a special assistant to then-Under Secretary Russell Train. Six months later, Watt was named Interior's Deputy Assistant Secretary for Water and Power Development, and from there was appointed Director of the department's Bureau of Outdoor Recreation in July 1972. After Nixon was forced to resign amid the Watergate Scandal, incoming President Gerald Ford named Watt as vice-chairman of the Federal Power Commission in 1975. He went to Mountain States Legal Foundation in 1977.

Once Reagan summoned Watt back to Washington to head Interior, he became the best fundraiser the Sierra Club ever had. His policies and pronouncements so infuriated Americans who identified with the environmental movement that memberships to national and local conservation organizations soared. People who had perhaps always held suspicions that pro-industry government officials were out to rape and ruin the land were suddenly convinced of it in Watt's case. Even lip service to the newly-strong conservation ethic would have been enough to convince many middle-of-the-road citizens that Watt had the environment's best interests at heart, but he refused even to pretend that he was a friend of Smokey and Bambi. By words and deeds, James Watt radicalized "the Average American" as no other politician had in recent times.

Or perhaps the word "politician" does not fit James Watt. By most standards, he was not at all "politic" in his tactics, demeanor or choice of words. He was unnecessarily abrasive and confrontational at times when a politician would have smoothed ruffled feathers. He spoke his mind, certainly, and that is what convinced millions of Americans that the man was dangerous and irresponsible. Try as they might, millions of middle-of-the-road citizens could not bring themselves to believe that Watt was really a conscientious, well-meaning federal official. Not only his actions, but he himself told them otherwise.

In the course of his three years at the helm of Interior, the Wyoming lawyer vowed to curtail environmental restrictions on ranchers, miners and timber companies operating on public lands in the West, and he did it. A flag-carrier in the "Sagebrush Rebellion" which would have turned public lands over to private owners, Watt set in motion programs within his department to sell off the public lands or otherwise turn control of them over to business interests. He gutted the federal Office of Surface Mining, which had been intended to watchdog the strip mining industry. And he took measures to curtail public scrutiny of the department's activities.

But the greater his effectiveness in eliminating the Interior bureaus' role in protecting the environment and recreational use of the public lands, the more he solidified opposition. Coalitions of citizen groups across the country that previously had little in common now saw mutual interests in working together to confront Watt's policies. Coalitions at the grass roots level led to ties and cooperation at the national level, and soon literally millions of people were fighting James Watt.

By the end of October 1981, more than 1.1 million Americans had signed a petition demanding Watt's removal as Interior Secretary. President Reagan kept him, and 18 months later it was revealed that taxpayers were spending well over $300,000 a year for bodyguards to protect Watt from an increasingly angry public.

It took three years, but Watt was finally beaten. The president was finally forced to axe the outspoken secretary, lest the errant bureaucrat prove too great a liability in the impending Reagan re-election bid. But the president's reluctance to fire Watt confirmed what many Americans came to suspect: Watt was not really doing anything the president disapproved of, except putting his foot in his mouth.

The underlying conservative ideology of the Reagan Administration explains why Watt's behavior at Interior was forgiven so easily in the White House . . . and why Watt's departure changed very little of substance at Interior for the remainder of Reagan's years in power. A westerner himself, Reagan is aware of generalized disapproval of restrictions on the use of public land, most of which is located west of the Mississippi River. Whether confronting dunebuggy drivers wanting to tear across open range, or weekend woodcutters headed for pinyon trees on public land, or cattle ranchers trying to make ends meet by adding an unauthorized cow or two to their allotted public rangeland, or miners seeking the most economical mineral beds, Interior's attempts to control the use of the public lands are often seen by many as obstructionist.

Ownership and control of the public domain has been controversial since the founding of the United States as an independent nation. New World territories were conquered in the names of kings and queens of Spain, England, France and other European states and (assuming the legitimacy of those claims) the newly acquired lands became the property of their respective governments. Similarly, when Thomas Jefferson added 530 million acres to the United States with the Louisiana Purchase in 1803, the acreage became "government property" which was later opened to private acquisition through homesteading, grants to railroad companies to finance rail lines to "open up the West", and other means of disposing of the public domain.

Government-owned (or publicly-owned) land has amounted to 1.8 billion acres, including the acquisitions of Florida from Spain in 1819, Oregon from the British in 1846, 338 million acres in the Southwest from Spain in 1848, the Gadsen Purchase from Mexico in 1850, and Alaska from Russia in 1867. Of the total U.S. land mass (2,313,678,000 acres) about 1,838,000,000 acres, or 79 percent, was at one time owned by the public through its federal government. But the intent from the beginning seemed to be to dispose of these government lands into private hands, starting with the Public Sale Act of 1796, which allowed settlers to buy government land for $2 an acre.

And dispose it did. Today about 760 million acres of the original 1.8 billion acres remains publicly owned, administered through the Bureau of Land Management (400 million acres), the Forest Service (187 million acres), the National Park Service (67 million acres), the Fish and Wildlife Service (46 million acres), military lands (31 million acres), and 29 million acres in assorted other federal agencies. The Bureau of Land Management, under the Department of the Interior, became known as the repository of "the lands that nobody wanted"; they were, for the most part, what remained of the public domain after repeated waves of homesteading, grants, transfers to park status, additions to Indian Reservations, and other methods of turning public lands over to private interests.

That disposal policy came to an official end in 1976, when Congress passed the Federal Land Policy and Management Act, introduced by Senator Henry "Scoop" Jackson of Washington State and Arizona Congressman Morris Udall. "The Bureau of Land Management had its mandate," commented Historian David Lavender, referring to the public lands act, "a decision for permanence. The nation was going to hold onto its public lands and manage them with an eye to the future."

The act called for the professional management of these BLM lands for the good of all citizens, under the principles of multiple use and sustained yield. It institutionalized government ownership of the remaining public domain and mandated specific guidance as to how the land should be managed for the public interest. It legitimized government ownership and control of the means of production (chiefly ranching and mining) in much of the West, where BLM lands account for a third or more of the total territory of some states.

From a right-wing ideologue's viewpoint, then, the very concept of federal management of public lands is anathema. It may have been all right for the government to provide some kind of guidance and order on use of public lands so long as the intent was to dispose of the lands when spoken for. But the notion of perpetual government ownership and control of a vast, mineral-rich portion of the West, as expressed in Congress' Federal Land Policy and Management Act , was an abomination. Watt the Ideologue would see the Interior Secretary job as an opportunity to undo federal management capability on the public lands and to turn control over to its industrial users, the miners, ranchers and timber interests.

In a series of steps, some blatant and widely-publicized and others subtle and still little known, Watt and the ideological cadre he assembled under him in Interior set about to crush public control of the public domain.

From his statements and policies, it seemed clear that Watt firmly believed the public had no business owning lands and mineral resources (possibly excepting national parks), and certainly the public should not interfere with productive use of those resources. Environmental laws and regulations which tended to restrict business uses were to be eliminated, or at least curtailed.

As one veteran Interior official put it shortly after Ronald Reagan's first presidential term began: "This may be the first time since Teapot (Dome Scandal) that deals were cut that explicitly turned over huge amounts of national resources to settle a political debt. It is a matter of scale, you see. I suspect that corporations that have a stake in this business of raping the West are already padding their executives' salaries so that their PACs will be mighty flush for the next (Reagan re-election) go-round."

The federal coal program became the lightning rod for Watt's pro-industry permissiveness and the public's counter-attack. It was a pivotal issue for both right-wing ideologues and environmental activists, since it involved "national security" dogma for energy independence from the Arab world, it involved billions of dollars worth of natural resources, and it involved the testing of pro-environmental legislation such as the 1977 Surface Mining Control and Reclamation Act, wilderness designation provisions of the 1976 Federal Land Policy and Management Act, and a wide variety of other business-hindering laws such as the 1966 Historic Preservation Act.

From the environmentalists' perspective, the federal coal program was also good terrain on which to drawn battle lines because it involved a clear, trackable process for making decisions about resource conflicts on public land. Coal companies' negligence and blatant disregard for environmental concerns in the East had become common knowledge (and had in fact brought on such regulatory requirements as established in the Surface Mining Control and Reclamation Act), so the coal program was one around which it was relatively easy to mobilize.

The 1978 start-up of the federal government's coal program, as concocted by an environmentally-oriented Carter Administration, set in motion a process leading to the leasing of publicly-owned coal with full environmental safeguards. But the process had only just begun when Carter left office and Reagan came in.

Having installed Watt to oversee the Department of the Interior, including the federal coal program, the Reagan Administration was determined to keep the momentum toward leasing of federal coal, while modifying the process in mid-stream to allow the coal industry as much free rein as possible.

These manipulations eventually led to unlawful acts on the part of high Interior officials, and to intimidation and removal of conscientious civil servants who resisted these deviations. Ultimately, the ideologues' subversion of the public interest led to a congressional shutdown of the coal program and the resignation of James Watt and several of his top colleagues at Interior.

How concerned citizens brought down Secretary Watt and halted or blocked some of his most controversial policies is the subject of this book. Watt's removal and the congressional ban on federal coal leasing in 1983-84 were very much a product of citizen activism, and the general public needs to realize that. The usual cause of citizen apathy is disbelief that individual and collective actions will have any appreciable result; that government will do whatever it wants anyway, despite an irate citizenry; that powerful corporations with briefcases full of campaign funds call all the shots, not the average citizen. Certainly there is reason for such cynicism. But now and again, when the public becomes sufficiently motivated, our representative form of government does perform as it is supposed to.

Of course it was Congress that actually imposed the coal lease moratorium, and it was Nancy Reagan who convinced the president that Watt really was the small-minded bigot that everybody said he was (after he had squelched a proposal that the Beach Boys perform at a Washington Fourth of July celebration saying they attracted the wrong crowd), and it was the governors of the states where federal coal was under consideration who demanded a thorough review of Interior's coal program. And it was Watt himself who bragged about the credentials of his blue-ribbon coal program investigating panel, the Linowes Commission, blurting out that it was composed of "a black, a woman, two Jews and a cripple".

All of those factors figured into Watt's resignation. But the real bottom line, the real power in the secretary's ouster was that the public demanded it. If it had been only the "environmental establishment" in Washington who called for Watt to be fired, he would undoubtedly have stayed. He would have survived his repeated gaffes. He could have withstood congressional ire, and probably even criminal investigations into the functioning of his department. But in the end, he couldn't withstand the "thumbs down" he continually got from the general public.

The mobilization of citizen energy which eventually toppled Watt and shut down several of his major programs actually began before Watt took over at Interior, and even before Reagan won the presidency. It seems to have begun with citizen backlash to the so-called "Sagebrush Rebellion", the conservative camp's drive to remove control of the public lands from the government and give it instead to private interests, primarily ranchers. As the Reagan campaign geared up in 1979, the "anti-public land" faction was also moving vigorously into action, introducing bills in state legislatures around the West calling for state take-overs of the public domain as a first step to transferring it eventually into private ownership. Stumping in the Mountain States, Candidate Reagan declared himself a "Sagebrush Rebel" and suggested he would oversee the end of public land management by the federal government.

But local conservation groups were already banding together to fight the rebellion. Groups which theretofore had found little reason to cooperate with one another suddenly made common cause to fight for retention of the public lands. Indeed, some of the local groups had despised other memberships, due to presumptions of elitism, anti-hunting biases and organizational policies regarding nuclear power. But all saw themselves losing if the public lands were sold out to the highest bidder.

Aware of the groundswell of opposition to selling off the public lands, Watt moved quickly to effect the disposal. At the end of his first year in office, he boasted that 7.68 million acres of public land had been offered for sale, more than triple the previous year. Even so, the heat he was taking from a sizeable and vocal part of the public began to alter his public statements about the land disposal effort. By July 1983, Watt pledged, "there will not be a massive land sell-off," asserting that such an action "was never intended." He bubbled, "If you're looking toward the 21st century, then you're willing to lease some lands for coal development, for oil and gas development; you're willing to invest in parks, to restore them; you're willing to improve the refuges because you believe that the people in the next century also should have the right and the privilege of enjoying these lands, which are their lands."

Shortly thereafter, Watt pulled the Department of the Interior out of the federal government's "Asset Management" real estate selling program (fallaciously heralded as the best means of reducing the national debt). Behind-the-scenes his instructions to Bureau of Land Management officials remained to proceed as quickly as possible with land disposals.

The attack on Watt and his policies was mounted in all parts of the country, on many issues. One of the first skirmishes was Interior's attempt to diminish requirements for public participation in federal land use planning. Watt wanted the federal regulations regarding land use planning changed because the (pro-environment) public had become too involved in determinations as to how public lands were to be used. From his experience as spokesman for the U.S. Chamber of Commerce, Watt's concept of positive public participation was more like an industry lobbyist badgering a bureaucrat or a congressman into favoring a business client, not a scruffy backpacker pushing to retain a scenic trail through public lands slated for strip mining.

But Watt inherited planning regulations developed in the pro-environment Carter years. They not only built in too many potential obstacles to exploitation of the public lands, but they also allowed, even demanded, that anybody who wanted to could see how the federal-industry deals were being struck. The rules of government in this country require that federal agencies follow the regulations as promulgated . . . at least until such time as they can be un-promulgated. Modifying the federal government's planning procedures became a top priority under Watt's administration.

With Watt's attempts to change or circumvent bothersome federal regulations and laws came the evidence that his opponents needed to hang him. If the archeologists, the wilderness advocates, the millions of citizens who enjoyed recreation on public lands, the supporters of wildlife and the defenders of Native American rights—if they all knew what Watt intended to do, it was still only after the cherubic, born-again ideologue began to bend and break the rules that they could challenge him legally.

One of the earlier, more substantive legal challenges came from the National Wildlife Federation, an organization more than four million strong nationwide. It sued to force Watt's Office of Surface Mining to prepare an environmental impact statement because of the drastic regulatory changes being proposed to make life easier on strip mining companies. The Wildlife Federation charged that under Watt's changes, the Office of Surface Mining was setting up a process whereby it would itself violate the 1977 Surface Mining Control and Reclamation Act.

The Natural Resources Defense Council joined with the Wildlife Federation on another suit challenging Watt's attempt to give away federal coal through a discredited "Preference Right Lease Application" process. NRDC and seven other conservation groups hauled Watt into court with a suit in September 1982, contending that the secretary's coal program permitted excessive leasing without adequate environmental protection, and with no assurance that the public would be paid the full value of its mineral wealth.

In yet another suit, the environmentally-oriented Powder River Resources Council and the National Wildlife Federation filed suit to invalidate the controversial 1982 federal coal lease sale in the Powder River Basin.

Still, at the end of Reagan and Watt's fiscal year 1982, Interior boasted that it had issued 39 new coal leases, involving 1.7 billion tons under 83,627 acres. Watt and his assistant secretary, Garrey Carruthers of New Mexico, had leased more of the public's coal in one year than the pro-coal Carter Administration had proposed to lease in four years. And, on top of that, Interior was poised to lease another six billion tons before the end of fiscal 1984.

Much of the additional coal was to have come from the relatively unopened coal fields of New Mexico's San Juan Basin, from the Chaco-Bisti region. More than two billion tons were to be provided in New Mexico to coal companies through a largely discredited and discontinued leasing system, while another two billion would be offered for competitive bidding. For several reasons, Watt and other high Interior officials considered implementation of the federal coal program in New Mexico to be of critical importance.

The New Mexico coal-bearing lands were strewn with archeological sites—far more than encountered in other coal regions. It was an article of faith for pro-business ideologues that one of the major stupidities of the federal government was its tendency to halt industrial developments when an archeological site is discovered. If ancient ruins and artifacts were permitted to thwart coal mining in New Mexico, it would set a bad precedent for coal leasing elsewhere.

Furthermore, the issue of reclaimability of western coal lands came into sharpest focus in New Mexico. The coal industry and the conservative ideologues at Interior insisted on proceeding with the assumption that any and all lands could be reclaimed after strip mining; the extremely arid lands of the San Juan Basin just might force them to acknowledge the uncertainties of mine reclamation in all the coal regions of the West.

And northwestern New Mexico's publicly-owned coal deposits raised still another large red flag: if the Indian people who lived on and around the federal coal there were able to block mining, it could have major implications for mineral production throughout the West. Paradoxically, the reservations onto which western Indians had been forced actually held some of the West's richest mineral deposits. An estimated 15 percent of all the strippable coal in the United States, 50 percent of U.S. uranium and four percent of the nation's known oil and gas are under Indian land. Much of these mineral reserves lies under lands owned, controlled or used by Navajo, the largest and perhaps most powerful of all the tribes. Coal companies' ability to get to minerals under Navajo lands could set a precedent for mining other Indian lands elsewhere.

In the overall picture for western coal development, the situation in New Mexico stood out for yet another reason. New Mexico had always been wide-open for the mining industry. In a state with few other economic prospects, the people had a reputation for being very tolerant of mining impacts. State officials, who depended heavily on mineral production royalties for their programs, had traditionally looked the other way when miners skirted their responsibilities. But now, there seemed to be a strong environmental movement coming to the fore in New Mexico. It was a challenge that Watt and his lieutenants couldn't ignore.

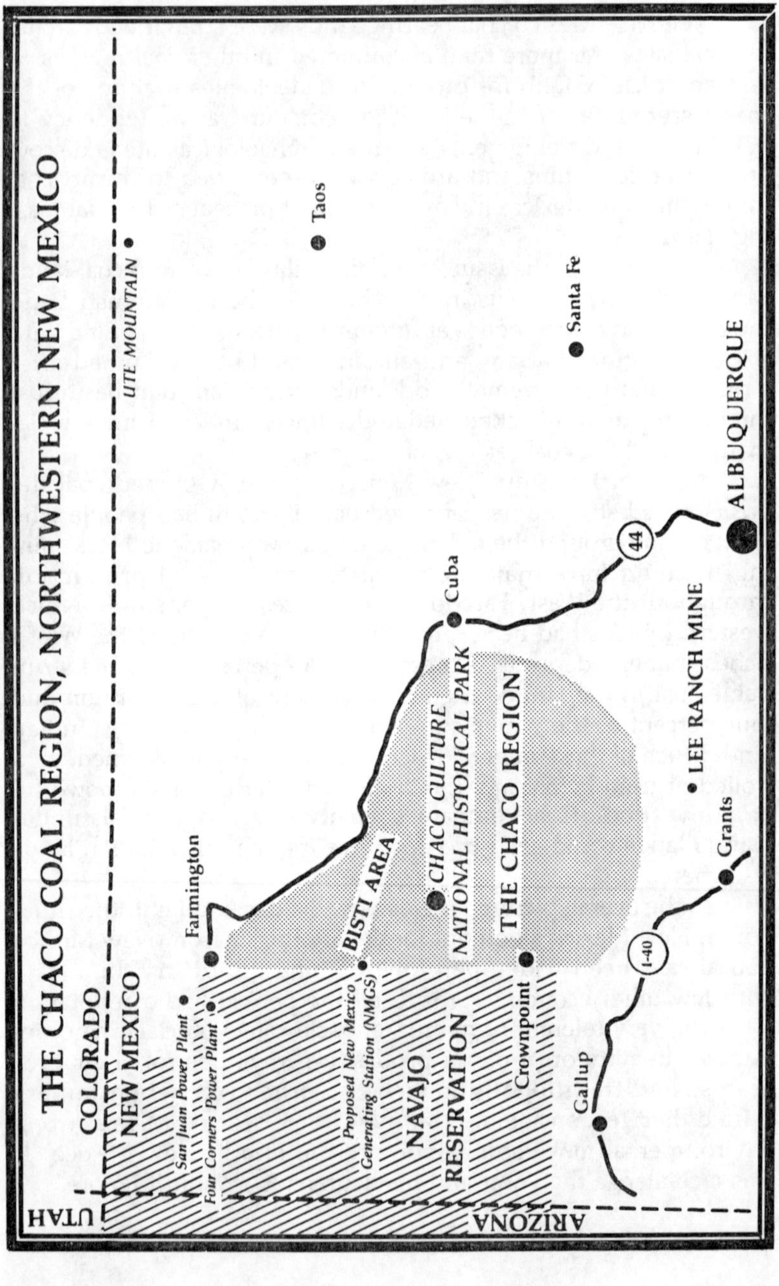

THE CHACO COAL REGION, NORTHWESTERN NEW MEXICO

CHAPTER TWO

PLAIN FACTS IN THE 'INCREDIBLY COMPLEX' SAN JUAN BASIN

Even in a world filled with sweetness and light, the strip mining of coal can be a nasty business. With the best of intentions, coal mining companies have wrecked irreparable havoc upon lands which formerly hosted meadow flowers, butterflies, chirping birds and big-eyed fawns. Only people forced to move from their homes to let the dragline's mammoth shovel rip up their family's land can fully appreciate the impact of surface mining. Not only is the topsoil and its vegetation stripped away to get at the black rock beneath, but people in the vicinity must condition themselves to the blasting and clamourous night-and-day operation of the giant machinery, and the incessant dust blown when the huge shovel is emptied onto enormous spoils piles.

Sooner or later, under ideal conditions, the ugly gaping mine trenches are filled in, trees and shrubs and grasses are planted, and the land returns once more to flowered meadowland with flitting birds . . . and maybe the mining company even creates a little lake which is stocked with fat and careless fish. Sooner or later the company will move its machinery elsewhere, leaving behind local folks now prosperous after working at the mine or selling toothpaste to the work crews.

But no one has ever said New Mexico's San Juan Basin offers ideal conditions.

Whipped by hot, dry summer winds and killing winter blizzards, the barren, semi-desert landscape in northwestern New Mexico does not start out as lush meadows. It is the most arid of the 12 coal regions nationwide where mining companies hope to secure coal from the federal government. It is the most difficult land to restore after strip mining, which is why a National Academy of Sciences report in 1974, "Rehabilitation Potential of Western Coal Lands", predicted that this energy-rich region may wind up a "national sacrifice area".

Lying within the triangle formed by Albuquerque, Gallup and Farmington, New Mexico's portion of the San Juan Basin is rich in oil, gas, uranium and coal. Its mineral resources are worth hundreds of billions of dollars, and energy companies operating there have already amassed large fortunes. Despite the land's wealth, the people living there are among the poorest of America's poor. Typically, the thousands of isolated homes there have no televisions, no dishwashers, no vacuum cleaners, no electricity, no gas, no indoor toilet, no running water, and quite often, no water at all. If that sounds like hard living, imagine what it would be like if the government then required you to give up what little livelihood you managed to eke out in this desert environment (herding sheep and hand-weaving rugs from the wool) so that the mining companies could dig up the coal.

If life is so tough out there, an outsider might ask, why not just take the mineral royalties and move to a city where you can get a paying job? Well, the government says the local people aren't entitled to payments from extraction of the coal. Besides, what are the chances of landing a good city job when you speak no English, can't read, and are only skilled at sheep herding and hand weaving?

"They'll never mine that coal out there," the Bureau of Land Management's Paul Applegate used to say. In Applegate's view, even if the government and the coal companies could figure out what to do about the Navajo Indians living over the coal in the San Juan Basin, other enormous obstacles still lay in the way. If the Indians didn't convince the coal companies to look elsewhere, then the world-class fossils imbedded in the coal would. And if the dinosaurs didn't scare the mining engineers off, then congressionally-required protection for the region's three Wilderness Study Areas would. And if the Navajos and the fossils and the wilderness areas weren't enough problems, then the existence of an estimated 250,000 archeological sites, many as yet undiscovered, scattered throughout the coal region would certainly give the mining executives long pause.

And then, of course, there is the law requiring post-mining reclamation. It would be easy enough for the companies' massive equipment to rip up the land, but would they ever be able to put it back together? Many experts, including company reclamation specialists, doubted that the already-desolate land would ever be brought back to an acceptable level of revegetation after strip mining.

For these reasons, the San Juan Basin has been considered the federal government's most problematic coal region. If other areas where the Department of the Interior administered large quantities of coal, in Wyoming, Montana, Utah and Colorado, had "Indian problems", they paled into insignificance along side New Mexico's coal region. If others had important fossils, it was only in New Mexico where popular interest in them had given birth to the first major museum of natural history anywhere in the United States in the last 100 years.

If other federal coal regions had problems reclaiming mined land when experts could count on 18-20 inches of annual precipitation to nourish planted seedlings, what would the results be in the San Juan Basin with four inches or less of usable precipitation?

The closer federal officials looked at the San Juan Basin as a coal-producing region, the more stymied they became. But the problems identified by lower-level public officials only made the asset-hungry coal executives more obstinate. Higher officials in Washington, especially when leaned on by corporate representatives, wanted a "can-do" attitude from their field bureaucrats, not hair-tearing, moaning, legal glitches and delays. And that was true even before James Watt came to power at Interior.

High-ranking Washington officials came to realize that the San Juan Basin really is "incredibly complex". Even so, a number of facts remain, plain and clear, which can be stated regarding prospects for coal mining there.

FACT: The San Juan Basin holds more than 200 billion tons of coal, of which 30 billion tons are owned by the U.S. public.

Not all of this coal is economical to mine; some of it is too deep underground to mine with methods that would be competitive with mining operations elsewhere, and some of it is in seams too thin to be worthwhile. Generally, the coal seams in the San Juan Basin are thin (rarely over 30 feet thick) compared to coal deposits in other regions of publicly-owned coal in Wyoming (up to 200 feet thick).

In 1979, at the re-start of the federal coal leasing program (after a 1971 leasing moratorium prompted by congressional recognition that far more public coal was already under lease than was needed in the foreseeable future), New Mexico coal mines produced 13.7 million tons a year. Yet there were 335 million tons of federal coal already under lease in New Mexico at that time, within 30 leases covering some 40,953 acres, most of it in the San Juan Basin. In addition, coal companies had laid claims to an estimated 2.3 billion tons more in the Chaco-Bisti region through the old Preference Right Lease Application (PRLA) process.

Federal and industry estimates predicted a dramatic increase in coal mining from the San Juan Basin in the 1980s and 1990s. Tonnages mined from New Mexico were projected to be 64.7 million by 1987, and 90 million by the year 2000, according to the McGraw-Hill trade publication *Coal Age.*

Much of the coal in the region is considered destined for the furnaces of electrical generating plants. The San Juan Basin is already the site for the largest concentration of coal-fired electrical generating capacity west of the Mississippi River, and other plants are projected.

FACT: The coal region is already heavily impacted by uranium mining.

The world's oldest, and perhaps largest, uranium mining region—the Grants Uranium Belt—lies within the San Juan Basin, and has already subjected the land and the people there to environmental health problems of major proportions. Although the widely-reported Three Mile Island nuclear accident in Pennsylvania was generally regarded the most serious radioactive contamination episode in the history of the nuclear industry, the 1979 collapse of a uranium mill tailings pond in the San Juan Basin actually exceeds the Three Mile Island near-meltdown in terms of radiation contamination. An estimated 1,100 tons of radioactive material broke through a retention dam for United Nuclear's Church Rock uranium mill, pouring some 94 million gallons of radioactive liquid into the nearby Rio Puerco which flows from Church Rock to Gallup and on into Arizona. A study by the New Mexico Environmental Improvement Division released three years later indicated that no long-term health hazards resulted from the spill, but the report went on to stress that "the Puerco River should not be used as a primary source of water for human consumption, livestock watering or irrigation", adding that "these waters contain levels of radioactivity and certain toxic levels that approach or exceed standards or guidelines designed to protect the health of people, livestock and agricultural crops."

Nevertheless, the contaminated stream remained the only practical source of water for many Navajo families. In 1985, the same tailings pond was still allowing radioactive seepage into the surrounding groundwater.

Fifteen such mill tailing spills occurred between 1959 and 1977.

Long-term contamination from abandoned uranium mill tailings is a major environmental health issue. As a 1980 Bureau of Indian Affairs Office of Trust Responsibilities report on uranium mining impacts in the San Juan Basin shows, "the problem of radon-222 exhalation from the tailings piles will continue for tens of thousands of years after the mines are played out. Stabilization of the tailings piles and reduction of radon exhalation to an acceptable level are, therefore, very long-term operations." Elsewhere in the report, it is stated that the greatest health threat is expected to be radioactive dust which gets into the food chain of Navajo Indians living in the region. "Maximized transfer of radionuclides through food chains might occur in the case of Navajo Indians who live near a uranium mill and eat sheep raised in the area," the report said. "The dust could be inhaled directly or it could settle on the earth, enter the food chain, and be ingested with foods."

Contamination from the uranium mills is only a small part of the overall negative impact of uranium mining activity in the San Juan Basin. Severe public health hazards exist from working conditions at the mines (especially during the earlier days of uranium mining when considerably less care was taken to protect workers from contamination), as well as from air- and water-borne contamination from abandoned, unreclaimed mine sites and unregulated mine water discharges.

Much of the uranium ore in the San Juan Basin occurs in water-bearing strata. To be mined, it must be "de-watered"; radioactive water is pumped out and, after minimal processing, is dumped into nearby arroyos. According to an Environmental Protection Agency study, the level of radium in such mine discharges is dangerous: "Whereas natural background radium concentrations are generally about several picocuries per liter, 100-150 picocuries per liter appear in the effluents of operating mines. The discharge of such highly contaminated mine effluents to streams and seepage from tailings ponds create a long-lived source of groundwater contamination."

In addressing concerns over reclamation of the awesome Jackpile-Paguate uranium mine on the eastern edge of the San Juan Basin, a March 17, 1983 Department of the Interior memorandum noted that "improper reclamation would result in more deaths from cancer than all 22 of the inactive uranium mills in the United States, combined. A conservative estimate is 248 deaths, plus a substantial number of genetic disorders over the next century."

In fact, analysis of a ten-year study period on birth defects in the Shiprock uranium region, conducted by Biologists Lora Shields and Alan B. Goodman and presented to the American Association for the Advancement of Science in 1984, showed a link between uranium and increased birth defects in the San Juan Basin. Examination of the medical records of more than 13,000 Navajo children born between 1964 and 1981 at Shiprock's federal Indian Health Service Hospital revealed exceptionally high rates of stillbirths and a wide variety of genetic defects. Shiprock is another major center of uranium mining activities in the San Juan Basin. Birth abnormalities were found to be two to eight times the normal level compared to the general American population, or to other Indian tribes. Among the defects found were rates of hydrocephalus (fluid on the brain) and malformed hips eight times the national average. Cases of club foot and cleft palate were three times the national average during the same period.

Navajo uranium miners who were exposed to high levels of radiation during the 1950s and early 1960s were also found to have high rates of cancer. Government studies have shown that uranium miners, both smokers and non-smokers, develop cancer at five times the expected rate. Normally, the incidence of lung cancer among Navajos is practically non-existent, except among uranium miners, for whom the cancer rate was 85 times the expected level.

FACT: The history of coal mining in this country generally demonstrates that companies have left devastated land after strip mining; the mining companies have shown routine disregard for regulations intended to safeguard the environment and community socio-economic well-being.

The track record of the uranium mining companies is disastrous in the San Juan Basin, and the record of the coal companies across the country is hardly any better. Roughly two-thirds of all the strip mined coal fields in the United States were found to require reclamation work when the federal government first assessed the overall environmental damage from this cause in 1965. A later study by the U.S. Bureau of Mines and the Soil Conservation Service in 1974 revealed that nationwide only 40 percent of the lands strip mined since 1930 had been reclaimed.

In 1979, the Department of the Interior reported that "Prior to development of control technology and evaluation of social and environmental awareness, many mining operations, both surface and underground, left ravaged lands and polluted air and waters. These conditions have had adverse impacts upon the safety and health of area residents as well as on the social and economic well-being of the nation's mining areas. . . . Outstanding problems attributed to uncontrolled coal-mining practices of the past include nearly 400,000 acres of abandoned, unreclaimed strip-mined land, 177,000 acres covered by burning and nonburning waste banks, 418,000 urban undermined acres threatened by surface subsidence, more than 10,000 miles of streams and rivers affected by mine drainage pollution, and over 250 abandoned coal mine and outcrop fires." The federal Office of Surface Mining estimated in a 1979 report that "the expenditure necessary for rehabilitation of all acres affected by past coal mining activities would total more than $30 billion."

It was public outrage at these strip mining abuses that led to the Surface Mining Control and Reclamation Act of 1977. But no sooner than the new law was on the books, the coal companies maneuvered to rid themselves of its restrictions. By 1983, an NBC TV special report on coal strip mining revealed that more than one million acres of land nationwide were left unreclaimed, and that the abuses that SMCRA was intended to halt were, in fact, a continuing national disgrace. The NBC "Monitor" program which aired August 6, 1983 reported that the mining companies owed more than $100 million in strip mine violation fines, which they were refusing to pay.

FACT: Post-mining reclamation in the San Juan Basin, where water is chronically scarce, is expected to be extremely difficult.

Reclamation of strip mines can be difficult even under the best of conditions. With ample precipitation to encourage revegetation on filled and contoured mines, major problems can still be encountered for such reasons as carelessness or disregard of proper reclamation practices by heavy equipment operators working at the mine, or by natural erosion of the unconsolidated fill material. Even in parts of the United States with ample topsoil and precipitation, reclamation results are often disappointing. But in areas of the arid West, with exceedingly thin topsoil and scant precipitation, reclamation prospects may be so remote as to be essentially impossible. Erosion occurs in the natural environment with great frequency; even when the earth has compacted and consolidated itself through eons, it can be blown or washed away with an amazing rapidity. Strip mine reclamation does not normally result in as thorough a compaction and consolidation as Nature produces over millenia.

The difficulties of reclaiming strip mined lands in the San Juan Basin have been recognized by the federal government for decades. Warnings have been voiced repeatedly about the likelihood of failure here, given the poor performance of reclamation in more forgiving environments.

In the Department of the Interior's 1979 Programmatic Environmental Impact Statement for the proposed federal coal program, the bleak prospect for reclaiming strip mined portions of the San Juan Basin are stated explicitly. "Arid and semiarid lands, particularly in the southwest (e.g. San Juan River Coal Region), have areas with average rainfalls of eight inches or less a year. While the amounts of water needed to sustain revegetation will vary with species requirements, areas receiving less than 10 inches of annual precipitation will likely require supplemental water. The question of whether initially irrigated plant communities can achieve and maintain densities similar to undisturbed native areas on reclaimed land has not been answered. Additionally, plant communities established under irrigation systems may be severely impacted if a drought year occurs after irrigation is terminated."

Local Bureau of Land Management offices in New Mexico agreed with this assessment in their coal-related studies. The 1982 Environmental Impact Statement for the San Juan Basin coal leasing proposal notes, "In general, the lack of moisture in the EIS region makes reclamation more difficult than in other parts of the country."

A more site specific evaluation of reclamation prospects in the heart of the coal region, offered through an Energy Mineral Rehabilitation Inventory and Analysis (EMRIA) report by the U.S. Geological Survey (Report 5-1976, "Bisti West Study Site, Bisti Coal Field: Resource and Potential Reclamation Evaluation") makes the point even more clearly: "The harsh climate at the study site, typical of arid areas in this region and characterized by low precipitation occurring in erratic patterns (spotty local thundershowers and some snow), will make revegetation difficult."

The Bisti West EMRIA report expands upon these expected difficulties: "Average annual precipitation, usually in the form of localized intense thunderstorms, is about 8 inches, with July, August, September and October each averaging about 1 inch. The remaining months each average about 0.5 inch. Up to 7 inches of the 8-inch total precipitation is effective. Average humidity is about 50 percent, and average annual pan evaporation is 50 inches.

"These averages fail to portray adequately the harsh climatic picture which emerges when the extremes of weather in this area are considered. The most severe restraint on vegetative growth is precipitation. The 8-inch average includes years with 4 inches and years with 20 inches. Typically, there may be a 3-month period with no precipitation, perhaps followed by a brief heavy thunderstorm, followed by another long, dry period. This erratic precipitation pattern and other climatic factors will largely contribute to the difficulty in revegetating the study site."

And if reliance on natural precipitation is unwise, so apparently is the expectation that the mined lands can be revegetated with irrigation. The area obviously has inadequate surface water to be tapped for irrigation, and shallow aquifers have very low yields as well. Going deeper for water is also futile. According to BLM geologists reporting in a 1981 environmental assessment for proposed coal development in the area, "The deeper aquifers may produce sufficient yields for reclamation, but water quality for irrigation is poor, particularly if the planting medium is fine-textured and has a high salt content. . . . Use of this water for irrigation would have to be on a very short-term basis and, even then, may require treatment."

Despite all the warnings, scientific studies and mounting evidence of a major disaster if these arid lands are stripmined indiscriminately, the U.S. Department of the Interior has continued with its plans for full-speed coal development.

FACT: Federal government officials, especially in the Reagan Administration, have colluded with industry so that companies need not comply with existing laws meant to protect the public and the environment.

The Reagan Administration, perhaps like no other, has encouraged business leaders to break the laws and regulations meant to protect the public and its environment. Since the earliest days of the American Republic, there have been presidents and department secretaries who felt their prime responsibility to be the unfettering of industry. Under the more pro-business presidents, America's natural resources—water, air, minerals, forests, soils and scenic areas—have been degraded or depleted for profit and development, often with local, state and national governmental officials assisting. Ronald Reagan rose to the presidency at the start of the 1980s with a widely-known commitment to "turn business loose" to "bring American back to greatness". Under Reagan, federal policy was clearly and unequivocably to relax and, if possible, abolish many of the governmental restrictions on how business is supposed to operate. Reagan's political appointments to high federal offices were meant to assure that federal agencies would cooperate to the fullest with business leaders who had long complained about restrictions stemming from such congressional laws as the National Environmental Policy Act and the Surface Mining Control and Reclamation Act.

But the zealousness of his political appointees, such as James Watt as head of Interior, James Harris as director of the Office of Surface Mining (OSM), and Anne Gorsuch Burford as director of the Environmental Protection Agency, quickly led to serious charges of criminal complicity to violate federal laws and regulations for the benefit of industry.

Scandals rocked the EPA, especially its industrial toxic waste clean-up "superfund". Perjury charges were brought against its director, Rita M. Lavelle, during investigations into manipulation of the fund for political purposes. She was sentenced to six months prison and a $10,000 fine. A contempt of Congress citation was handed down against her boss, EPA Administrator Gorsuch Burford, who was later forced to resign.

Similarly, top officials of the Office of Surface Mining deliberately set out to render the agency powerless to impede strip miners, through drastic budget cuts, re-definitions of agency objectives, staff reductions and deliberate non-enforcement of federal laws and regulations. Strip mine violations were routinely ignored, and fines previously levied against the mining companies were deliberately allowed to remain unpaid. The NBC-TV "Monitor" program in August 1983 revealed that the Office of Surface Mining had as a matter of policy not collected more than $100 million in violation fines.

Shown in the NBC documentary, former Interior attorney Carole Nickle made it clear that it was official policy to "go easy" on the mine violators. "Under the Reagan administration and under Secretary Watt, the Office of Surface Mining has been gutted of its enforcement power," she said. She served in the OSM Knoxville, Tenn. field office until she resigned in protest. "Basically, my client, the Department of the Interior under Secretary Watt, I felt was committing illegal acts and was planning to do so in the future." The documentary pointed out that a federal judge agreed with her assessment of Interior's collusion with the coal strip mining industry. The judge stated that "the Interior Department was flouting the law and Secretary Watt was showing a disregard for it."

The 1983 documentary included the following interview with a former government fraud investigator, Vince Laubach, who was harassed by higher Interior officials when he tried to crack down on strip mine violators. Said Laubach: "Conceivably well over a hundred million dollars (in fines against stripminers) could have been collected, that we knew about. As to the reclamation fee cases, I recommended that we try to uncover as many of those who are cheating the government as we can. And to prosecute the most serious, outrageous cases. And on the smaller cases, I recommended that we give these cases to private collection agencies to collect. . . . They didn't think much of any of my recommendations.

"I had heard from people who had been there some time that I was sticking my neck out by trying to vigorously collect this money, because this is a very political issue. And, as I went to the Inspector-General, asking for help in confidence, the person I saw said that he would hold it in confidence, think it over, and would talk about it in a week or so. He did not keep that confidence, however."

Lauback was fired by Reagan lieutenants because he insisted on enforcing the strip mining laws.

It seemed that the officials running OSM were trying to subvert the very laws they were sworn to uphold. But that came as no surprise to those who knew the background of the people Watt assigned to head the agency. OSM Director James Harris had worked hard as a state senator in Indiana to overturn the 1977 Surface Mining Control and Reclamation Act, the law which created and directed OSM. Harris helped launch the effort to take the matter to the U.S. Supreme Court, challenging the strip mine law's constitutionality. The Supreme Court ruled unanimously in favor of the law.

FACT: The people who would be most directly impacted by the mining of federal coal in the San Juan Basin are Navajo families living off of the land.

In the Chaco-Bisti coal region, the people most directly affected by federal-corporate plans for mining are Navajo Indians who have special problems arising from the stripping away of the earth's surface.

The Chaco-Bisti coal region has more than 22,000 Navajo, with varying degrees of dependence on the land for subsistence. Nearly all of them live in isolated areas, in hogans or modern equivalents, where they herd sheep, cattle, horses and goats. While few of them actually own title to the land they occupy and use (record title to much of the land is held by the U.S. government), their families' traditional use of this off-reservation territory substantially pre-dates the U.S. Constitution.

In ways unlike those of the average American, the Navajo in the coal region have a deep dependence on the land and its natural productive capacity. As with any people making a livelihood from livestock, they require the topsoil to produce forage; they feel as crippled as any other rancher when the surface is stripped away for coal mining. But the Navajos' disruption is far deeper and more pervasive. For them, the land's vegetation not only provides meat and cash from the sale of livestock, it also yields medicinal herbs, natural dyes for cash-producing Navajo rug weavings, trees for home construction, corrals, cooking and home heating, nuts and berries for diet supplements, and an endless variety of other uses poorly understood by non-Indians. Similarly, in ways unlike other Americans, the more culture-bound Navajo have a strong emotional and psychological attachment to specific geologic formations, such as mesas, buttes, valleys, arroyos, eagle-catching sites, or watering holes, some of which are imbued with mystical or religious significance. And beyond that, they have a world-view, an underlying philosophy, of the sanctity of the life-giving "Mother Earth".

An estimated 65 percent of the Navajo living in the coal region do not speak English, and are ill-prepared to make a living by non-traditional means. The 1978 per capita income for Navajos was estimated at $2,500, less than a quarter of the national average.

Many of them have had no schooling at all; the average Navajo of this region has received no more than a fifth grade education. The Navajo Treaty of 1868 required the federal government to provide schools for them, but the government's effort was halfhearted at best, despite the importance that many Navajos attached to education.

FACT: The Navajo people have consistently opposed coal strip mining in the San Juan Basin.

Although large-scale coal mining has occurred on Navajo lands since 1960 when Pittsburg & Midway started New Mexico's first major coal strip mine to feed the Cholla power plant in Arizona, there has always been deep and widespread local opposition to it. The Navajo Tribal government was created initially by the federal Bureau of Indian Affairs in 1923 precisely so that energy mineral developers (oil companies) could have a formal Navajo body to ratify their plans to exploit the Indian lands. (In fact, it was Interior Secretary Albert Fall of New Mexico who ordered the creation of a Navajo tribal government. Fall is better known as the Interior Secretary who accepted half a million dollars in bribes to exploit federal minerals in the infamous 1923 Teapot Dome scandal.) The tribal government has customarily agreed to such mining against the wishes of local communities. The massive Navajo Mine was opened on the reservation in 1963 to feed the heavily-polluting Four Corners Generating Station. That mine operates on a 48-square-mile lease from the Navajo Tribe to Utah International coal mining company. Terms of that lease, signed in 1957, gave the Navajos a royalty rate of slightly more than one-twentieth of the value of the coal. In 1968, the Navajo Tribal Council signed another coal lease for the Burnham Mine, near the eastern border of the reservation, in New Mexico. Other coal strip mines were opened at Black Mesa, in the central part of the reservation, and just off the reservation in New Mexico, at the San Juan Mine, which feeds the San Juan Generating Station built by Public Service Company of New Mexico.

Local opposition to these strip mines has taken the form of armed confrontation in the past. After more than 10 years of voicing objections, local residents and other Indian activists took control of the Burnham Mine by force of arms. In late July 1980, a small group of Indians armed with high-powered rifles and handguns, staged a mid-afternoon take-over of the mine and demanded that it be closed permanently. Their six-hour shutdown of the mine resulted in the arrest of eight men, and a heightened awareness of the how strongly local people felt about strip mining. Among the Burnham residents' major complaints was the fact that the miners were dynamiting ancestral burial sites.

Opposition has continued relentlessly since that time. Navajo chapters (local governments) in the Chaco-Bisti region have repeatedly and consistently opposed any additional coal leasing or mining in their areas, and have submitted written petitions to the Department of the Interior seeking a halt to the federal coal program in the region. They have sent delegations to Washington, and traveled to Denver, Albuquerque, Santa Fe and other cities to testify against the proposals.

While a few Navajo have favored the mining proposals, primarily to gain employment, the overwhelming majority of Navajo residents in the San Juan Basin have consistently and strongly opposed it.

FACT: Navajo families living in the off-reservation coal region are poorly-represented in local, state and national decision-making arenas.

Navajos had trouble getting their own tribal government to respect their wishes when it came to strip mining on the reservation. But those who lived off-reservation, in the Chaco-Bisti coal region, had even less chance that the governmental bodies responsible for coal-related decisions would abide by their wishes. Racial discrimination by Anglos and Hispanics against Navajos is well-documented. Navajos are systematically denied fair representation in county and state legislative bodies, and are denied equal employment opportunities, according to recent findings by the U.S. Civil Rights Commission.

A federal court ruling in August 1984 found that the New Mexico State Legislative district reapportionment two years earlier had conspired to deprive Indians of representation. According to the court ruling, "It is apparent to the court that racially motivated gerrymandering exists in the state redistricting plan." The court went on to say: "Although Indians account for 8.13 percent of the population of New Mexico, only one of the 70 members of the New Mexico House of Representatives is an Indian. This figure would not be remarkable if the Indian population were widely dispersed across the state. But that is not the case. The great majority of New Mexico's Indian population resides in Cibola, McKinley, San Juan and Sandoval counties. The populations of these counties entitles them to 11 representatives."

The report also analyzed the general lack of Indian participation in state and local governments, suggesting the underlying reason is that Indians were actually prohibited from voting in New Mexico state elections until 1948. "An even more devastating result of the prohibition is the belief it created among some Indians that voting was a privilege not accorded to Indians who were perceived to be second-class citizens. Perceptions and attitudes change very slowly in Indian country, being passed on from generation to generation."

"Finally, we note an abiding sentiment among the Indians of New Mexico that the state is an enemy of the tribes. . . . These perceptions, grounded in large part in the discrimination of the past, are the single biggest factor in the depressed political participation of Indians in New Mexico."

The U.S. Commission on Civil Rights issued a 216-page report in February 1982, on the effects of racial and cultural discrimination in energy development in northwestern New Mexico. The report noted that "many Navajos feel that they have little or no involvement in decisionmaking which, from their point of view, critically affects their lives. Decisions, whether they have to do with social, cultural, economic or technical concerns, are made in distant places in a language and process they cannot understand. . . . There is a sense of being manipulated, of having one's destiny taken away."

FACT: The Navajo Tribe was authorized by Congress to select 35,000 acres of public land in the San Juan Basin to relocate tribal members away from lands in Arizona designated for rival Hopi Indians. The 35,000 acres picked by the Navajo Tribe included much of the most coveted land sought for coal strip mining.

The Navajo Tribe has always contended that its proper reservation boundary should extend far the to east into New Mexico, encompassing all of the Chaco-Bisti region. Historical analysis would seem to support the Navajo claim. But in addition to these long-standing claims is another, more recent one, stemming directly from acts of Congress designed to resolve a land dispute between the Navajo and Hopi tribes in the so-called Joint Use Area in Arizona. Through legislation in 1980, the Navajo Tribe was allowed to select 250,000 acres of public land on to which its people would move after vacating a large portion of the Havajo-Hopi Joint Use Area; 35,000 acres of that total were to be chosen from public lands in New Mexico, and Congress required that the selected lands be within 18 miles of the existing Navajo Reservation boundary. The lands selected by the tribe in 1982 included a large portion of the lands overlying the most easily strippable federal coal.

However, the Department of the Interior refused to approve the tribe's selection, and sought to have critical portions of those lands transferred instead to the major utility company in New

Mexico, Public Service Company of New Mexico, through a land trade of questionable value to the public.

FACT: The San Juan Basin coal region holds little-understood remnants of the most impressive prehistoric civilization in North America.

Cultural resource protection is a major limiting factor on the federal coal program in the San Juan Basin. In the heart of the Chaco-Bisti region lies Chaco Canyon, the cultural and administrative center of the most impressive prehistoric civilization in North America.

Archeologists have found evidence of human occupation in the San Juan Basin dating back to 10,000 B.C., but the most spectacular accomplishments of these earlier residents were produced by the Chacoan Anasazi between 900 and 1200 A.D. Nowhere else in North America had prehistoric Indians developed engineered roadways and masterplanned cities of multi-storied buildings enclosing 800 rooms or more.

While the imposing ruins in Chaco Canyon had attracted attention since their discovery by Europeans in the late 1800s, it was not until the mid-1970s that archeologists realized that the canyon was only the "capital" of a much larger empire extending more than 60,000 square miles, and that 80 (and perhaps many more) outlying towns were part of the civilization in Chaco Canyon. And more marvelous yet, the "Chacoan Outliers" were apparently linked to each other and to Chaco Canyon by carefully engineered and constructed roads.

After a decade of intense study, archeologists are still unable to explain why such a complex civilization arose in the Chaco region, what sustained it, why they required 30-foot-wide roads when they had not invented the wheel and had no pack animals. Archeologists are still at a loss to explain what caused their society to collapse suddenly about 1250 A.D.

Answers to these mysteries can only come from detailed analysis of the archeological remains—which are scattered far and wide over the lands intended for strip mining.

FACT: Fossils in and above the coal beds constitute one of the world's most important paleontological zones, containing rare

clues to why Earth's dominant life form succumbed to extinction 65 millions years ago.

Since coal is a fossil fuel (the remnant of vegetative matter produced ages ago) it is not uncommon to find fossils of dinosaurs, mollusks and other long-vanished creatures within or over coal seams. But the fossil concentrations, types and combinations in San Juan Basin coal region represent a unique opportunity for scientific study. More than 200 different kinds of organisms have been identified within the San Juan Basin coal region, and new life forms are being discovered every year, making this one of the most important Late Cretaceous terrestrial biosystems in the world. About one-third of the plant and animal fossils found are unique to northwestern New Mexico.

Fossils in the Chaco-Bisti region are uniquely important also because of their ecological context. Stumps and logs are preserved in their original positions, with remnants of insects and animals found in the context in which they related to one another 70 million years ago.

Explains Dr. Barry Kues, University of New Mexico paleontologist: "The fossils in the coal-bearing formations and in nearby slightly younger strata represent a sequence that documents one of the most important events in the history of life—the transition from dinosaur-dominated terrestial communities to those dominated by the primitive mammals that replaced dinosaurs after they became extinct.

"Northwestern New Mexico is one of only a few places in the world where this transition is well displayed. Understanding this abrupt change, and the reasons for the extinction of the dinosaurs, is of more than just academic interest. Among the mammals that evolved during this time were the first primates, our remote ancestors."

Stripmining for coal in this fossil-rich region would destroy much of the paleontological context, if not the fossils themselves.

FACT: The San Juan Basin coal region includes two congressionally-designated federal Wilderness Areas and a third which probably would have been designated except for coal lease applications filed for it.

Public support for preservation of the scenic, other-worldly badland areas of the Bisti (a corruption of the Navajo word for badland, "bistahi") had been strong since 1970. Following an intensive inventory of public lands which might be suitable for inclusion in the National Wilderness Preservation System, as required by the Federal Land Policy and Management Act, three areas totalling more than 28,500 acres were designated as federal Wilderness Study Areas in December 1979. All three, the Bisti (3,968 acres), De-na-zin (18,554 acres) and Ah-shi-sle-pah (6,563 acres) overlie coal seams.

Nearly all of two of these areas, Bisti and Ah-shi-sle-pah, had been leased or claimed for strip mining by coal companies through the since-discontinued "Preference Right Lease Application" system. But land use planning conducted by the Albuquerque District of the Bureau of Land Management in 1980-81 concluded that Bisti and De-na-zin should be preserved and added to the federal Wilderness Preservation System, while Ah-shi-sle-pah should be destined for mining.

All three areas, within the larger Bisti region, are important for their fossil deposits, with Ah-shi-sle-pah having the greatest concentration.

Bisti and De-na-zin were formally added to the Wilderness Preservation System by an act of Congress October 30, 1984, becoming the first BLM Wilderness Areas in New Mexico.

Other tracts surrounding the Bisti and De-na-zin Wilderness Areas have been leased or targeted for strip mining. The two areas, plus a third area preserved by the 1984 San Juan Wilderness Protection Act, Fossil Forest, cover barely 0.3 percent of the San Juan Basin's coal reserves.

FACT: The real battle over federal coal is for control of the resource, not for mining production to meet the public's demand for energy.

Although coal companies have been relentless in their drive to acquire the publicly-owned coal in the San Juan Basin for the past 20 years, their primary objective has been control over that resource, rather than mining from it. The companies have a great deal to gain by merely acquiring rights to mine the coal. In fact, the coal market has been bleak during much of the 1980s. But by obtaining leases from the federal government during a depressed coal market, the companies hope to acquire assets at substantially less than their true value.

Already coal companies hold federal leases with enough coal for an estimated 180 years of production. According to the Department of the Interior's Fiscal Year 1982 Coal Management Report, the coal industry in the United States already holds 616 federal leases on some 18 billion tons of coal. And of the 616 federal leases held, only 111 were in production. Clearly the companies were not pushing for leases in the San Juan Basin because they desperately needed them to meet the public's demand for coal-fired electrical generation or any other pressing consumer demand.

But acquiring a new lease accomplishes at least two important objectives. Most importantly, it gives the company control over the resource. The company gets the right to use the land for mining, rather than let the tract remain as unencumbered public property, open to multiple uses. Secondly, the coal lease becomes a bankable asset, even if the company has no immediate intention to mine from it.

And leases acquired under President Reagan's Interior Department could be expected to have far less stringent environmental stipulations than a lease on the same tract acquired during an administration that gave more weight to environmental protection.

FACT: The coal-related resource conflicts in the San Juan Basin took on a high level of political importance as a test of wills for Reagan administration ideologues.

The federal coal leasing program in the San Juan Basin achieved a level of importance far exceeding the relative economic value of its meager coal seams, partly because similar land use issues in other western coal regions were already fairly well decided, and partly because the environmentalist and state government rebellion against Watt's coal program in New Mexico was so startling coming from a state steeped in the "rape and ruin" mining tradition.

The political context in New Mexico was threatening to right-wing ideologues who swept into Washington to lead a national conservative crusade only to find that people of New Mexico had just elected a man being labeled as "the most liberal governor in the nation". It was clear that New Mexico Governor Toney Anaya had won due to the vigorous campaign efforts of environmental activists.

Then, too, there were the political aspirations of the Assistant Secretary of the Interior in charge of the coal program, Dr. Garrey Carruthers, a former New Mexico Republican Party chairman who intended to run for governor in the 1986 elections.

For those and other reasons, the San Juan Basin coal battles were perceived in Washington as bellwether episodes.

CHAPTER 3

STRIP MINING NAVAJO LANDS

The grey hills on Chaco Mesa are nearly bare. In the strong overhead sun, colors are obliterated and few shadows give definition to the desert landscape.

Along the dirt road north of Pueblo Pintado, in the heart of the coal-bearing San Juan Basin, there is little evidence that the surrounding countryside could support life, although a circling eagle apparently expects to catch a lizard or desert rat some time soon. Mile after mile, one sees no indication that humans have altered anything in the environment, save the road and power line that follow a natural gas pipeline through some of the most desolate, inhospitable land in the United States.

Here, the chalky white surface of the earth barely supports two small clumps of grass per square yard. No trees, no sagebrush, no cactus, a few tumbleweeds. Occasionally the surface blackens, creating a sharp contrast with the blanched, wind-swept powdery soil around it. The dark stripes are coal outcrops, proof of the billion-dollar treasure lying a few feet below.

For more than 50 years, perhaps a hundred, the federal government has known of these coal seams lying near the surface of the Chaco region. But until now, the burnable black material has attracted little interest from coal companies or the federal government which owns the land surface and the minerals estate below. Still, one might easily conclude that if there is a need for coal in the United States, for fueling power plants or for marketing abroad, these lands might be an appropriate place to mine it. In the middle of "nowhere", there are few townfolks on Chaco Mesa to be disturbed by the mining draglines; scooping off the surface overburden would not despoil virgin forests, or scenic lakes or rivers. The land appears empty, unused for anything else, so why not get coal here?

Just when the casual visitor to the Chaco is convinced it would cause no harm to strip mine the area for coal, suddenly a herd of sheep and goats appears over the horizon, followed by a sheep dog and a Navajo woman on horseback.

These bleak lands are home to some 22,000 Navajo Indians who live off the land, people whose per capita income is about $2,500 a year. The Navajo in the Chaco area of northwestern New Mexico depend on the sparse vegetation, the medicinal herbs, the mutton, the wool, the watering holes, the prayer offering points . . . their entire environment in order to continue their way of life.

Year after year, in one public meeting after another, these tough, independent Indians have strongly opposed federal plans to lease their homeland to coal companies. Drawing on the lessons of past oppression by the white American invaders, they repeat the warnings of their ancestors that the whites' greed will take away their land, their heritage.

"In the year 1620, these white people came from across the ocean and asked us, the American Indian, for a small plot of land to live on. A place where they could raise their children. Since then, they have pushed us pretty much off of our land. My ancestors are buried here on this land. I am not going to give up Pueblo Pintado. I don't care what happens. When we pray, we pray to our sacred Mother Earth. If we let them dig it up, who is going to fix it back to the way it was? No one is going to do so. We don't want our Mother Earth destroyed. We cannot be left standing

around among mounds of dirt that once used to be our land, trying to herd our sheep. That picture is just not acceptable to me. There was an old man who lived here named Tall Medicine Man. He was my father. That is why when I say I am not going to give up Pueblo Pintado, I mean this. Our water that used to flow clean and plentiful will become contaminated, and our air will also become darkened with pollution." So said Nancy Dennison, in her native tongue.

"I want to make my speech short because every time these people come here to ask us what we think about proposed coal mining, we give them the same answer every time. No. How many times do we have to tell them no? Maybe they do not know the meaning of the word no. Maybe they are not going to listen to what we say, or they are not going to do what we want. This electricity that is going to be put in, I do not want. I oppose it. They are talking about digging up our land for coal and also taking our water . . . we will be left with just our belongings and no place to go. This is where this coal development can lead to. After the coal has all been dug and all the water has been sucked up out of the ground, our land will be left destroyed. They who destroyed our land will just leave. They will never once look back. We will be the ones who will have to live here among the remains." So said Bert Mescal, wearing his turquoise pendant.

"I have never attended school in my life, not even half a day have I ever spent in school. This is the case with the majority of us. We are open to trickery of the white people who have education. Their laws permit them to take advantage of us because we do not understand their ways. The white people have examined all the possibilities of this coal development. We are asked if we understand this. We, the Navajo people, have a difficult time understanding their ways of thinking. We can be manipulated very easily by them. We are very easy to be persuaded to follow the plans they have for us. We can be easily led like sheep. This was not always like this. Our ancestors and our leaders from a long time ago were not like this. They were suspicious of even one piece of paper handed to them. They warned us of the day when these white people could easily control us. I think these white people are going to cheat us in any way they can, even if we say no. They will throw us a pile of money thinking that we won't be able to resist, and we will grab the money and give up our land. We are told that we are living on top of this coal they want to mine. They are not telling us where we are going to move our homes and our sheep and other livestock when they begin to dig up our land. . . .

They are just concerned with one thing, and that is coal, coal. If they make us leave our homes and sheep, where are we going to get meat to eat? We need our sheep. I am sick over what will happen to us. I cannot sleep at night because I think about his. A long time ago my grandmother told me this. She was three years old when she returned from The Long Walk. She said that in the future, the land will be taken because of greed. The people will be bribed and their land will be gone. They will even lose custody of the children. This is where we are headed. We will not have a home any more if we allow them to take our land. We will be left wandering around homeless. This was what was foreseen by my grandmother years ago." And so said Alice Lopez, who speaks no English.

The Long Walk that Alice Lopez referred to was a traumatic episode more than 100 years ago that remains fixed in the Navajo mind, and it equates with BLM plans to remove them from the coal lands. Rounded up by Colonel Kit Carson in 1863 and herded into a concentration camp 300 miles from their homeland, the Navajo spent four years in confinement at Fort Sumner. Over 2,000 Navajo died in the long forced march across New Mexico and the imprisonment which awaited them at the fort. Survivors were allowed to return to "Dinetah" only after they agreed to give up almost 90 percent of the territory they claimed as their aboriginal lands.

Navajo creation stories tell of the tribe's beginnings here in the mesa country of New Mexico and Arizona, where they were made custodians of the lands between their four sacred mountains. Although ethnographers and anthropologists say with certainty that the Navajo are relatively recent arrivals in this part of the Southwest, arriving from the Canadian West perhaps 500-600 years ago, it is with equal certainty that the present day Navajo consider themselves inextricably attached to the land here.

The federal government tells them they are living on public land in the off-reservation area where the coal lies buried. To Interior officials these people are "unauthorized occupants", trespassers, whose use of the public domain has been tolerated for generations because nobody else had any desire to use the meager rangelands where they built their hogans and corrals. The government tells them they must move off of the land because the laws and federal regulations give the coal companies rights to the black rock beneath their homes.

To which Navajo Cecil Werito replies: "We were here before the laws were made."

Although the land north of Pueblo Pintado, and much of the rest of the Chaco-Bisti coal region, looks desolate, uninhabitable and unused, it is in fact, used as intensively as possible, given Navajo traditional lifestyles. Navajo customarily do not congregate into towns; more typically, there will be one family per square mile, and often no other dwellings within view. The surrounding "empty" land is the basis for their livelihood, their culture, their survival.

If the Indians are in the way of an imperative for coal development, there would seem to be at least two options: move them onto other nearby lands while the mining is under way, or move them into towns. But the first option is untenable because all the lands in the region are already under maximum use to support other subsistence families. Moving Navajo families onto adjoining lands would only impose them on another family just barely eking out a minimal living. The second option, relocating Navajo into towns and cities bordering the coal region is a strategy which has resulted in death, mental illness, and total inability to retain their sense of independence. More than enough evidence has been gathered with similar relocations to say that option two constitutes genocide.

Navajo history from shortly after the first contact with Europeans in the late 1500s is one of forced relocations and encroachment onto aboriginal lands by the whites. As in other parts of the Americas, the Spanish conquistadores rounded up Indians as slave laborers and confiscated their lands. By the mid-19th Century, an estimated one-half of the entire Navajo tribe was held in chattel bondage by Spanish colonizers based out of Mexico.

When the "manifest destiny" of the Anglo-Americans brought much of the Southwest into the United States by means of a military victory over Mexico in 1847, included in the conquered territory was some 35 million acres of Navajo land.

Navajo author and activist John Redhouse explains the federal government's claim to Navajo land this way: "According to European occidental reasoning, the Navajos were 'discovered' by the Spanish who were later defeated by the Mexicans who in turn had just surrendered to the Americans. Somehow the Navajos were alienated from their land, and title was transferred in succession to the United States via the Right of Discovery, Right of Conquest, Manifest Destiny, and a legal treaty which precluded the tribe as an indispensible party. In other words, the Americans could now steal Navajo land fair and square, and this theft would be painted 'legal' under the color of international law and earlier colonial precedents. In 1849, Navajo lands were officially declared part of the public domain and subject to the concurrent jurisdiction of the provisional territory of New Mexico and the United States government. Legal fiction defied reality as the Navajos were suddenly considered trespassers on their own land. . . ."

White settlers were soon homesteading the Navajo lands recently designated as 'public domain' and moving livestock onto the Indians' grazing areas. The resulting conflicts prompted Kit Carson's round up of the Navajos and their Long Walk to Fort Sumner in 1863. Upon their release, families returned to their original territories, including the lands which Washington and local white settlers considered public domain . . . the traditional Navajo lands in the coal-rich Chaco-Bisti region.

During the next 50 years, as the Navajo population and livestock herds grew, the original land base their leaders had agreed to as the price of freedom from Fort Sumner was patently inadequate. Navajo delegations to Washington produced repeated expansions of "Navajo land" into New Mexico, but these gains were routinely reversed by later administrations responding to political pressures from whites in New Mexico angered by such denials of their right to homestead and use the public domain rangelands for themselves.

In the early 1900s, the Navajo pressed hard to expand their land base to the east farther into New Mexico to accommodate the growing population. Their case won approval from Interior officials and, more importantly, President Theodore Roosevelt. But at about the same time, the president also was pushing hard to have the U.S. Geological Survey determine which of the vast western public lands were coal-bearing. He wanted to avoid turning over valuable coal deposits to speculators, since coal was becoming increasingly important to fuel the new transcontinental railroad engines. A 1906 mission by the U.S. Geological Survey demonstrated that much of the Chaco-Bisti region was coal land.

President Theodore Roosevelt signed an executive order in 1907 reserving 1.9 million acres—surface and minerals—for the Navajo east of the reservation, in New Mexico. This constituted only a part of the lost homeland, but half a dozen influential non-Indian sheepmen in the Territory of New Mexico were outraged by the order. They set about to sabotage the president's action by initiating an act of Congress which attempted to open up the lands again to white use and settlement. Less than half the Navajos who were entitled to gain lands from the 1907 executive order actually did so before the president's decision was effectively reversed. Said Roosevelt: "I strongly protest against opening up or cutting down the Eastern Navajo Reservation Extension. Such an act would be a cruel wrong and would benefit only a few wealthy cattle and sheep men. The movement to throw open the Eastern Extension and to ruin the Navajos is merely in the interest of a few greedy white adventurers and a few wealthy men who wish to increase their already large fortunes and who have much political influence."

Roosevelt's attempt to expand the Navajo Reservation essentially failed, and the Chaco-Bisti lands were again opened up to homesteading and other public domain uses. When those Navajos who had formally claimed land in the region were finally given trust patents to their holdings, the documents showed that the coal under their lands had been withheld and remained government property.

Through a variety of legislative and executive procedures, the Navajo Tribe has attempted to regain its former territory in New Mexico, but with each success came a withholding of mineral rights to the federal government. It is the coal under those lands regained by the Navajo, as well as under the remaining public domain (BLM lands) used almost exclusively by the Indians, that now threatens the lifestyles and livelihood of Navajo in the Chaco-Bisti region.

Some of the regained lands are owned outright by the tribal government, some are "held in trust" for the tribe by the Department of the Interior, administered by the Bureau of Indian Affairs, and relatively little is owned outright by individual Navajo. Still other lands in the area are public lands, the grazing rights for which are leased to the tribal government, or to Navajo communities or to individual Indians. But only in the relatively rare case where an individual Navajo owns the land outright (through homesteading or allotment procedures) is the Navajo user of the land allowed the same kind of legal protections written into the federal laws to benefit landowners over federal coal elsewhere in the United States.

Because Congress felt it was unfair for landowners to have their property stripped away by holders of federal coal leases, the 1977 Surface Mining Control and Reclamation Act (SMCRA) introduced the "right of surface owner consent" into the federal coal leasing program. According to that law (originally intended to protect the interests of large ranchers in Wyoming, Montana and elsewhere who saw coal companies making hundreds of millions of dollars off of publicly-owned coal under their grazing lands) any landowner who lives on a parcel to be offered for coal leasing by the federal government, or who makes a significant portion of income from that land and who had done so for at least three years, is entitled to halt the coal lease by refusing to sign a consent statement for companies interested in bidding on that particular coal tract. Or, the landowner may consent to the leasing of federal coal under this property, usually for a royalty on the value of the coal produced and/or a lump-sum payment. The "surface owner consent" provision permitted the owner of the surface to reject the government's plan to lease public coal under his property, or to claim a piece of the action if he so chose.

That was how Congress intended to protect the ranchers in Wyoming from stripmining, but the lawmakers were obviously not thinking about protecting the Navajo in the Chaco-Bisti region. The surface owner consent provision fails to protect the Navajo in the off-reservation area because only a small percentage of them actually hold legal title to the land through homesteading or the 1907 allotment process. Instead, most of the lands used by Navajo in the Chaco-Bisti coal region are owned by the tribal government or are still "government lands" administered by the Department of the Interior.

In 1981, when the Navajo Tribe attempted to file a "refusal to consent" to coal leasing for lands it owned in the off-reservation area, Interior responded that the tribe was not a "person" as required by the surface owner consent provision, and furthermore, the tribe did not earn a significant portion of its total income from the particular tracts of public coal which the federal government planned to offer for lease.

Protection for the Navajo over federal coal is further diminished (compared to non-Indian ranchers in other federal coal regions) by the fact that a large portion of the publicly-owned coal in the Chaco-Bisti area is claimed by companies through the old "Preference Right Lease Application" (PRLA) process—which is specifically exempted from surface owner consent by federal coal laws written in the late 1970s. Under the now-discontinued preference right leasing procedures, coal companies could claim leases based on their prospecting for coal in areas where the government did not know that valuable coal deposits lay. Applicant-prospectors were entitled to leases there if they could prove to have found commercial quantities. While the PRLA process was discarded in the 1977 law, the bill grandfathered in all existing applications, including the 26 PRLAs running through Navajo land.

The bulk of the strippable federal coal in the Chaco-Bisti region is under Preference Right Lease Application, which provides no protection for the surface owner at all, except that damages must be paid to the landowner when the mining equipment tears up the land.

If there would be no royalties generally, and practically insignificant payment for damages, neither could the local Navajo residents expect to earn wages from the mining activity that would disrupt their livelihood. Because of racial discrimination against Indians, alcoholism and the incompatibility of Navajo traditions and punch-clock workday routines, local residents knew they could not count on jobs at the mines and related operations. Besides, BLM's own analysis estimated "local hires at no more than 25 percent of the workforce," and hinted that even those jobs would be at the lowest end of the pay scale.

Little wonder, then, that the Chaco-Bisti Navajos had been steadfastly opposed to the plans to mine coal in their region. The strength of that opposition grew more apparent to industry in the mid-1970s, when the Indians mounted a sustained legal battle to prevent acquisition of right-of-way through their lands to build a railroad needed to haul the coal to market. In 1976, the Atchison, Topeka and Santa Fe Railway Company submitted a right-of-way application to BLM to cross 290 acres of public lands with its proposed coal haul line. But even more Indian land would have to be crossed, and the company set out methodically to gain approval from Indian landowners. The proposed Star Lake Railroad was intended to take off from Santa Fe's main line at Prewitt (between Gallup and Grants, New Mexico), and then snake its way through the mesa land to Pueblo Pintado in the coal region, at which point one branch would head east another 10 miles to the Star Lake coal area, and a second branch would run 43 miles to the west to the Bisti area, bordering the Navajo Reservation.

With the help of legal aid attorneys, Indian landowners in the path of the rail line sought to quash attempts by Santa Fe Railway to gain the needed right-of-way. With arguments in court and before the Interstate Commerce Commission (which would have to approve the new rail line as a common carrier), the Navajo were able to stall the project for more than five years, at which time the depressed coal market further slowed momentum for the proposal.

The Navajos' attorneys alleged "a staggering variety of misrepresentations made by Star Lake Railroad right-of-way agents" in trying to obtain permission for the haul line. The landowners allegedly were told that the papers they were asked to sign only gave permission for surveying, when, in fact, the papers gave right-of-way. Others were alleged to have been told they would be jailed if they did not sign their consent. In other instances, amounts of money offered for right-of-way consent were drastically less than would likely be acceptable to other, better-informed and educated landowners.

When these allegations were called to the attention of the U.S. Attorney's Office, an official there wrote to the attorneys for the railroad, complaining, "We were dismayed to learn that many of our clients were totally unaware of how the right-of-way would affect their (land) allotment. Apparently the railroad representatives obtained the consent of our clients without informing them that they were entitled to compensation and with little or no discussion of where the rail line would be built on their property or how it would affect such things as access and drainage."

The District of Columbia Circuit Court ruled that the Interstate Commerce Commission's approval of the Star Lake Railroad was unlawful because, "by ignoring the serious charges of misconduct and violations of statutes designed to protect Indian lands, the ICC failed to consider (A) the evidence of bad faith in Star Lake's promises to preserve sacred and historic Indian sites and (B) the public policy of avoiding unnecessary disturbance of the Indians' quiet possession."

Whether Indian lands are involved or not, the Bureau of Land Management by law must assess the socio-economic problems which might be caused by any actions which it might take—such as the leasing of federal coal. Presumably if its action would mean the death of a living culture, such as that of the Chaco Navajo, then that fact would have to weigh heavily against the relatively less significant positive impact of leasing public coal there to add to the speculative assets of a few coal companies.

Beyond that general obligation to assess the socio-economic impacts of its actions, the Department of the Interior is specifically charged as guardian for American Indians. The Secretary of the Interior and the agencies under him (including the BLM, the BIA, the U.S. Geological Survey, and the Office of Surface Mining) are bound by the "trust responsibility" doctrine which requires them to look after the Indians' interests. An honored and legally effective doctrine, Interior's trust responsibility is much the same as a private fiduciary responsibility where a legally assigned administrator is required to promote the interests of the beneficiaries of a trust fund.

While leasing publicly-owned coal in the Chaco-Bisti region might be in the interest of a particular utility company eager to burn coal to generate electricity, and in the interest of a few coal companies eager to claim as much of the potential supply from this region as possible, and perhaps even in the interest of the economy as a whole in New Mexico, the Interior agencies are still legally committed to protecting the interests of the Indians.

Although the Navajos had said 'no' to the plan to lease coal in the Chaco-Bisti area, not once but hundreds of times, in all parts of the region, Interior could and did justify its intentions to continue with massive leasing in their area. Under James Watt and Garrey Carruthers of New Mexico, Interior in Washington was less concerned about what the Navajo said they wanted than whether the Indians would be able to stop them. The routine in Washington was to give industry what it wanted: whatever industry wanted was de facto in the best interests of all Americans. So much for the trust responsibility.

Still, federal laws like the National Environmental Policy Act and the Federal Lands Policy and Management Act required BLM and high Interior officials to jump through the hoops of assessing a federal proposal's negative impacts, not only on the environment, but on the people most heavily affected.

How reliant were the Chaco Navajos on the land covering the coal which Watt wanted to turn over to industry? What really would happen to them? Of course they didn't want their land torn up, especially if they would get no monetary benefits from the mining, but those are the breaks that anyone would have to take in a similar situation.

The Watt mind-set held that people who opposed mineral development, especially energy mineral development, were soft-headed traitors, obstructionists, anti-American liberals. If these people were living over coal, why didn't they start a coal company, earn a lot of money on it, and go into Florida real estate?

Interior's attitude toward Navajo opponents to coal development in the Chaco-Bisti was simplistic: the Indians were in the way of progress and, besides, this was their chance to take part in the American Dream. It implied that the Indians had no valid culture of their own.

But to some field level Interior officials, the question of coal leasing impacts to the Chaco Navajo depended on how committed the Indians were to living within their existing pastoral culture. Would their lives be destroyed by strip mining away their territory, or would they be able to accommodate such a disruption with more or less the same flexibility of an average citizen?

Obviously the degree of commitment to the old culture varied greatly. Navajo men who joined the armed services in World War II and in the Korean War were much more acculturated to the dominant American society than those who had remained on their ranches and had never held jobs in the white man's world. The children tended to be more Americanized than the older people. Those who had been educated at boarding schools—one of the greatest acculturating influences on the Navajo people—tended to be 'less Navajo' than others who had lived at home during their schooling. College educated Navajos who may have taken classes in Berkeley, Boston or Albuquerque were naturally less dependent on the land and its abilities to provide subsistence livelihood. By and large, Navajo women seemed to be more tied to the land than the men, not an unusual sociological finding among indigenous peoples, and very predictable for the Navajo since their traditional society is matrilocal, meaning that the husband in a marriage goes to live in his wife's area, rather than the other way around. Lands tend to be inherited through a wife's side of the family.

One measure of the commitment held by individual Navajos to their old culture is, of course, their fluency in any other language; most women and many men living in the Chaco-Bisti coal region at the time of James Watt's scheme for massive leasing spoke only their native tongue.

But an even greater indicator of the Chaco Navajos' retention of the old cultural lifestyles—and hence a measure of their ability to deal with the dislocations inherent in strip mining their lands—was the extent to which traditional medicine men still played a role in everyday life. Given the number of people in the area (and the length of time the Indians had been living in the proximity of cities like Gallup, Farmington and Albuquerque, as well as the mobility provided by the ever-present pickup trucks, the number of church missions, and the penetration to such remote areas by radio) one might have expected to find only one or two practicing medicine men in the Chaco-Bisti area, serving elderly, culture-bound clients.

But when an informal survey by BLM field personnel tallied up more than 55 practicing medicine men in the coal region, it seemed clear that preservation of the old culture, the old way of life, would be of major importance to area residents. These people could not be expected to merely pick up their belongings and move away to let the coal be dug out.

The Navajos' continued reliance on medicine men as an integral part of society was solid evidence that a significant number of them were tied closely to the land emotionally and culturally. Strip mining the landscape would obliterate their cultural setting, eliminate the medicinal herbs from some areas, change the topography of landforms which served as religious sites and prayer offering points, render meaningless the functions of many age-old clan structures.

Massive strip mining would, in fact, mean a hideous attack on Mother Earth.

But few BLM or Interior officials were impressed by the Navajos' continual invocation of "Mother Earth". Some had heard it all a thousand times before: save "Mother Earth" from the wicked white rapist. To many federal officials, the cry for Mother Earth was nothing more than a ploy to gain an advantage at the negotiating table. If the Indians said 'no' to coal development it was because they were holding out for a bigger percentage of the take from marketing the coal, they argued. Perhaps the jaded federal officials had spent too much time in the company of coal and utility executives who totally rejected the Navajos' purported attachment to the land, too much time with people who knew that an alcoholic Indian would sell anything for the price of a bottle of whiskey.

"How can they expect us to believe that they have this great respect for Mother Earth . . . that mining coal would be such a horrible thing?" asked utility executive Bud Mulcock. "They've been backing their pickups up to coal outcrops for years and shoveling in coal to burn in their homes."

The pro-coal development mentality among some Interior officials and most industry representatives completely ignored the scale and impact of a few Navajos digging coal by the shovelful, a little at a time, compared to the cataclysmic effect of a 24-hour stripping dragline which drastically and irrevocably changes the face of the earth and destroys the meaning of life.

But questions involving the depth of Navajo culture, or the degree of dependence on the old ways, were not aspects given much attention in BLM land use planning, or during other decisions in the federal coal program. The psychology of the Navajo was, to be sure, not a major point on which plans for leasing billions of dollars worth of federal coal hinged. Instead, BLM veterans recognized that addressing the cultural and spiritual needs of the Chaco Navajo could only yield trouble. Such issues were deliberately ignored, or broad-brushed with such statements as: "Traditionally, they (Navajos) consider the earth sacred and many of their ceremonies were established to maintain the balance between their lives and the earth."

With a presumed mandate from Watt and Carruthers to clear obstacles out of the way of federal coal leasing, BLM officials at the field level easily persuaded themselves to ignore or downplay the negative impacts to the Navajo living over the coal. Instead of talking about sheep with no grass to eat, talk about the jobs, the paychecks, improved access to health care facilities, the opportunities to enter the mainstream of American life.

Not all Navajo, of course, wanted to depend on raising sheep all their lives. In fact, pressures on Indians, especially males, to get salaried jobs was great. Increasingly caught up in a cash economy, if only to pay the higher price for gasoline to maintain their mobility, Navajo families in the coal region recognized the need for expanded employment opportunities. New jobs were seen as necessary to keep children living in the area, rather than having to seek work in Albuquerque or other urban centers. But the same people who wanted new jobs for the Chaco-Bisti region were among those who vehemently opposed coal strip mining. That might seem contradictory to people who have never depended on subsistence livestock grazing; most BLM officials and energy company executives haven't. To the Navajo accustomed to living off the land, it's one thing to want and need a job, and quite another to be willing to tear up the land to gain the paycheck.

An essential point in understanding the Navajo's strong opposition to strip mining is the central role of family ranching as the mainstay of survival in a harsh world. As cash became increasingly important to Navajos, wage earning jobs naturally were in demand. But for many reasons the jobs rarely lasted very long, and the formerly employed Indians were back living off the land again, raising sheep and cattle for food and cash, weaving wool into Navajo rugs, cutting wood or digging coal to heat their homes. For the Navajo, livestock grazing was the safety net; they had the land to fall back on when their jobs didn't work out for reasons of work ethic, cultural obstacles, racism, or alcoholism.

Jobs were important, but it was the land that insured survival. What, then, if the job required destroying the land, as strip mining did?

The prospect of coal strip mining in the Chaco was widely recognized by local people as a looming disaster.

CHAPTER 4

PROFITEERING ON THE PUBLIC LANDS

It is hard to overestimate the manipulative power of Public Service Company of New Mexico (PNM), the state's largest utility. The effectiveness of its scheming is best known by people and groups it targets as enemies.

In early 1982, reportedly at the request of one of the utility company's subsidiaries, undercover agents with the New Mexico State Police began spying on environmentalists fighting the company's plan to open a strip mine in the Bisti Badlands, immediately bordering the now-designated federal Bisti Wilderness Area. The agent, son of a New Mexico Supreme Court Justice, infiltrated public meetings disguised as a news photographer to capture photos of PNM opponents, to be inserted in State Police files on potential sabotage of mining operations in the San Juan Basin.

Intimidation set in as soon as the targeted environmentalists (all highly-respected individuals within the New Mexico environmental community, and none with any history of political violence) learned of the State Police investigation. What citizens would want to speak out against a PNM project if it meant police undercover agents would be set loose to stalk them?

Topping off the feelings of intimidation, within eight weeks of learning they were targets, one of the most persistent and outspoken of these PNM critics was bludgeoned in her bed as she slept, by an unknown, 3 a.m. intruder who stole nothing, did not attempt rape, and got away after pounding her head and face more than four times, leaving a "message" of contusions and lacerations.

No one has accused PNM executives of instigating the severe beating. The targeted environmentalists now treat the police investigation and the brutal attack as unrelated. But the effect was certainly chilling.

Intimidating federal bureaucrats is much easier, considerably less risky, and undeniably effective.

Generally, civil servants in the Bureau of Land Management were dismayed when James Watt became their chief as Secretary of the Interior, shortly after Reagan won his first term. Many were recent converts to "environmentalism", important tenets of which were written into the bureau's first real statement of mission in the 1976 Federal Land Policy and Management Act (FLPMA). Two important implications of the act were that Congress told the career bureaucrats in no uncertain terms that their past management of the public lands had been overly-permissive, that they had abetted deterioration of the public domain, that they should clean up their acts and be more responsive to the public interest, not just accommodating to special interests. After the 1976 "organic act" spelled out their new responsibilities, many of the career BLM personnel took the environmental message to heart, and admitted to themselves and to co-workers that they had, in fact, been overseeing industry's pillage of the public wealth. The second implication of the 1976 act was a major expansion of BLM personnel, many of them young and idealistic professionals, to carry out the bureau's newly-defined mission. These new recruits, already steeped in environmental consciousness through natural resource management training at universities around the nation, injected a strong reinforcement for their superiors' freshly-instilled commitments.

For the veteran BLM officials, who had risen to positions of field-level decisionmaking by virtue of longevity if not competence, Watt's taking over at Interior meant they would now be forced into the old mold of accommodating industrial pillage; they would have to go against their consciences and their internalized commitments to the public interest as spelled out in FLPMA.

Besides, Watt the avowed "Sagebrush Rebel" would work to take away their turf, literally, and no bureaucrat would be expected to like that.

So there was considerable coffee-break complaining from BLM officials at all levels when Watt began sending down directives which the bureaucrats considered contrary to their FLPMA responsibilities. And the more dedicated of them were even inclined to balk in their official functions when directives from Watt and his underlings required them to break laws and regulations.

There was a need, therefore, to intimidate the bureaucrats as well as the environmentalists. How this intimidation worked and its effectiveness are described throughout this book. But an example here illustrates how PNM exercised its influence to this end.

Shortly after Watt's confirmation as Secretary, BLM Albuquerque District Manager Paul Applegate was called to visit the office of one of PNM's more influential vice-presidents, ostensibly to discuss one of the many pending utility company projects which required BLM approval. The meeting took place in the executive's plush, power-establishing office. Discussions covered many topics, but when the District Manager returned to his own office, the primary information he relayed to his staff was how much pull PNM had with Watt. The biggest impression Applegate received from the meeting, he said, was that he had been told by the PNM executive that Watt was their man; that PNM had, in fact, been responsible for Watt's being hired as director of Mountain States Legal Foundation, the pro-industry, Colorado-based organization which had been Watt's stepping stone to the secretariat.

The implication Applegate imparted to his staff was that Watt would make sure PNM got whatever it wanted, and that foot-dragging and problem-making in the local BLM office would be dealt with severely. Once the local BLM decisonmaker was convinced that the deck was thoroughly stacked in PNM's favor, through that incident and hundreds of others, the bureaucrats' survival instincts dictated how decisions would be made for the remainder of Watt's time in office.

Similar manipulations by PNM occur in other branches of local, state and federal government which can impact PNM's plans. Of course, powerful companies exercising their influence is as American as apple pie; the public has come to expect it. But what the public may not know, and would not condone if it did know, is the extent to which this use of influence by PNM largely dictates not only what happens to publicly-owned mineral wealth in the San Juan Basin, and to the long-term economic well-being of the people of New Mexico, but controls the state's cultural, scientific and academic life as well.

New Mexicans know, of course, about the new Museum of Natural History constructed in Albuquerque to display the state's treasure of dinosaurs and other fossils . . . but do they know the extent to which PNM controls the museum and why?

To understand the utility company's exercise of power, one must know what it has at stake in northwestern New Mexico and throughout the Southwest.

In the national economic context, PNM is a large frog in a small pond . . . or more accurately, a large horned toad in the arid Sunbelt. In the late 1970s and early 1980s, when PNM began its conquest of the San Juan Basin in earnest, the utility's executives were headstrong with bulging profits. PNM's after-tax profits in 1979 were $54 million, a whopping 120 percent increase from two years before. In 1979, when other utilities around the country were looking at profits of only 10 to 12 percent of total revenues, PNM hauled in 22.4 percent. It was, in fact, one of the fastest growing utilities in the nation.

PNM listed assets of $1.7 billion at the end of September 1981, most of which came from supplying electricity to half a million customers in New Mexico. The company owned 13 percent of two generating units at the Four Corners Generating Station outside Farmington, as a partner with Arizona Public Service Company, Southern California Edison, Salt River Project, Tucson Gas and Electric and El Paso Electric. PNM also owned half of each of three units in its San Juan Generating Station, and some 92 percent of a fourth unit there. The company was already diversified, with a coal company subsidiary, a water utility, a real estate subsidiary, a fiberboard manufacturing plant and other ventures, before it acquired the largest natural gas utility in the state, Gas Company of New Mexico, in 1984. PNM reported total operating revenues of $203.3 million for the quarter ending March 31, 1985.

Compared to other utility companies, and comparing its coal mining subsidiary to other coal companies, PNM could show itself to be an enlightened, even progressive firm, fully measuring up to its corporate responsibilities to the community at large. The company has made a point of distinguishing itself from Arizona Public Service Company (APS), prime operator of the heavily-polluting Four Corners power plant outside Farmington. With appropriate hoopla, PNM installed expensive anti-pollution devices on its smokestacks when it built its San Juan Generating Station in the early 1970s, near APS's Four Corners Station. Company officials publicly urged the management of APS to do its part by installing pollution control equipment as well. APS, by contrast, had to be hauled into court after repeated violations of air standards, and would install the air cleaners only on court order.

And unlike APS, PNM has gone lightly on its commitments to nuclear power, a corporate choice which has pleased environmentalists and investors alike. It owns 10 percent of Arizona's Palo Verde Nuclear Generating Station, and has no other direct interests in nuclear power production. Instead, PNM has concentrated on coal, and on coal that it controls in its own immediate area. PNM has carved out the San Juan Basin as its sphere of influence.

It may be just a toad in the desert, compared to New York's Consolidated Edison, or Los Angeles' Southern California Edison, but this toad has millions of tons of coal that it owns or has high expectations of controlling. And it has that coal right next to its power plants, so that it isn't at the mercy of rail freight increases like those two giant utilities on the coasts. It has cheap labor and relatively clean air that it expects to be able to pollute before exceeding total clean air standards.

But PNM needs a partner to take full advantage of these corporate pluses. That partner is the Bureau of Land Management.

In large measure, PNM's strength in the power generating business depends on the degree of cooperation it receives from six bureaus within the Department of the Interior: the Bureau of Land Management, which administers much of the land surface and minerals in the San Juan Basin; the Bureau of Indian Affairs, which administers other public lands in the coal-rich area held in trust for the Navajo Indians, and provides high-leverage counseling to the tribal government; the Office of Surface Mining, which monitors mining companies' strip mining activities to assure that the lands are reclaimed; the U.S. Fish and Wildlife Service, which works to protect threatened and endangered species from development proposals over which the federal government has some authority; the National Park Service, which manages parks and works to assure compliance with laws and regulations regarding cultural resources (archeological sites) which might be possible additions to the the park system; and the U.S. Geological Survey, which determines the value of publicly-owned minerals to assure that the U.S. Treasury gets full price for minerals made available to mining companies.

Of these agencies, it is the Bureau of Land Management that most shapes PNM's future. The Albuquerque District of BLM (which administers 2.8 million acres of public land and the mineral estate under 8 million acres, most of which is in the San Juan Basin) is inextricably linked to PNM's plans. As guardian of the public's land and minerals in the San Juan Basin, BLM's Albuquerque office:

- Administers more than 30 billion tons of coal;

- Controls the land surface in the areas closest to the most economically mineable coal where PNM would therefore like to build its mine-mouth, coal-fired power plants;

- Controls the surface over which PNM must construct powerlines to carry that electricity from the power plants to its customers;

- Must protect eagles and other endangered wildlife species that would be disturbed by PNM's industrial activities;

- Must protect the thousands of archeological sites on public land that would be torn up by strip mining;

- Must protect important fossils lying over and amid the public's coal;

- Must protect pristine areas for possible inclusion in the National Wilderness Preservation System; and, of course,

- Must protect the people in a given area from adverse socio-economic impacts which might result from its approval of industrial proposals.

In blunt terms, it can cost PNM many millions of dollars if BLM attempts to force strict compliance with federal laws and regulations. Conversely, BLM can save PNM millions if the federal agency is lenient and tends to see matters from the corporation's point of view.

PNM's market position in the growing Sunbelt, then, depends in large measure on how cooperative its junior partner is.

In 1970, the company began its move away from gas- and oil-fired generating stations in favor of coal, and specifically, mine-mouth power plants. Vice-president for Engineering and Operations Jerry Geist was tapped to oversee this transition, and six years later Geist took control of the company as president. Fifteen years later, PNM's generating capacity was 90 percent converted to coal.

And who owns this coal on which PNM pinned its future? The public. It is mostly a publicly-owned resource; some is administered by the State of New Mexico through the State Land Office, and some is privately-held, but by far the largest portion of the easily strippable coal in PNM's self-designated sphere of influence is owned by the U.S. public.

The San Juan Generating Station on the northern edge of New Mexico's San Juan Basin was the big step along PNM's route to coal dependency. Planned by Geist, the power plant gave the Farmington area the distinction of hosting the largest concentration of coal-fired electrical generation west of the Mississippi. Under contracts with the Navajo tribal government, the Four Corners plant was fed by the huge, open pit Navajo Mine on the reservation, while Geist's San Juan plant on private land burned coal from its San Juan Mine, using mostly federal coal leases.

With its first units completed in 1973, the San Juan plant provided almost 60 percent of the electricity sold in PNM's service area. Once all four units were in operation, at a cost of more than $1 billion, the plant would produce 1,600 megawatts daily. But that much electricity takes a lot of coal; with only two units operating, the San Juan Mine was feeding 7,500 tons of coal a day to the furnaces. In the early 1970s, PNM was already hungry for additional federal coal leases to keep the new generators turning.

PNM's coal acquisition activities at that time were led by Western Coal Company, a PNM joint venture with Tucson Electric Power Company, which began acquiring leases on federal coal deposits in northwestern New Mexico. Western acquired several more federal leases around the new power plant, and three federal coal leases in the Bisti area, some 45 miles southeast of the San Juan Generating Station.

It was soon clear that PNM had designs far grander than simply assuring an adequate coal supply for its San Juan Generating Station. Even before the four generating units at the new plant were in operation, PNM was maneuvering the Albuquerque District of BLM into a position where public land in the Bisti, next to its new coal leases, would be turned over to PNM for yet another large power plant.

From the mid-1970s on, PNM left no stone unturned in attempting to coerce BLM into turning over public resources in the San Juan Basin, land and minerals, for the unfolding of PNM's power trip.

By 1985, 15 years after then-PNM Vice-president Geist began the company's reorientation away from oil and gas to coal as PNM's fuel of preference, the utility had control over more than 75 square miles of coal lands in the Bisti region. PNM had plans for a company town of 20,000 people, again on land it expected to get from BLM, and plans for an aluminum manufacturing plant (using aluminum content in the flyash waste from its furnaces), and it had a 55,000-acre ranch in the area, most of it coal-rich rangeland leased from BLM.

There were, to be sure, many pitfalls along the way, and many opportunities for BLM and other Interior agencies to demonstrate their responsiveness to industry needs.

For example, PNM faced a formidable problem posed by the rich archeological heritage that lay atop the coal seams it wanted. In the heart of PNM's sphere of influence in northwestern New Mexico were the ruins of the great and mysterious Chacoan Anasazi civilization, lost cities of which were still being discovered even as the coal lease acquisition process was under way.

BLM cultural resource specialists estimated that PNM's coveted San Juan Basin contained 250,000 archeological sites, not all of which were considered important enough for *in situ* preservation, but from which research should certainly help piece together answers to lingering archeological puzzles. As the company was grabbing up coal assets during the 1970s, archeological research in the area (some conducted by PNM's own specialists) was unfolding a cultural resource treasure never before realized. Although attention had been focused on the spectacular ruins in Chaco Canyon for half a century, it was only in the mid-1970s that archeologists began to realize the true extent and significance of what had taken place there and in the surrounding area for hundreds of years before Europeans set foot in the San Juan Basin. Mounds of rubble that ranchers and sheep herders had stumbled upon years ago were suddenly discovered to be "Chacoan Outliers", or satellite towns linked administratively to an imperial headquarters in Chaco Canyon. And the archeologists kept finding more of these outliers. Then, using aerial photography and ground checking, the researchers stunned the archeological community nationwide by announcing that these prehistoric towns—not cliff dwellings, not pit huts, or tipi concentrations, but towns of multiple-storied buildings and complex master planning—were in fact linked by engineered roadways.

Nowhere else in North America had prehistoric civilizations developed such highly-planned and carefully-engineered cities and causeways. And they were being discovered right over the coal beds that PNM wanted to strip mine.

Clearly PNM had a problem. Federal laws and regulations already on the books required agencies like BLM to pay careful attention to archeological sites, especially sites on public land. Across the country, discovery of cultural resource sites where companies wanted to locate projects, even on private land, had already stopped many a project cold. As BLM archeologists read their responsibilities, their agency could not approve such projects as federal coal leasing, land exchanges, or powerline right-of-way easements on public land without thoroughly evaluating the cultural resources on the lands in question. That included strong possibilities that a project might have to be abandoned entirely, or relocated, so that important sites would be undisturbed. Well-established procedures required that BLM study such sites and recommend important ones for inclusion in the National Register of Historic Places. Federal regulations stated that even a finding that such a site was "suitable" for inclusion on the National Register was sufficient to halt agency approval for projects which threatened the site.

What would become, then, of PNM's grand design if the federal coal it wanted was no longer available due to archeological discoveries?

The company's response took several forms. The most positive and effective strategy was to enlist the help of New Mexico's congressional delegation in pushing for passage of legislation which drastically upgraded Chaco Canyon from "national monument" status to that of a national historic park which specifically included several of the major Chacoan Outliers. Naturally supported by the National Park Service, the measure passed and the Chaco Culture National Historical Park was designated in 1981.

From PNM's perspective that cleared away a big part of the archeological problem. To the demand that archeological sites in its sphere of influence needed to be preserved, PNM could now respond, "That's already been taken care of." The effect, then, of the legislation expanding and re-designating Chaco Canyon National Monument was to leave the rest of the San Juan Basin open to coal exploitation . . . never mind that many of the region's archeological sites had yet to be discovered, much less thoroughly evaluated.

Another part of PNM's strategy was to pressure BLM to go easy on surveys to find new archeological sites. Just go ahead and lease the coal, PNM said, we'll take care of the archeological surveys later, when our people work out the mine plans.

A 1979 incident at an internal BLM meeting on cultural resources in the coal region illustrates the attitude among high-ranking BLM officials regarding archeological obstacles to coal development. In a conference room in Santa Fe's Federal Building, then-Assistant State Director of BLM Larry Woodard, already notorious internally for favoring PNM's interests, listened to a delegation from the Albuquerque District Office making a plea for increased effort in identifying cultural resource sites in the San Juan coal region. In the course of technical recommendations on what might be done, Albuquerque District Archeologist Randy Morrison suggested an initial agency-sponsored attempt to evaluate the significance of the prehistoric road network linking the Chacoan Outliers in order to determine what protective measure would be required if federal coal were to be leased under the ancient roads.

Assistant State Director Woodard interrupted to assert that the prehistoric roads did not exist. A bristling confrontation developed, with the BLM archeologist insisting that the roads were real, while the Number Two BLM official in New Mexico was adamant that the Chacoan roads were fiction. The archeologist, who had himself discovered and followed several of the road segments leading to Chacoan ruins, finally sputtered that the ancient roads did exist, in fact, whether Woodard admitted it or not. To which the BLM Assistant State Director replied: "Look, it doesn't matter whether they exist or not, because we're going to mine through them anyway."

That was the pro-industry attitude prevalent at BLM New Mexico headquarters even before James Watt headed Interior.

BLM did eventually conduct a two-phase study of the Chacoan road system although top officials were exceedingly reluctant to fund it, and did so only with the understanding beforehand that the study itself constituted the only mitigation measure which would be given to the prehistoric roads; that is, it was decided at the outset that there would be no preservation of the amazing road system.

Even after PNM's successful tidying-up strategy supporting an expanded Chaco Culture National Historical Park, a bundle of potential problems remained. For one, there was the federal Clean Air Act and its amendments and regulations which called for maintaining clean air in national parks. The vistas of our national parks are to be preserved by discouraging smog and haze from industrial activities. PNM, of course, intended to build a new four-unit, coal-fired, smoke-producing power plant just 13 miles from the newly-designated national park. Again, an accommodation was worked out to permit a degradation of air quality in the new park.

Similarly, when PNM executives saw they faced a challenge for use of these coal-rich public lands from wilderness preservation enthusiasts, they sought congressional help to limit the challenge. At a time when other pro-industry groups were arguing against the validity of the concept of federally-protected wilderness areas in general, and against protection for the heavily-eroded Bisti Badlands specifically, PNM officials were collaborating with New Mexico Senator Pete Domenici to obtain congressional approval for exchanging federal coal leases they already had in the Bisti for other federal coal leases outside the BLM-drawn boundaries of the proposed Bisti Wilderness Area. In 1980, with the support of the Sierra Club, PNM and BLM announced that the Bisti Coal Lease Exchange proposal had been approved by Congress. A 3,590-acre portion of the Bisti, which already had PNM coal leases on it, would be kept available for congressional action to designate it part of the National Wilderness Preservation System.

The action also provided congressional blessing for strip mining other parts of the Bisti, still in the vicinity of PNM's proposed mine-mouth Bisti power plant.

But again the question of air quality arose from this action. Now that part of the Bisti was as good as saved for federal wilderness designation, would a future PNM power plant be allowed to degrade the air, and thereby the scenic vistas, in a federal wilderness area? Would BLM agree to trade away public land to be used for a smoke-producing power plant a scant three to four miles from pristine land it intended to preserve as a federal wilderness area? The 1977 amendments to the Clean Air Act had strengthened efforts to maintain air quality in regions where the air was already relatively clean, and held there should not be any "significant deterioration" in Class I air quality regions which specifically were to include federal wilderness areas as well as national parks. BLM studied the matter and decided it would be all right to pollute; that the soon-to-be Bisti Wilderness Area would not be designated a Class I air quality area, because it had not been a wilderness area at the time of the 1977 amendment.

PNM's solution to the fossil dilemma took a different course.

Shortly after passage of the Federal Land Policy and Management Act (FLPMA) of 1976, and noting the eighth point in its 13-point declaration of policy (". . . the public lands [shall] be managed in a manner that will protect the quality of scientific, scenic, historical, ecological, environmental, air and atmospheric, water resource and archeological values; . . ."), the District Manager of the BLM's Albuquerque Office hired a paleontologist to evaluate the fossil resource in the San Juan Basin and to make recommendations on how the bureau should treat them.

If coal was to be mined in northwestern New Mexico, it was certain that dinosaur bones and remnants of many other extinct species would be unearthed in the process.

Fossils from the late Cretaceous Period (65-70 million years ago) extracted from the San Juan Basin were important to the overall study of paleontology around the world. Demonstrating as they did the species mix and ecological context at the time of the demise of Earth's large reptiles and the assumption of dominance by the early forms of mammals, the fossil-laden strata in northwestern New Mexico had already yielded important specimens studied and exhibited in museums and laboratories nationwide.

Fossilized dinosaurs and other ancient creatures had been dug up and hauled out of the San Juan Basin for more than 100 years when Dr. Keith Rigby joined the BLM in Albuquerque in the late 1970s and began delineating areas of high paleontological potential—much of which coincided closely with the best coal strip mine areas.

BLM recognized its FLPMA-mandated responsibilities to protect those scientific resources and not let them be destroyed deliberately or inadvertantly by federally-approved strip mining. But clearly the coal companies and PNM would do their best to see that federal coal areas were not ruled off limits to them due to the presence of some old bones.

Just as public and professional excitement about the Chacoan ruins was building at the same time that the companies sought to nail down their claims to the public coal in the San Juan Basin, so, too, was public support coalescing for a New Mexico-based museum to display dinosaurs from the basin. A public outcry against exploitation was being voiced by local paleontologists and the abundant rockhound clubs, demanding an end to the tradition of New Mexico fossils being shipped off to museums in New York, Chicago, London and elsewhere. Nowhere in New Mexico, they rightly pointed out, was there a home-grown dinosaur displayed. A privately-organized "Dimes for Dinosaurs" fundraising effort captured the public's imagination and commitment.

Faced with a growing movement to "save the dinosaurs", PNM set out another containment strategy: downplay the importance of the fossils while hammering out a loose, nonmandatory state-federal-industry agreement as to how the mining companies were to react upon discovering fossils during mining. A third prong of the strategy by PNM and some mining companies was to throw their weight behind plans to build a state-run (PNM-controlled) museum of natural history to display fossils extracted from the basin and elsewhere. When PNM Chairman Jerry Geist turned over a $250,000 check to the museum's directors in April 1985 as a contribution to the building fund, some saw it as a payoff for museum policies which would not hamper PNM's plans to mine coal.

And lastly, the companies touted the importance of mining to acquisition of bones to fill the proposed museum. Coal executives claimed that nothing could boost paleontological research like a good coal mining dragline. More fossils would be found by digging up and exposing the hidden bones in the course of mining than would be found by generations of paleontologists who waited for the fossils to expose themselves by natural erosion, they argued.

BLM's shifting position in the midst of the fossil controversy illustrates the results of industry influence.

Initially, under Dr. Rigby's recommendations, BLM was to designate certain areas of the San Juan Basin as FLPMA-authorized "areas of critical environmental concern", calling for special management plans to maximize (or at least avoid minimizing) the study or recovery of paleontological resources in those specific areas. Next, BLM would conduct rigorous field work to identify and possibly excavate important fossil locations, particularly in areas that might be jeopardized by strip mining. Also, any coal leases issued in the coal zone would contain strict stipulations for notification of BLM and others in the paleontological community in the event that fossils of a specific nature were uncovered during mining. And BLM was to establish a permanent, on-the-ground presence in the coal area, by means of a BLM "Bisti Multiple Resource Center" (to include paleontologists, archeologists, wilderness specialists, geologists and other staff) so that BLM experts could respond quickly to fossils found during mining to evaluate, and extract, them if necessary.

In addition, BLM was to preserve intact a specific paleobotanical area known as "Fossil Forest", to serve not only as a permanent research site, but as a scientific benchmark for other Cretaceous Period research around the world.

None of that happened, and Dr. Rigby was forced out of the BLM for his efforts, largely through pressures brought by PNM and coal company executives.

In 1984, BLM signed an agreement allowing the coal companies to monitor themselves while digging through paleontological areas; the natural history museum was opened in Albuquerque in

1986 with the coal industry dictating who would be selected to head it; the sophisticated paleontological equipment which Dr. Rigby had acquired for the Albuquerque District BLM was given away to New Mexico State University in Las Cruces at the insistence of then-Interior Assistant Secretary Garrey Carruthers (who held a tenured professorship there); the plan for a Bisti Multiple Resource Center to monitor industry activity in the area was totally scuttled; and by 1985, the BLM Albuquerque District had no paleontologist at all.

If BLM was prepared to accommodate PNM's plans in these relatively minor ways, the turn over of more than 7,000 acres of publicly-owned land in the Bisti to the utility company for a power plant was a somewhat more difficult task. How could BLM agree to give PNM this public land when the implications of such a transaction meant major degradation to a national park and a high-priority federal wilderness area, probable destruction of a central part of one of the most intriguing archeological districts in the nation, certain devastation to paleontological areas of worldwide significance, and dislocation of hundreds, if not thousands, of Navajos?

With James Watt on its side, PNM certainly had a fighting chance. Anyone reading the newspapers knew—and certainly BLM field level managers knew—that if Watt were asked to choose between coal mining and wilderness areas or national parks or fossils or dirt-poor sheep ranchers, he would not hesitate to call in the draglines. Still, BLM would have to find a way to justify giving up some 7,700 acres of public land in the Chaco-Bisti so that PNM could have private land (next to the federal coal) on which to build its pet project, the New Mexico Generating Station. That justification was to be the public interest that presumably would be served by BLM acquiring a piece of privately-owned land along the canyon rim above the BLM-managed Rio Grande Wild and Scenic River next to the Colorado border north of Taos, New Mexico. The land is a mostly bare, non-descript bump of a hill known as Ute Mountain.

How BLM and PNM contrived to foist off Ute Mountain in exchange for the Bisti lands sought for a power plant is a lesson in political corruption and deceit. It required the distortion of a federal land use plan, violation of the National Environmental Policy Act, violation of the American Indian Religious Freedom Act, violation of the Freedom of Information Act, and disregard of numerous other federal regulations. That story is told in Chapter 9, "Land Grab for a Power Plant".

The successfulness of PNM's manipulations are largely due to its relative financial strength in a state with little economic clout, and to its recruitment of politically influential people into its corporate hierarchy. PNM's corporate offices in Albuquerque are now home for people who were formerly string-pullers with the Department of the Interior in Washington. Joe Browder, for example, was formerly special assistant to Interior Secretary Cecil Andrus, involved in federal coal leasing matters, and before that, directly involved with the Washington-based Environmental Policy Institute which specialized in coal leasing matters; he became a special assistant to PNM President Geist. Similarly, Joellyn Murphy, former assistant director of BLM in Washington headquarters, joined PNM's staff and became vice-president for governmental and regulatory affairs; the daughter of former BLM New Mexico State Director Art Zimmerman is now the official PNM spokesperson; former Albuquerque Mayor David Rusk, son of former U.S. Secretary of State Dean Rusk, was hired on as head of PNM's Issues Analysis Section, and later became director of corporate communications.

But the influence interlockings go much deeper and are more subtle than that. The company's board of directors displays the normal links throughout the New Mexico economy, yet some of the other hidden ties are especially revealing: PNM's director of industrial development, Joe Zanetti, for example, also served as president of the new Museum of Natural History's policy advisory committee, which was the primary body responsible for selecting the museum's director. The museum's policy on whether to halt coal mining operations in the Chaco-Bisti to retrieve fossils is a matter of grave importance to PNM. The utility company's financial contributions and policy-setting role have given the firm a far greater influence over the museum than most New Mexicans realize.

When the museum opened in 1986, the thousands of people who had contributed to the "Dimes for Dinosaurs" campaign which originally launched the natural history project had ample reason to feel cheated. After expenditure of millions of tax dollars, they still had no New Mexico dinosaurs on display. As a product of museum policy, what they got instead were Disney-like plaster castings of dinosaur bones. The new facility had razzle-dazzle educational gimmicks, but very few real fossils from the Bisti region or anywhere else.

In a published review of the museum opening, Spencer Lucas, curator of geology at the University of New Mexico, found the general absence of New Mexico fossils disturbing: "My most serious criticism concerns the almost total absence of real fossils in the displays. Instead, casts—plaster and plastic replicas—populate the many exhibits devoted to the fossil record."

Zanetti resigned from PNM in May 1986, but continues to serve as an industrial development consultant to the utility company and is still head of the museum's policy advisory board.

CHAPTER FIVE

BUT THE PUBLIC EXPRESSES ITS 'PUBLIC INTEREST'

What's so wrong about a private company manipulating a government office to get what it wants? Nothing really, as long as the agency does not succumb and begin acting against the public interest. If civil servants respond as well to a wide range of other legitimate interests as they do to corporate interests, then the governmental process works as it is supposed to. A big reason why the public has come to accept as normal civil servants who bend over backward to accommodate corporate interests is that frequently there is no other "interest" being expressed. That is, sometimes the public defaults through apathy or indifference, so that the bureaucrats have only one sector making demands—the corporations' public relations and governmental affairs officers pushing for favors.

But the public did not default on its land and other resources in the San Juan Basin.

For many reasons, the public did not just sit back and forfeit whatever interests it might have in the public lands of northwestern New Mexico. Instead, people throughout the state, and from around the United States, took exception to the view that the seemingly barren lands were good for nothing better than indiscriminate strip mining. Groups organized for other purposes, like the New Mexico Wildlife Federation, the Audubon Society, the Sierra Club, the American Indian Environmental Council, New Mexicans for Clean Air and Water, the New Mexico Archeological Society, the Rio Rancho Rockhound Club, the New Mexico Mountain Club, school teachers, sheep herders, botanists, retirees and many other segments of society at large brought their opinions to bear.

That's what is supposed to happen in a democracy, and when it does, it puts a conscientious civil servant in an enviable situation; he or she can weigh the common good, strike compromise positions for balanced decisions, and notify competing interests (and superiors in the bureaucracy) that they got the best they could hope for given the degree of opposition. Without that competition, the bureaucrat must nearly always buckle to the sole pressure group making demands; without competing demands he has only his conscience and professional judgment to help him withstand the often ruthless pressures exerted by corporate interests.

Public pressure, then, specifically vociferous and persistent public pressure, is what allows a dedicated federal bureaucrat to do what he knows is right.

That's the human nature side of the "public involvement" process. There's also the legal side. If traditionally big corporations got what they wanted from the government, at the expense of the public at large, it was the recognition of that fact that led Congress to write into law requirements for citizen participation in federal decisionmaking. Although requirements for public involvement are mandated across the board (in regulatory agencies as divergent as the Nuclear Regulatory Commission and the Federal Trade Commission) in no governmental bailiwick did this seem more appropriate than in the Bureau of Land Management. Here, after all, was a agency that was charged with managing the public's land and resources.

The Federal Land Policy and Management Act (FLPMA) of 1976 says in the fifth sentence of its declaration of policy that "in administering public land statutes and exercising discretionary authority granted by them, the Secretary [of the Interior] be required to establish comprehensive rules and regulations *after considering the views of the general public,* and to structure adjudication procedures to assure adequate third party participation, objective administrative review of initial decisions, and expeditious decisionmaking." In its third section, the law spells out what it means by "public involvement" in BLM's activities: "The term 'public involvement' means the opportunity for participation by affected citizens in rulemaking, decisionmaking, and planning with respect to the public lands, including public meetings or hearings held at locations near the affected lands, or advisory mechanisms, or such other procedures as may be necessary to provide public comment in a particular instance."

Repeatedly, the senators and congressmen who passed FLPMA stressed the importance of public involvement in BLM's programs, particularly relating to land use planning; "the Secretary shall, *with public involvement* and consistent with the terms and conditions of this Act, develop, maintain, and when appropriate, revise land use plans which provide by tracts or areas for the use of the public lands." Further: "The Secretary shall allow an opportunity for public involvement and by regulation shall establish procedures, including public hearings where appropriate, to give Federal, State, and local governments and the public, adequate notice and opportunity to comment upon and participate in the formulation of plans and programs relating to the management of the public lands."

It is entirely clear, then, that Congress intended for the public's expression of its wishes to be weighed carefully and thoroughly as BLM went about its business. It was written into BLM's organic act that the agency was not to assume as a foregone conclusion that whatever industry wanted, industry got.

From the start, BLM officials directly responsible for management of public lands in the San Juan Basin were hearing from the public. Since the 1960s, members of the public were pushing for preservation of the scenic Bisti Badlands, thousands of acres of other-worldly geologic formations on public land where normal traces of man's intrusions are systematically erased by severe natural erosion. And dinosaur hunters had expressed an interest in these public lands even earlier. Public support for preserving the vanishing habitat for America's Bald Eagle added to the interests competing for the use of the public lands. But perhaps more than any of these, it was the American Indians' use of the lands, prehistorically and contemporaneously, which weighed in most heavily when BLM officials began to consider the demands made by the coal companies.

Relative to other states, New Mexico may have more 'archeology' than any other place in the nation. Given its dry, preservative climate, the general lack of thick, obscuring vegetative cover, and above all the existence of still-inhabited Pueblo Indian towns dating back hundreds of years, it is easy for today's residents and visitors to be reminded of archeology in New Mexico. As tourist visits to the spectacular Anasazi ruins in Chaco Canyon rose dramatically in the 1960s and 1970s, so did public opposition to coal strip mining in this fascinating archeological region.

Likewise, public sentiment favoring the American Indians' right to be left alone, to live traditional lifestyles if they so chose, played an important part in public involvement affecting BLM as it addressed corporate interests. It was not so much that the Indians' wishes had to predominate as it was that the government should not be seen by the public to be an oppressor of the Indians. From the start, what the general public thought of the Indians' plight was more important than what the Indians themselves thought.

Still, through countless local Navajo chapter meetings, chapter resolutions, legal aid lawsuits and other means, the Indian residents of the federal coal region had made it abundantly clear they opposed a federal coal program which would convert the land they used for subsistence grazing into strip mines.

Even as the over-all coal program was being hammered out in Washington in 1980, Indians on the eastern edge of the reservation staged an armed takeover of a coal mine to protest draglines raking through Indian burial grounds.

That was the context in which the Albuquerque District BLM found itself at the start of its land use planning process in 1979. The Federal Coal Leasing Amendments Act of 1976 and the Surface Mining Control and Reclamation Act of 1977 required that lands overlying mineable federal coal not be leased to coal companies without first undergoing comprehensive land use planning. The Code of Federal Regulations implementing those laws amplified the procedures to be used prior to offering public coal for lease, and the regulations further institutionalized not only the land use planning process but the public involvement process as well.

Knowing he would encounter substantial public interest in the coal-related land use planning he was about to initiate for the San Juan Basin, BLM Albuquerque District Manager Paul Applegate in 1979 hired a public participation specialist as his public affairs officer, the first such officer assigned at a district office level in New Mexico. Over the next five years, covering the two-year planning process and three years of maneuvering toward the first competitive coal lease sale to come from the land use plan, "the public" expressed its public interest repeatedly and well, and it called for BLM caution in selecting lands it would offer to coal companies.

Rapport between local BLM officials and non-industry groups like Sierra Club, The Wilderness Society, and New Mexico Wildlife Federation had rarely been better than at the time when the San Juan Basin land use planning effort got under way. This was in the after-glow of environmentalist successes such as the National Environmental Policy Act, the Federal Land Policy and Management Act, and other legislative and administrative measures which made such groups feel they could be a part of the process, rather than forever fighting pre-ordained decisions. Through its various acts in the mid-1970s, the federal government had promised it would be responsive to the public interest, and to a wide range of "publics" with special interests. Groups at the national and local level were optimistic that real achievements had been made, and that they could, in fact, participate in federal decisionmaking when their interests might be affected.

Combining with that positive attitude was the opportunity for such groups and BLM to work together for a common cause: retention of the public lands in public ownership. In the West, the "Sagebrush Rebellion" made allies of BLM and the Sierra Club. If the BLM took a dim view of the movement by ranchers and mining companies to take the public lands out of the government's hands, so did the hunters, the rockhounds, the pro-wilderness advocates, the dirtbikers, the hikers, the archeologists, the paleontologists and a full spectrum of other users of the public lands who foresaw themselves being shut out literally and figuratively if the "Sagebrush Rebellion" were successful. In 1979, a N.M. Public Lands Coalition was formed by such groups, led by Will Ouellette, a Sandia Laboratories engineer, of the New Mexico Wildlife Federation, and Jean Herzegh, a Sierra Club member active in the fight to preserve the Bisti Badlands. The local Albuquerque District of BLM provided important, if furtive, assistance to the counter-rebellion.

When a "Sagebrush Rebellion" bill was introduced in the New Mexico Legislature in 1980, aimed at turning control of federal lands in the state over to the state government (and thence, presumably, over to private owners), it was soundly defeated. But the more important results of that short-lived coalition were the personal relationships developed between BLM officials and these non-industry activists. Built on the feeling they had fought a battle together and won, a sense of trust and cooperation lingered long after the coalition ceased to exist.

Working with this rapport among citydwellers experienced in asserting their needs for recreation on public land, the BLM Albuquerque District launched its public involvement effort for land use planning in the San Juan Basin. However, it was easy to see that while the Sierra Club and other interest groups were concerned about the possible outcome of coal-related planning for the San Juan Basin, other groups would be even more directly affected by the results. Coal mining interests, including mining employees and people engaged in support industries in Farmington and Gallup, needed to know what might happen under various plan scenarios. And of course, there were the Navajo who inhabited the coal region. A public participation plan was devised to draw all of these groups, and others from the amorphous "general public", into the BLM planning process starting in early 1980.

One of the first steps taken in trying to gauge the breadth and depth of the public interest in the coal-related issues was a series of field interviews with individuals and members of organizations known to be, or expected to be, interested in the outcome of the planning effort. Opinions varied, naturally, depending on whether the impacts from mining were seen to be favorable or unfavorable. Community leaders in the towns on the periphery of the San Juan Basin generally viewed a startup of the federal coal leasing program as a boon to their economic well-being, while subsistence Navajo ranchers saw the program as likely to destroy their way of life.

One of the people interviewed in early 1980 was the president of a bank in Grants. For him, the federal program would breathe new life into the sagging local economy. Grants' economic future had been tied to the uranium mining and milling industry since the 1950s, and the uranium bust cycle had set in hard in 1980. The banker saw increased interest in coal extraction as the lifesaver Grants sorely needed. As far as he was concerned, coal would become more important to Grants than uranium ever was.

Another person interviewed, a teacher at a Bureau of Indian Affairs school in Pueblo Pintado, in the heart of the coal region, saw little positive resulting from the mining of coal in his area. He was worried that the mining would destroy significant archeological sites. Pointing to the impressive Chacoan Outlier ruin a short distance to the west, silhouetted on the horizon, he said the ancient ruins were an inspiration to current Navajo residents of the region. "Life can be very hard out here," he said. "But we have these Anasazi sites around us to remind us that we can not only survive, but can thrive and achieve great things."

A coal mine reclamation specialist working west of Gallup expressed serious doubts about the ability of the land to recover permanently from strip mining. That was not the company point of view, he hastily pointed out, because according to the executives, reclamation would be no problem. Drawing on several years' experience with different mining companies, he said the poor soils and scant precipitation were only part of the difficulties. A big deterrent was that company officials generally have no real commitment to reclamation. Their lack of seriousness about rehabilitating the land trickles down to the heavy equipment operators who knowingly drive through "reclaimed" areas, destroying or compromising the rehabilitation work. "They know that the company is in business to dig coal out, not to grow plants."

A Navajo tribal government official in Crownpoint directing a program to develop jobs for Navajo workers was expected to be pro-mining since it would create jobs for area residents. He was, instead, deeply concerned about the disruptions that strip mining would have for his people. "We keep telling you (the federal government) that we don't want strip mining here, but you don't seem to understand the word "no". We say "no" and they send somebody else out to ask us again. And we tell the new person "no". But you only hear the word "yes". Let one Navajo out here say "yes" just one time, and that will get heard." Tears welled in his eyes as he spoke.

Then in the summer of 1980, working with a public participation budget of more than $10,000, BLM initiated a series of public meetings throughout the coal region and in Farmington, Gallup and Albuquerque to allow the public to inform the BLM planning team what issues should be dealt with in the plan, and what they thought the plan should provide. Special effort was made in communicating with the Navajo residents of the coal region; discussions at meetings in Crownpoint, Ojo Encino, Lake Valley, Pueblo Pintado, and other communities were translated English to Navajo and Navajo to English.

The BLM planning team working in its Farmington office began to gain insights on where federal coal leasing, if any, should take place. Parts of the planning process seemed relatively cut-and-dried; they were required to subject all of the potential coal lands to the 20 "Unsuitability Criteria" derived from the Surface Mining Control and Reclamation Act. Cemeteries were to be off-limits to leasing for coal, as were nesting areas for federally-protected threatened or endangered species such as eagles and falcons. Also to be considered unsuitable were archeological sites eligible for inclusion on the National Register of Historic Places, and areas under consideration for inclusion in the National Wilderness Preservation System. Presumably a good-faith effort to screen out those areas and others covered by the Unsuitability Criteria would be a relatively simple matter.

The guts of the planning effort would be the more subjective land use trade-off decisions. Given that a specific tract of land could be used for grazing sheep, or for long-term paleontological study or for coal strip mining, which use or uses should BLM planners decide to allow? And if it disallowed some usage, was there a substitute tract of public land elsewhere that could be used instead?

BLM sought to involve the public in that trade-off process by financing and helping organize a "Public Forum of Experts" on coal-related topics, and a follow-up "Public Brainstorming Session" where members of the public could sort through the options facing BLM and come up with their own recommended solutions. The BLM public participation specialist arranged for members of the Farmington League of Women Voters to invite national experts of their choosing to address a day-long conference on the issues involved in stripmining the Chaco-Bisti region. The idea was for the general public, proponents and opponents of the coal program, and BLM officials and members of their land use planning team, to hear first-hand from leading authorities what might be expected if a massive federal coal leasing effort were in fact started. Conference organizers brought in the following experts: Daniel Jackson, western editor for *Coal Age* magazine; Professor of paleontology William Clemens Jr., of the University of California, Berkeley; Ted Birkedal, Branch of Indian Cultural Resources, National Park Service in Santa Fe; University of Arizona Professor Helen Ingram, to discuss water resources; Pat Geehan, deputy director of the Office of Coal Leasing, Interior Department, Washington; Sociologist Judith Davenport, University of Wyoming; Reclamation Specialist Ed Kelley, New Mexico Department of Energy and Minerals; Sterling Grogan, Utah International (Mining Company) environmental supervisor; Vice-chairman of the Navajo Tribe Frank E. Paul; and Al Henderson, director of the Navajo Tribal Division of Economic Development.

Utah International's Sterling Grogan discussed reclamation efforts at his company's Navajo Mine, and sought to disspell any doubts about the effectiveness of reclamation. "In my opinion, the most unfortunate part of the propaganda that you people are being bombarded with by the BLM and some other federal agencies in this particular basin is this incredible statement that reclamation of mined land in the San Juan Basin is questionable. How any human being who knows anything about ecology can make that statement is absolutely and totally beyond my comprehension. I can take you in my car to the Navajo Mine and I can walk you—for the next week because it will take that long to do it—over more than 2,000 acres of reclaimed land that was strip mined for coal in the San Juan Basin. Now, none of that land has been grazed yet, and it won't be until we have approval from Ed Kelley and from the Navajo Tribe to release it for grazing. In my opinion . . . there is no way to concoct an ecologically defensible argument that in a few years, on the order of 10-15 years from the date of seeding, that that land will not be capable of supporting at least the same level of economic use that it was supporting before mining."

On the other hand, Grogan admitted that little is known about reclamation in the arid West. "I think that's stretching it, personally, to call anyone today an expert in reclamation. Why? Reclamation as an art (and only parts of it are scientific today) is, when it comes to reclaiming coal strip mined lands in arid environments, is maybe 10 years old as an art. There has been mine land reclamation going on in the United States since 1922—documented reclamation since 1922. That was primarily in the Mid-west and the East in the early days. We are learning a lot right now. We're still in the process of making some fundamental changes in reclamation plans essentially from year to year."

He said the cost of reclamation had been drastically underestimated when his company first began at Navajo Mine. "When we first started out, we thought we were looking at costs in the neighborhood of $5,000 per acre for reclamation of the Navajo Mine. . . . We're looking at a range of $8,000 to $12,000 per acre today."

"Our goal is to restore a cold desert ecosystem to a condition where it will support at least the pre-mining level of economic activity. The first and most significant decision we made was that we would have to use supplemental irrigation water to provide for the plants in this extraordinarily harsh environment. As you know, in the San Juan Basin, we receive what some researchers say amounts to about six inches of precipitation per year, which in reality according to the data that we've been gathering since the early 1970s, really amounts to an average of about three-and-a-half to four-and-a-half inches of effective precipitation per year during good years. I don't think in 1980 we received three-and-a-half inches of effective precipitation. By effective, I mean precipitation that eventually becomes available for plants to use for growing. In order to get plants started to revegetate that land, we decided that we'd have to use supplemental irrigation, and so we are using this."

Helen Ingram, University of Arizona political scientist specializing in water resources, observed: "Someone once said that every recipe for energy development has 'add water' somewhere in the introduction. A lot of people feel that the Colorado River is already overcommitted, that the water planners who first divided the water between the upper basin and the lower basin, and then to plan development, were enormously over-optimistic and in recent years, tree ring analysis at my university indicates that the long-term dependable flow of the Colorado is much less than what was expected. . . . As most of you know, the San Juan River (which feeds into the Colorado River) is currently under litigation. There is a real question about whether or not the San Juan is itself overcommitted by the number of water rights. But if (energy development does not take) surface water, then it's got to be ground water. . . . Aquifers are funny things, and some of them are replenished from the surface and many ancient aquifers really are not renewable. Once they are gone, they are gone forever. We are talking about a trade-off with the present use of ground water for coal development, traded-off against all the other aspirations and hopes which people may have at times in the future. I think the question is one that really needs to be seriously addressed before commitments are made."

Al Henderson, director of the Navajo Tribe's Economic Development Division, spoke briefly of the human costs of mining the Chaco-Bisti region. "I read somewhere the (coal mining in the San Juan Basin) was expected to relocate about 10,000 to 15,000 families. If the families have to move to urban centers, hidden costs are involved. They have never had to pay insurance, and they never had to pay utility bills. All these costs are new things to them, and I think that the social upheaval has become very apparent. . . . Seventy to 75 percent of the Navajo families (throughout New Mexico and Arizona) still live in rural settings."

Fossil expert, Dr. William Clemens, Jr., of the University of California, Berkeley, stressed the importance of the paleontological resources of the San Juan Basin. "Here within the basin there is a record of life going from a period about 70 million years ago up to about 40 million years ago. This is a period in earth history in which major changes were witnessed in the flora and fauna in the area. It starts at a time when dinosaurs . . . populated the area. Then we have the record of the extinction of these animals about 64 million years ago, and records of change in the faunas immediately after that extinction. This is one of the few areas of the world where there is a record of organisms living just prior, during, and after that extinction. . . . The fossil record here says something about a major extinction that occurred 64 million years ago. Although the newspapers carried accounts of hypotheses involving comets or a whole variety of other kinds of catastrophes that might have caused this extinction, I think it is fair to say that this area of research and questions along this line remain unanswered. We say that our fossil record in the San Juan Basin, particularly the record of the last dinosaurian forms . . . would be immediately affected by strip mining operations."

Clemens added: "The preservation of bone or shells or leaves is an unlikely event. One generous estimate is that out of every million animals that ever lived at one time, maybe one of them is represented somewhere in the fossil record. Of that, maybe one in a million has been exposed at the surface and collected in time before it was destroyed by erosion. . . . I feel strongly that certain areas should be reserved as research areas."

He discounted the coal company argument that coal mining is advantageous for discovering fossils. "Having looked at a strip mine, the faces (mine walls) of a strip mine are the last places I'd go to look for fossils, even with a hard hat."

Ted Birkedal, with the National Park Service, said he felt existing federal laws were adequate to protect the archeological resources of the San Juan Basin . . . if they were stringently enforced. "With strip mining, which I believe is the primary mining that is going to take place, there is no way to protect all the sites. The site density out here is too great. Either you stop strip mining—and that's the only alternative you have, which I don't believe Mr. [Sterling Grogan of Utah International] would agree to—or you have to accept a very important loss."

The Park Service archeologist added: "The San Juan Basin contains some of the most significant cultural resources in the United States, and particularly important because the physical record of those archeological and historical sites is largely impacted there. There are over 10,000 years of prehistory and history in this area. . . . The Chacoan cultural system which developed in the 10th century and continued into the 12th century, probably represents one of the highest points in North American Indian culture in terms of development. This we call a system, which was centered in Chaco Canyon, and it had outlier communities, communities which extended clear up to Dolores, Colorado, . . . and clear over to the northeast where you can see outliers at Chimneyrock and clear to the south to the Zuni area. These communities were interlinked by road networks. This then covers the area of a small country like Belgium. We don't have a similar impact system in the rest of the United States to look at.

"We also have a record here of several interesting groups that have their histories in the basin; the Indian Pueblo people, and of course, the Navajo people. Now, posed against this is always the significant threat of development. It would be, I think, a significant threat, but one thing we do have in the San Juan Basin is that 80 percent of the land is either Indian-owned, state, or federal land. There is a whole gamut of legislation that we have for archeology now, and regulations . . . tribal, state and federal . . . which if properly implemented should reduce the threat to cultural resources should mining proceed on a significant scale."

The BLM-League of Women Voters "Public Forum of Experts" in April 1981, served the important function of legitimizing and publicizing the various concerns that certain special interest groups, like those interested in archeology, paleontology, wilderness and Indian lifestyle advocates, had in relation to federal proposals for coal strip mining in the Chaco-Bisti area. Subsequent BLM "public brainstorming sessions" in Farmington and Albuquerque produced recommendations from some of those special interest groups and members of the general public who began to see the coal conflicts as a classic lesson in civics.

These public events also had the effect of drawing together opponents of the federal coal program. Environmentalists heard, met and made common cause with paleontologists, archeologists, wildlife advocates and Indian rights activists. By the end of 1981, a coalition had formed to monitor and challenge the federal government's plans to turn the San Juan Basin over to coal mining and electrical generating interests. Formed initially by members of the Rio Grande Chapter of the Sierra Club, the anti-uranium group known as The Mount Taylor Alliance, Taos Environmental Action, The Crownpoint Citizens Alliance, and the American Indian Environmental Council, the Committee on Coal eventually grew into a major obstacle for James Watt's plans to hand the public's Chaco-Bisti property over to industry to do with as it pleased. Members of the committee became more familiar with federal laws and regulations than many of the civil servants whose job it was to implement them.

The Committee on Coal had as its stated objectives: "To stop or limit needless exploitation of people and resources in the San

Juan Basin; to promote alternative energy technologies which reduce the perceived need for extraction of nonrenewable resources; to support Native Americans and other residents of the San Juan Basin in their effort to determine their own destinies."

In one of its early documents, the committee indicated one of the chief keys to its later successes. "This (committee organizational) structure and the functions it serves reveal a central assumption of the Committee on Coal. It is that issues as broad and long-term as those joined in the San Juan Basin may be won securely only in the hearts and minds of the people. Laws and regulations may be good, even visionary, but it is only when there is a consensus demanding it that they will be enforced consistently (i.e., over decades rather than just during enlightened administrations). . . . This assumption, that power really does reside with the people (if they will decide to exercise it), leads obviously to the central long-term strategy of the Committee on Coal. The strategy is to build a consensus on land use in the San Juan Basin. It will be necessary to engage in staying actions, through technical comments and legal action, to fight many brushfires, and even conflagrations, but such actions should be recognized for their true purposes; postponing destruction of what we aim to save until a consensus can be achieved, and secondly, attracting more people to that consensus."

Within a short time, the Committee on Coal, primarily through the Sierra Club, was receiving financial aid from southwestern landscape painter Georgia O'Keeffe, then America's greatest living artist; public opinion support from Taos novelist John Nichols (author of "The Milagro Bean Field War"); and videotaped public service announcements by film superstar Robert Redford.

The Committee on Coal's tenacious monitoring of BLM activities raised the blood pressure of many Interior officials in Washington and in New Mexico.

As one Albuquerque District BLM coal planning supervisor noted in April 1983: "They know more about what we did and why we did it than we do ourselves."

CHAPTER 6

A PLANNED DISASTER

With the federal coal program set in motion, and the general public watching closely, it was only a matter of time before the Bureau of Land Management in New Mexico ran smack into a major scandal.

Ranking Reagan Administration Interior officials working with company officials embarked on a long campaign to subvert the public interest and deny the public fair value for its property. With the clarity and deliberateness derived from ideological commitments, they pursued their goals by intimidation, by collusion with federal officials to favor their interpretation of critical laws and regulations, by fostering latent racism among civil servants, by manipulating politicians to exert pro-industry pressures on the bureaucracy, by direct pressures on local officials to circumvent federal laws and regulations, and by suppressing the public's right to know.

The realities of industry dominance in our form of government do not depend on an aggressively pro-business president. How far the industries can go in optimizing their advantage is determined by the chief executive and his political appointees, but the clear trend in American history has always been for government to give industry a free rein. Without doubt, it has been this freedom (one might say license) that has given American industry its vitality.

Industry had paid relatively little attention to federal coal reserves until the 1960s, although Congress had passed laws governing its availability as far back as 1920 (the Mineral Leasing Act of that year established the Department of the Interior as the agency responsible for leasing publicly-owned coal). By 1950, only 88 federal coal leases had been issued; 166 federal coal tracts had been leased by 1960. But in the 1960s, the number of federal leases almost tripled, with 485 federal coal leases in effect in 1970. However, that jump in no way reflected an increase in public consumption of coal, nor a dramatic rise in coal exports. Instead, coal companies were acquiring the federal leases for speculation. They bought the leases cheaply then traded on their new assets. It became obvious that the public was not getting fair value for its resource, if the lease holder could turn around and assign it to another party at an enormous profit. Under heavy pressure from Congress, the Department of the Interior under President Richard Nixon imposed a federal coal leasing moratorium in 1971. The shut-down lasted almost ten years, as Congress enacted a series of environmental and natural resource laws which had major impacts on the federal leasing process. Chief among these were the Federal Land Policy and Management Act, the Federal Coal Leasing Amendments Act, and the Surface Mining Control and Reclamation Act.

The coal leasing moratorium in 1971 had stopped one scandal, but Watt's rise to power at Interior in 1981 set the stage for another. After a decade of attempts to assure that the public received fair market value for its coal resource, and that the public lands and other resources were protected in the event of coal mining, Watt set out to thwart those protections. If the public and Congress had been alarmed at the leasing of federal coal for speculative purposes in the late 1960s and early 1970s, Watt set out to encourage exactly that. His objective was to provide as much public coal to the companies as they could possibly want, regardless of how much they might need for mining to meet consumers' demand for energy from coal.

In the San Juan Basin, Watt's policies meant a de-emphasis on environmental protection, a disregard for how much coal would likely be needed from the coal region to meet demand, a negative attitude toward other resources which conflicted with coal development, such as archeological and paleontological sites and potential federal wilderness areas, and a smug assurance that coal mining jobs would be the best thing that could happen to the poor Navajo families living over the coal.

In the 1980s, the federal coal scandal in New Mexico was highlighted by the following elements:

- Deliberate skewing of the land use planning process to favor coal interests at the public's expense.

- Imposition of a pre-determined plan by Public Service Company of New Mexico (PNM) to use public land in the Bisti to build another coal-fired power plant.

- Direct violation of the National Environmental Policy Act by BLM officials trying to accommodate PNM's power plant, regardless of its adverse implications for other public resources and the public interest.

- Fraudulent procedures by BLM in developing a justification for approving PNM's Bisti power plant.

- Deliberate failure to comply with required screening out of lands unsuitable for coal lease consideration.

- Disregard of impacts to Native Americans living over the federal coal beds, and violations of regulations designed to protect their occupancy rights.

- Deliberate failure to screen out lands with questionable reclamation potential.

- Deceit and fraud in determining the amount of public coal to be offered for lease.

- Attempts to defraud the public out of fair market value for its coal resource.

At the outset of the federal coal program in New Mexico, the big agenda item for business was to assure that the most lucrative coal-bearing lands were handed over to them without the risks inherent in land use planning. Eleven coal companies or individuals already had a claim of sorts on most of the easily strippable public coal in the San Juan Basin before the planning process began, and, generally, they demanded the right to it regardless of the outcome of land use planning. Through a discredited and discontinued federal process known as "Preference Right Lease Applications", the best coal in the San Juan River Coal Region (that lying close to the surface just north of Chaco Canyon, running from Bisti, just off the Navajo Reservation border, some 70 miles southeast to Star Lake near Cuba, New Mexico) had been spoken for prior to start-up of the federal coal program in 1979. A total of 75,510 acres, believed to hold about 2.3 billion tons of mineable coal, were claimed within 26 application areas.

Preference Right Lease Applications (PRLAs) as a way of obtaining federal coal had their origin in the Mineral Leasing Act of 1920. That act stipulated that ". . . the Secretary of the Interior may issue, to applicants qualified under this Act, prospecting permits . . ." and that if "the permitee shows to the Secretary that the land contains coal in commercial quantities, the permitee shall be entitled to a lease under this Act for all or part of the land in his permit. . . ." Naturally, prospecting permits were to be issued only in areas where coal deposits were not known to exist. It was assumed that coal companies could help in locating workable quantities of public coal through financing their own exploration work. If a company was willing to spend its own money prospecting for coal in areas that were not known to be federal coal lands, they could make application for a lease on what they discovered. And should their discovery be borne out by government verification of the applicant's geologic reports, then it was deemed only fair that when and if a lease was issued for those lands, the successful prospecting company would be given the lease preferentially; that is, without having to bid against other companies for the lease.

Prospecting permits for all of the PRLAs in the Chaco-Bisti region were granted between 1967 and 1970 . . . during the last four years before Congress cracked down on federal coal leasing abuses. After widely varying amounts of prospecting work, the lease applications were filed between 1971 and 1973, mostly during the period of the leasing moratorium.

As the Interior coal program started up again in the Chaco-Bisti region in 1979, a crucial question was whether the PRLAs were to be subject to land use planning, or whether the use of those particular tracts of land had already been decided by the lease application process. The Federal Coal Leasing Amendments Act of 1976 established quite clearly that only those lands which had undergone "comprehensive land use planning" should be leased. The Bureau of Land Management's decision, as influenced by Washington-level officials during the pro-coal Carter Administration and by industry lobbyists, was that the PRLAs should go to coal leasing, not some other potential use, although the PRLA areas were to be subjected to the "Unsuitability Criteria" established by the Surface Mining Control and Reclamation Act of 1977.

Assuming, then, that the 26 PRLAs were "as good as already leased" to the applicants, these 75,510 acres of public, private, tribal and state land surface over federal coal beds were not fully subjected to the legally required land use planning. BLM staffers and inquiring members of the public were informed that the PRLAs were "grandfathered" into the federal coal program, and BLM could use no discretion in deciding whether to lease the coal there.

That was a false assumption, an example of industry's success in seducing the civil service into misinterpreting the laws and regulations to benefit the coal interests. BLM was not, in fact, required to issue PRLA leases in those areas, and could not even determine at that time which of the applications, if any, deserved a lease based on demonstrated commercial quantities of coal in the areas. Yet the congressionally-mandated BLM land use plan essentially skirted those areas as being "as good as leased already".

More damning, however, was BLM's failure to investigate the validity of the PRLAs in question. Ignoring a U.S. Geological Survey staffer's challenge to the validity of some of the San Juan Basin PRLAs, BLM passed up the opportunity to declare all or some of the applications void, thereby foregoing the millions of dollars that would have been paid to the public in bonus bids had the coal tracts been offered competitively rather than through the application process. By challenging the validity of the PRLAs, BLM might have gained an additional $100 million or more for the public's minerals had they been offered competitively.

Historic and geologic evidence generated within the Department of the Interior itself, and available to BLM, makes it clear that the government knew of the existence of these coal formations more than half a century before the PRLA companies went prospecting for it. How then could BLM in good conscience claim these lands were qualified for preference right leasing?

In 1906, a U.S. Geological Survey team investigated the Chaco region for minerals, and its report a year later, "Bulletin 316", describes the coal resource as being in workable quantities. The report was sufficiently detailed that it included a map showing the direction in which the coal strata were said to tilt.

A 1912 memorandum from the director of the U.S. Geological Survey to the Commissioner of the General Land Office (later to become the Bureau of Land Management), references this 1907 report, and adds: "The accompanying sketch illustrates the condition. From east of Durango, Colorado, the coals of the lower Mesaverde have been traced westward about fifty miles to a point south of Cortez, Colorado, then southward to Gallup, New Mexico, a distance of more than 130 miles, and from Gallup east to San Mateo, seventy-five miles, at which point it disappears beneath the Mount Taylor lava flow. Northeast of San Mateo, however, at Casasalazar, and northward, the same horizon has been mapped. In every direction from the land included in this entry the lower coal is found to outcrop, and at no place is it of less than workable thickness.

"All of this land is, therefore, undoubtedly coal in character.

"This area was examined by geologists of the Survey in 1906, and the Government was at that time in possession of knowledge of the coal character of the land. The results of this field work were published and accessible to the public in 1907."

Two agencies of the Department of the Interior, then, the General Land Office/Bureau of Land Management and the U.S. Geological Survey, knew of the workable coal deposits in the Chaco-Bisti region as far back as 1906. Yet BLM issued coal prospecting permits to companies in 1967-70.

Apparently the 1906 minerals survey was not even the first to document the coal in the Chaco region. An earlier exploration commissioned by the U.S. Geological Survey in 1879 resulted in a map which refers to this region as a federal coal area.

In a sense, it would have been far more remarkable not to have discovered the coal beds even in the most cursory survey, because in many places the black coal seams reveal themselves in stark visual contrast to the sparsely vegetated, light-colored sandy soils. In few other places around the country are the geologic strata so visibly displayed.

Government knowledge of the Chaco region coal deposits is further demonstrated by the official justification by which the federal government denied a homestead application filed by Chaco Canyon archeological pioneer Richard Wetherill.

On May 14, 1900, Wetherill applied for land in the Chaco as a homestead. The application caused some consternation among certain archeological preservationists who feared that Wetherill would use his title to the land to loot the treasures of the Chaco. In any event, in 1901, the Government Land Office (BLM) sent S.J. Holsinger from its Phoenix office to investigate. Holsinger recommended that the government create a 795-square-mile national preserve around Chaco Canyon, including the paleontological and archeological sites to the north, over the coal deposits, and including what would later become the BLM's Ah-shi-sle-pah Wilderness Study Area. He urged the General Land Office to deny Wetherill his homestead based on the fact that the lands sought were coal lands.

A June 1, 1912 General Land Office document regarding Wetherill's homestead application also notes that the Chaco lands are "coal lands". Page 3 of the document, from the Director of the General Land Office to the Department of the Interior's Board of Equitable Adjudication, states: "The records of the General Land Office show that the land embraced in this entry is included within coal land withdrawals of October 13, and November 7, 1906, and that the same was classified as coal land, minimum price, June 15, 1907. . . ."

Given this history, why would BLM have issued coal prospecting permits for this region in the late 1960s? Why would the bureau have accepted Preference Right Lease Applications in an area it should have reserved for competitive lease sales where the public would be paid bonus bids to obtain the lease?

The answers are far from clear. But there is no doubt that BLM accepted Preference Right Lease Applications in the Bisti area as late as 1973 when it had already issued leases competitively in the same area in 1961.

BLM coal leases NM 0186612 and NM 0186613, issued August 1, 1961, for more than 2,000 acres in the Bisti area were issued competitively to Public Service Coal Company, a subsidiary of Public Service Company of New Mexico, the state's leading utility. The fact that they were issued competitively is an acknowledgment that the area is a "known coal area". Asked why the two leases would have been issued competitively, a BLM geologist explained, "Apparently it was already in a known coal area, so they couldn't apply for it as a PRLA."

Why, then, were 26 PRLAs accepted by BLM in the Chaco-Bisti region as late as 1970-73?

The same issue erupted among U.S. Geological Survey officials in 1966-67, as the applications were being made. The acting Farmington District Geologist for USGS, Jim Fassett, argued that a coal prospecting permit should not be issued to a company that wished to file a PRLA in the Star Lake vicinity (toward the eastern end of the coal outcrop zone in the Chaco region). In a detailed, four-page memo to the USGS Regional Mining Supervisor in Carlsbad, dated January 10, 1967, Fassett contended, "It is my opinion that since a continuous coal bed averaging more than 10 feet thick crops out across most of the permit application area, the area is clearly known to contain large quantities of coal and thus should be properly offered at a competitive lease sale."

To support his conclusion, Fassett quoted an assessment of the area made by a private geologist considered the foremost authority on coal in the San Juan Basin, E.C. Beaumont, who maintained that the area concerned contains coal reserves of 39 million tons at overburden depths of less than 100 feet.

However, Fassett's questioning of the validity of the PRLA prospecting permit led nowhere, since superiors persistently quashed his assertions. In a memo dated July 18, 1967, Regional Mining Supervisor R.S. Fulton wrote:" (The Carlsbad Office) has never denied the existence of coal in at least part of the lands involved, but Carlsbad does deny that the coal has been determined to be workable—the mere existence of coal does not prove the coal is workable." Fulton goes on to note: "On March 1, 1967 . . . after examining the area, the outcrops, and noting the lack of cover over the coal seam, all were of the opinion that the workability of the deposits had not been determined, and that the deposits were properly subject to prospecting."

When the federal coal leasing laws were rewritten in 1976, 1977 and 1979, existing PRLAs were specifically grandfathered in while the process itself was entirely abolished. The Preference Right Lease Applications in New Mexico were accepted. The only reason the coal in the PRLA areas was not already leased to the applicants was that the entire federal coal program was shut down (except for so-called emergency and bypass leasing) in 1971 due to abuses Congress perceived back then.

And so it was that in the 1980s the public's most valuable coal deposits in the Chaco-Bisti region were made available to coal companies for the asking, without competitive bidding for leases.

BLM's acceptance of the PRLAs had other implications, besides creating the unlikelihood that the public would be paid full value for its resource. It also meant that families living on the surface above federal coal would not have "surface owner consent" rights to reject or, in effect, sell their approval for a percentage of the coal's value. In the Chaco-Bisti region, Interior determined that most of the residents, Navajos, would be forced to abandon their homelands with little or no compensation since their tenure on the land was typically based on traditional usage rather than legal title as required by federal "surface owner consent" terms. Furthermore, acceptance of the PRLAs in New Mexico led to woefully inadequate land use planning and environmental protection since the PRLA process itself seemed to have already determined that those areas would be sacrificed for mineral production.

Again in 1983, Congress called into question the validity of many of the existing PRLAs. In its report on the "Coal Leasing Program of U.S. Department of Interior", in April 1983, the Surveys and Investigations Staff for the U.S. House Appropriations Committee charged there had been apparent irregularities in BLM's handling of PRLAs. The report noted: "In the rush to meet the self-imposed December 1984 deadline for processing all pending preference right lease applications, BLM is failing to examine the validity of the prospecting permits upon which these applications are based, even though the court, in NRDC v. Hughes, indicated that Interior had the right to look behind the preference right lease applications and examine the validity of prospecting permits. The decision of the Secretary to issue a prospecting permit is clearly a discretionary action. The authority of the Secretary to deny permits, at his own discretion, has been consistently upheld. The discretion, however, is bound by the nondiscretionary limitations of the statute that permits be issued only in areas where the existence or workability of the deposits was unknown, and by the Secretary's determination that issuing a permit is in the public interest. The Secretary has no authority to issue prospecting permits in areas where the existence and workability of coal was known, or could be reasonably inferred. He has a duty to carry out the intent of Congress in passing the Mineral Leasing Act. The Secretary is not restricted by previous errors made either by BLM or Geological Survey in initially approving, continuing, or extending prospecting permits. It is well within his power to reject pending preference right lease applications which were invalid at their inception.

The report continued: "A 1950 report by Geological Survey entitled 'Coal Resources in Wyoming', so thorough that it is still used as the primary source in the compilations of Wyoming's coal reserve base, includes clear descriptions of coal resources in locations for which there are now pending applications for preference right leases by holders of prospecting permits that were granted well after the publication of this report. Geological Survey apparently knew that substantial amounts of coal existed at these sites, yet continued granting prospecting permits. Studies with similar results have also been conducted on preference right lease applications in Colorado. A study conducted by the Colorado Open Space Council concluded 'it is evident that nearly every preference right lease and preference right lease application in Colorado is in an area where the existence and workability of the coal was well-known and should have been identified as such by the Department of the Interior.' The report stated that its research found evidence of 'wide scale abuse' of the prospecting permit/preference right lease system in Colorado."

But in New Mexico in 1979, with the existing PRLAs grandfathered into the revised federal coal program in 1979, and the validity of the 26 Bisti region PRLAs no longer questioned, it seemed that most of the really valuable federal coal was already locked up by specific companies at the start of the land use planning process.

Except for the PRLAs entirely within the BLM three Wilderness Study Areas (which were temporarily stymied by the Unsuitability Criterion that unequivocably ruled out coal leasing in areas under consideration for federal wilderness designation), each of the PRLA areas passed through what was supposed to have been "comprehensive" land use planning, and were found most appropriately used for coal mining.

All that remained then was for BLM to draft lease stipulations for the PRLAs and have the applicants demonstrate that they did, in fact, have commercial quantities of federal coal in their application areas. If BLM, with aid from the U.S. Geological Survey, confirmed the companies' final showings, the leases were to be issued. There remained, however, the nagging problem of how to demonstrate that the coal beds were marketable when no transportation existed to haul the black rock to market. The coal deposits would certainly be more marketable, more "workable", if a railroad were there, but the long-proposed Star Lake Railroad remained a distant dream, hung up in court by Indians who opposed it crossing their land, and by squabbles among coal companies seeking competitive advantage over the others.

A year and a half after completion of the Chaco-San Juan land use plan, in the midst of the national coal leasing scandal, some BLM officials began to worry that the validity of the PRLAs might be questioned. "Apparently in the early or mid-1970s, Jim Fassett produced a paper which might invalidate some PRLAs," said a former USGS official, then working for BLM in its Santa Fe office, "but the USGS mining engineer ignored it. But if somebody like Mimi (Lopez, of the Committee on Coal) gets a hold of it, we could be in for trouble. We could get hung on Freedom of Information Act requests."

Even so, treatment of the PRLAs was only one of the points of compromise for the BLM coal-related land use planning exercise. Besides skewing the Chaco-San Juan Management Framework Plan by erroneously assuming the PRLAs were "as good as leased", BLM irreparably compromised its land use plan by warping the decisionmaking process to favor Public Service Company of New Mexico's proposed power plant in the Bisti. PNM was proposing a land trade with BLM; the public was to give up land in the Bisti in trade for the Ute Mountain tract adjacent to the Rio Grande Gorge near Taos.

The land use planning process entailed analysis by bureau specialists to maximize use of the various resources or values located on or within any given tract. Thus a BLM wildlife specialist would recommend a management strategy to enhance habitat for such high-interest species as falcons or eagles as might be discovered on lands undergoing planning. Likewise the bureau geologist would recommend an optimal strategy for mineral leasing on the same lands, should the two public resources exist on the same tract. Similarly, the agency wilderness or outdoor recreation specialist would propose management to enhance those potential uses of the area, and archeologists would outline optimal management for cultural resources found there. Following a multiple use analysis to determine which of the many potential uses could be compatible with other uses, the BLM decisionmakers are supposed to make the land use trade-offs to decide how specific tracts should be used, based on the Federal Land Policy and Management Act principles of multiple use and sustained yield.

In the summer of 1981, when BLM Farmington Area Manager Bob Calkins came to the land use decision on trading off Bisti lands to PNM, he balked. He said he could not see how, in good conscience, he could recommend the Ute Mountain Land Exchange, when turning over the Bisti lands to the utility company would threaten the other resources he had already opted to preserve. Endorsement of the land exchange with PNM was especially worrisome because Calkins knew there was no real public demand for the Ute Mountain tract near Taos that PNM was offering in trade.

If the Bisti land were given up for PNM's use for a large power plant, for other industrial uses and for a company town of up to 20,000 residents, then proper management of the other publicly-owned resources would be much more difficult. The existence of a power plant in Bisti would obviously detract from the area's wilderness characteristics (the plant site was only three miles away from the proposed Bisti Wilderness Area). And a power plant and company town would expose archeological sites and fossil beds to vandalism and theft; by permitting such a private inholding within what was chiefly public domain, BLM would be exposing all the lands to greater deterioration through recreational off-road vehicle use, pot hunters, and thoughtless damage by operators of heavy equipment. In a land where water was already scarce and strip mine reclamation was sure to require large amounts of water, the decision to give up public lands in Bisti for the power plant and town site was an obvious contradiction.

With the planning nearly complete, BLM District Manager Paul Applegate paid a routine visit the Farmington office. As Applegate stood over the map-strewn tables, Calkins told him he didn't see how he would be able to recommend approval of the Ute Mountain Exchange. Applegate seemed stunned. Calkins went on to explain how the land trade would adversely affect management of the other resources, but Applegate insisted that he keep the land exchange option open. You don't have to say the land exchange is a good idea, Applegate told Calkins, just don't recommend against it. Off the cuff, Applegate suggested that Calkins' decision should say something like, "if the Ute Mountain Exchange is found to be in the public interest, then the following lands should be made available for exchange with PNM".

Against the Area Manager's better judgment, the land use plan did, in fact, hedge its recommendation regarding the Ute Mountain Land Exchange.

Imposition of PNM's plans for the Bisti lands into BLM's land use plan was a shock to several bureau specialists who had assumed the resource conflicts were clearly perceived. BLM specialists in the Farmington, Taos and Albuquerque offices were certain that the proposed land swap was not in the public interest, based on the analyses they had been assigned as part of the processing of the Ute Mountain Land Exchange proposal. Laws governing exchange of public lands require that such trades be clearly in the public interest, and the specialists' analyses had shown just the opposite. There was no real need for the acreage that the public would be acquiring from PNM north of Taos, and loss of public control over the lands in the Bisti would jeopardize many resources which had already been identified as important.

The core of BLM's land use planning for public property in the Chaco-Bisti region had been corrupted by that warped decision. With Applegate's commitment in favor of PNM's grand design to turn the Bisti lands and its coal reserves over to industrialization, the stage was set for countless other illegalities and irregularities over the next five years which significantly compromised the public interest.

Even portions of the land use planning process that seemed relatively straight forward and specifically mandated by Congress encountered trouble when applied on public lands in the San Juan Basin.

In addition to the land use trade-off process described above, the planning process for coal lands was supposed to entail three other methods for screening out public land as unsuitable for coal leasing consideration. The first screen was that only lands with moderate to high coal-producing potential were to be considered for leasing. Second, the planners were to apply the 20 "Unsuitability Criteria" called for in the Surface Mining Control and Reclamation Act of 1977; the criteria covered such off-limits areas as cemeteries, habitat for threatened and endangered species, floodplains, occupied dwellings, federal Wilderness Areas and areas under study for official wilderness designation (Wilderness Study Areas), outstanding natural areas, and archeological or historic sites deemed suitable for inclusion in the National Register of Historic Places, among other exclusions.

The third screen was to be serious consideration for the desires of people residing in the potential coal-producing areas.

The intent of each of these screens was subverted, sometimes as a result of misinterpretations of the coal program and other times due to strong pressures brought by industrial interests.

Initially, BLM planners focused on coal lease offerings only for areas considered to have moderate to high potential for coal extraction, as the first screen required. Generally, it meant that the lands to be carried forward for consideration for leasing were those within or adjacent to the PRLA zone of easily strippable coal running from Bisti to Torreon, north of Chaco Canyon. A few coal areas more distant, such as those north and east of Crownpoint and others north of Farmington, were solidly included in the land use plan, but known coal areas of lesser potential such as those around Gallup were essentially excluded as not complying with the requirement for moderate to high potential. Of course, BLM archeologists, wildlife specialists, and others working on the plan concentrated their efforts on those areas which were likely to have conflicts with coal development, so they, too, largely ignored outlying areas such as those around Gallup.

However, when James Watt took over Interior in 1981, near the end of the Chaco-San Juan planning schedule, one of his primary objectives was to push as much public coal into corporate hands as possible. So the BLM planners in the San Juan Basin were directed to bring additional thousands of acres of lower potential coal lands into the plan. The result was that lands about which very little was known were at the last minute thrown in for land use decisions. Hurried assessments were made as to what other public resources might be lost in areas around Gallup and other places if they were strip mined.

This demand by Watt to throw all known coal lands into consideration for leasing had other, even more serious, repercussions later as government geologists attempted to determine (as required by law, but without adequate data) what the fair market value of those added coal deposits might be.

The effectiveness of the second land use planning screen, application of the Unsuitability Criteria, was jeopardized by BLM's acquiescence to coal industry demands that the coal under public lands could be leased to them before the criteria were fully applied. While it was clear that the federal coal program called for applying the Unsuitability Criteria during land use planning, the companies were able to convince BLM officials at the Albuquerque office that some of the criteria could be partially applied and deferred to a later stage . . . after the coal lands had already been leased.

Although some BLM planners objected to that interpretation, the plan was completed before BLM officials finally admitted that deferral was improper. The deferral of the criteria was explained this way: "Application of the Coal Unsuitability Criteria was partially deferred, pending completion of surface owner consultation and other research. The criteria which were found applicable at this stage included those dealing with wildlife, archeological sites, and Wilderness Study Areas. Those which were deferred included rights-of-way, buffer zones for such things as rights-of-ways, cemeteries and institutional buildings. Full application of these deferred criteria will be done when more site specific data is available."

The most tumultuous of these conflicts between resource specialists and industry pressures for misinterpretation of the planning procedures involved the bureau's archeologists. As they read the laws and regulations, BLM could not offer for coal lease lands that had not been screened for archeological sites . . . especially in a region which was known to have thousands. BLM Albuquerque District Archeologist Randy Morrison insisted verbally and in repeated memos that full cultural resource surveys would be required before lands could be offered for lease, and that the surveys should be done prior to or during land use planning. He warned repeatedly that failure to do so would violate federal laws and state-federal agreements. He was invariably ignored.

A Morrison memo dated January 22, 1980, spells out his concerns clearly; "I believe we may have a problem with our coal leasing program—especially in the San Juan Basin. It appears that we are leaving ourselves open to lawsuit. It is my understanding that we intend to require Class III (100 percent) cultural resources inventory of the selected [coal] tracts after the lease is signed. My considered opinion is that we are treading on thin ice by taking this approach. . . . There is little doubt in my mind that if large-scale leasing of coal in the San Juan Basin is instituted in 1983 that the Bureau will be faced with lawsuits precisely like NIYC [National Indian Youth Council] vs Andrus, et al, or at a minimum a judicial review of our actions under the Administrative Procedure Act. My expert advice is, suits would be successful. Because the laws, regulations and interpretations since 1974 are so clearly against our intended approach, I cannot understand why we are running this unnecessary risk.

"In summary, we are moving into a major program in apparent violation of the required procedures in 36 CFR 800 [federal regulations], which involves compliance with three laws and an Executive Order. We are doing so in the face of a volume of information indicating that we are proceeding from an unsupportable position. Personally, I do not understand the reasons for such an apparent evasion of procedure."

Morrison was forced to resign in May 1981.

Similarly, when other cultural resource specialists insisted that planners needed to know ethnographic data about Native American usage of the lands under consideration for coal strip mining, they were ignored.

Perhaps the most important criterion established in the Surface Mining Control and Reclamation Act (SMCRA) is that which would exclude from coal leasing lands considered unreclaimable. Although not one of the 20 criteria spelled out in regulations implementing SMCRA, the requirement to rule as off-limits to strip miners those parcels where reclamation is considered technologically or economically unfeasible is an integral part of the 1977 law, Section 522(a)(2). None of the potential coal lands in the Chaco-San Juan were determined unreclaimable, even though the 1979 Programmatic Environmental Impact Statement for the entire federal coal program says specifically that the San Juan River Coal Region is the most arid and where reclamation will be most difficult.

Studies on reclaimability of coal lands in the Chaco-Bisti area produced by the U.S. Geological Survey revealed serious scientific doubt about prospects for reclamation. But, under political pressure, the USGS researchers tried to be as optimistic as possible. "In light of the difficulty of only partially revegetating the [Bisti West] study site, total revegetation of the site is unrealistic. In addition, partial revegetation of the study site is consistent with the guidelines for this report (Agreement between BLM and Bureau of Reclamation, FY 76 Work Order No. 10) which states, 'For planning purposes the Bisti West site will be returned as near as possible to its natural condition. For these reasons, the alternative of total revegetation of the study site is not considered further in this report.' "

Because of their bleak predictions, most of the Geological Survey's Energy Mineral Rehabilitation Inventory and Analysis (EMRIA) studies were effectively suppressed. Copies of the documents were kept in draft form for long periods of time, and were therefore unavailable to the public. In other ways, the critical EMRIA reports were prevented from having wide distribution. For example, a copy of the 1981 EMRIA report on the Kimbeto area, north of Chaco Canyon, was not even made available to its principal author until 1984.

Instead of publicizing the difficulties expected in reclamation, BLM attempted to present as positive a picture as even rudimentary knowledge of the area would allow. A document distributed by BLM stated, "Several coal companies, including Western Coal, Pittsburg and Midway and Amcoal, have carried out reclamation efforts in the San Juan Basin which are considered successful. . . ." This rosy statement brought a reply from the Navajo Tribe's director of the Environmental Protection Commission who complained: "I believe you should qualify the terms 'reclamation efforts' and well as 'successful'. Apparently you are not aware that revegetation, which is an important and integral part of reclamation, at Western Coal [mine] is currently heavily dependent on irrigation and that at Amcoal [mine,] revegetation has not been achieved. Neither company has assured itself that their revegetation efforts will endure the climate of the region, nor that the vegetation will repropagate itself without the artificial instruments presently used by these companies. It should be noted that the companies are experimenting with seed mixtures and soil types to provide this assurance. Thus, it appears that your statement will mislead an uninformed public as well as falsely encourage prospective federal lessees."

But such warnings received precious little recognition within BLM. The land use plan noted only in general terms that reclamation will be difficult; it made no assertions as to the prospects of reclamation on specific coal-bearing lands. Essentially, this important criterion was ignored, for political reasons, in the federal coal region where it was most likely to have ruled out some lands for coal leasing.

The third planning screen to rule out lands from consideration for leasing was intended to be consultations with local residents to determine whether strong objections existed. Since the Navajo residents of the coal region had so much to lose and so little to gain from federal coal leasing, and had, in fact, already repeatedly denounced the government's plans for coal leasing there, the consultation screen was essentially ignored as a planning factor.

Only one area within the Chaco-San Juan planning unit was ruled off-limits to coal leasing in reference to the required consultations: that around Torreon, at the extreme eastern part of the planning unit. Even there, the land use planning decision notes that the real reason for excluding those lands is that they had low coal mining potential to begin with. The land use recommendations document noted: "Development of federal coal in the Torreon vicinity was also not recommended, due to the existing high population density, local opposition and the fact that the coal in this region is of marginal value. Most of the surface in this area is Indian trust land or homesteaded lands."

In fact, residents around Torreon were neither more vocally nor more consistently opposed to coal leasing there than Navajo residents elsewhere had been. All Navajo communities in the coal region had sent to BLM formal resolutions opposing the leasing, or had spoken out forcefully at hearings in their respective chapter meetings.

BLM's task of "formally" consulting with well over a thousand potential Navajo surface owners was almost insurmountable for several reasons. First, BLM had only one field staffer who spoke Navajo at the outset of the planning effort (later one more was added) and many, if not most, of the residents spoke no English. Second, determining who owned what land in the Navajo area was exceedingly difficult, if only because Navajo heirs were more likely than not to hold undivided interests in the same parcel; a 160-acre tract might have 20 or more family members holding equal interest in it. Third, establishing the place of residence of a people with a traditional pastoral background can be frustrating; it is not unusual for a Navajo in that region to claim as his mailing address some business or institution 30 miles or more from his home. And fourth, BLM officials responsible for the planning effort were reluctant to upset every family in the entire planning area with the prospect that they would lose their lands and homes when not all would face that wrenching fate.

Although consultation with surface owners was supposed to have taken place during the course of land use planning, BLM officials admitted their failure to incorporate this kind of data into their land use plan. Almost three months after completion of the plan, BLM's Acting Farmington Resource Area Manager, Rich Watts, reported that his staff had received responses from only 240 of the 1,831 Navajo who might be "qualified surface owners" over lands which might be offered for federal coal leasing.

The BLM's Chaco-San Juan Management Framework Plan was formally approved in September 1981. "Consultations" were still going on as late as March 1984.

Not even the firm opposition of Navajo Tribal Chairman Peter McDonald to additional federal coal leasing in the planning area served to screen out any lands based on consultation. In a letter dated November 21, 1981, McDonald spoke for the tribe itself as a major property owner in the coal area and on behalf of individual Navajo families, when he formally stated the tribe's refusal to consent to federal coal leasing on Indian lands in the Chaco-Bisti region.

McDonald's letter said: "This is in response to the subject notice of the Bureau of Land Management requesting statements of consent or refusal to consent from qualified surface owners for surface mining or leasing of Federal coal underlying those lands. . . . The Navajo Nation firmly refuses to consent for surface mining activities and/or leasing of Federal coal underlying its lands. This includes all trust lands and fee lands of the Navajo

Nation. . . . The Navajo Nation also firmly refuses consent for surface mining on Public Law 2198 lands on behalf of the Navajos residing on such lands. These Navajos are qualified surface owners under 43 C.F.R. [Code of Federal Regulations] 340-0-.5(pp)."

BLM State Director Bill Luscher responded to the tribal chairman saying that the refusal to consent was rejected because, under strict interpretations of the provisions for surface owner consent in SMCRA, the tribal government is not a "qualified surface owner" in that it does not physically reside on the lands meant to be covered by the refusal. Luscher cited the definition of "qualified surface owner" under the code of federal regulations, 43 CFR 3400.0-5 (1980). The regulations require that to be a qualified surface owner, the person must: 1) hold legal or equitable title to the land; 2) must personally farm, ranch or otherwise derive a significant portion of income from the lands in question; and, 3) must have met the other two conditions for at least the past three years. Although Luscher's reply to McDonald was technically correct, the Navajo chairman's letter could have been used as a consultation input to screen out certain areas had BLM been so disposed. At least the letter should have carried some weight given the trust responsibility that the Interior Department has for Native American interests.

Over all, the lack of concern for Native American uses of the land and their opposition to federal coal leasing is perhaps the most vulnerable aspect of the land use plan.

A basic principle of land use planning (for BLM, just as for any other agency responsible for planning) is that one needs to know as comprehensively as possible what is out there on the ground. That is called "inventorying", and it includes the necessity of thorough understanding of how the land is currently being used. If one is going to make decisions about changing a land use . . . perhaps especially when the change is to be strip mining . . . then it is only responsible to take into account what current uses are being made of the land in question.

In the Chaco-Bisti area, one cannot escape knowing that the land is being used by Navajo Indians. Much of the land is owned outright by the Navajo Tribe, through purchase or concessions made by Congress or Executive Order; much of the remaining land is publicly-owned and leased to Navajo people for grazing sheep, cattle, goats and horses, often through the Bureau of Indian Affairs. There is very little private land in the region, and relatively little State-owned land. Essentially, the land that is not owned by the Navajo Tribe there is leased to the tribe or to individual members of the tribe. And there is federal coal under almost all of it.

While BLM planners had no trouble "inventorying" the grazing land being used by Navajos, the agency was totally stymied by other "exotic" uses of the land by the Indians. A general reluctance to deal with such issues as potential destruction of land forms with cultural and religious significance, and human use and consumption of the vegetation on the rangelands, eventually led to a seriously flawed land use plan, since it ignored the current uses it was about to change.

BLM even had difficulty making the connection between grazing land for sheep and the production of Navajo rugs. The typical rancher out West raises livestock to sell to meat packers, not for raw materials from which to produce works of art. Rug weaving by Navajo residents of the Chaco-Bisti for years has been a leading cash product, essential to economic well-being, but BLM's planning analysis could not tolerate such an obvious cultural difference.

Imagine, then, the amount of serious attention given in the plan's inventory phase to medicinal herbs on the land used by Navajos—herbs which, of course, would be obliterated during coal strip mining, and ignored in coal company's post-mining revegetation efforts. Imagine the weight given by planners to a Navajo sweat lodge, used for purification ceremonies, or areas of black sand from which medicine men collect ingredients for healings and religious sand paintings.

In short, BLM planners knew little about contemporary Navajo use of the lands overlying public coal. But more importantly, attempts to learn more were actively discouraged by BLM officials. When Cultural Resource Specialist Carol Thompson, who had taught school on the Navajo Reservation, attempted to incorporate into planning and environmental assessment work some ethnological information pertinent to those projects, she was reprimanded; when she insisted, she was threatened, and when she persisted further, she was forced out of her position.

Nevertheless, some sketchy information on Navajo religious sites, grave sites and herb gathering areas did find its way into the planning document. A few sites eventually were delineated as off-limits to strip mining. While the data incorporated was sufficient to give the appearance that these types of contemporary land uses were included in the plan, BLM also admitted that it had barely scratched the surface in attempting to identify such cultural sites. In fact, BLM had made no serious effort to determine where those sites might be.

Cultural and racial bias prohibited BLM from achieving an inventory base from which to begin planning. The general attitude of BLM officials and many of the resources specialists was that the Navajos living over the coal were strange, backward people living in primitive squalor. They didn't speak English. It was difficult or impossible to communicate with them, so why try? Besides, veteran bureaucrats can sense power, and these people seemed to have none.

CHAPTER 7

WATT'S GIVEAWAY

James Watt took over at Interior for newly-installed President Ronald Reagan early in January 1981, and quickly called in former New Mexico State Republican Party Chairman Garrey Carruthers as his Assistant Secretary for Land and Water Resources. At that point, the Bureau of Land Management in New Mexico was on the brink of making the difficult land use planning decisions for the Chaco-Bisti region.

Carruthers, a professor of agricultural economics at New Mexico State University in Las Cruces, had grown up along the Colorado-New Mexico border, and his mother still lived near Farmington, the oil and coal boomtown in northwestern New Mexico. He wasted no time in manipulating the BLM land use planning process in the San Juan Basin.

Along with Watt and Carruthers came a brigade of other right-wing true believers, some of whom had helped formulate the conservative agenda of Reagan's first term as associates of the conservative think-tank, Heritage Foundation. Seeing themselves as saviours of the American free enterprise system, the team at Interior set out to overturn or render ineffective the many laws and regulations that had been passed by Congress in the 1970s to protect the environment and the public health and welfare.

Now the public's wealth and welfare would be looked after by Corporate America; the only trouble with the United States was the shackles on the feet of industry, they reasoned. For years, business had complained that government red tape, all the federal rules and regulations, were strangling the American money-making machine, and now Reagan, Watt, Carruthers and the other ideologues at Interior saw their solemn duty and seized the opportunity to strike loose those inhibiting regulations . . . never mind that in their zeal they would subvert the U.S. Constitution, break federal laws and perpetrate fraud on the American people.

During the last six months of land use planning for public lands and minerals in the Chaco-Bisti region, Watt's policy changes were beginning to be felt at the BLM field level.

The Reagan-Watt "Sagebrush Rebellion" (privatization of public resources) was being forced into the decisionmaking process at the local level. One of the first implications of that policy in the San Juan Basin was the shift from offering federal coal leases in order to meet projected national demand to offering leases to meet the coal companies' demands for leases. It was no longer enough for the BLM offices to find coal-bearing lands where companies could go to mine coal to meet the market demand for coal for power plants or even for exports . . . instead, the BLM managers had to find enough coal amid the heavily-conflicted lands to meet the companies' desires for cheaply acquired assets, regardless of how much coal might actually need to be mined to meet expected consumption.

The immediate effect of that "lease for reserves" policy in the San Juan Basin was that BLM managers were required to throw much more acreage into a pool of leaseable lands. BLM planners in the Farmington Resource Area Office were stunned when they were instructed to include in their "coal lands carried forward for further consideration for leasing" those additional lands around Gallup and east of Crownpoint. They had effectively eliminated those coal deposits from lease offerings due to the planning criterion which called for only high to moderate coal potential lands to be included. In the eleventh hour, the planners had to attempt land use trade-off decisions without knowing what might lie over the coal beds that the Reagan Interior Department wanted to offer to the coal companies.

BLM was already worried that it had insufficient archeological surveys, for example, in the areas it had "planned" to lease for coal, but it was embarrassingly ignorant about cultural sites on lands where it hadn't expected the coal companies to want coal leases.

Directives came down from Watt and Assistant Secretary Carruthers that there was no problem offering these other lesser known areas for coal leasing, because if any presently-unknown resource conflicts were found after the lands were already under lease, the additional conflicts could be dealt with at the mine plan stage; that is, once the lease holder applied for a mining permit. The policy of deferring such land use decisions until after the lands were already leased brought howls of outrage from the general public, especially from the archeologists and citizens interested in archeology, and from environmentalists and others concerned about Native American rights to use the lands in question.

How could the Department of the Interior satisfy the requirements for comprehensive land use planning, they asked, if it waited until after it had already given the companies the right to mine the coal to identify what conflicts may exist on the leased tracts?

The reason the Reaganites and the companies insisted on having the leases issued, regardless of what conflicts might be found later, has to do with mineral economics, with control over the resource. A lease establishes that a company has the legal right to get the coal. Prior to lease issuance, a coal company is but one of several competing potential users of the land in question. From the companies' standpoint, to hold the lease was to control the land and the coal under it. And from the Reagan ideologues' viewpoint, the central issue was always a question of control: would the public, through the federal government, control the mineral-bearing lands, or would industry have that control?

Even considering these important ideological interventions, what came out of the Chaco-San Juan Management Framework Plan was a flawed, but still somewhat useful basis for making initial determinations as to where federal coal should be sought, and where perhaps it would be better not to seek it.

The plan made such obvious decisions as avoiding strip mining in the Chaco Culture National Historical Park, avoidance of coal leasing in those three areas which had been designated as federal Wilderness Study Areas (to be preserved until such time as Congress decided whether those areas should be added to the National Wilderness Preservation System), and leaving undisturbed those sites known to be nesting areas for eagles. In effect, the land use plan made major decisions as to how specific tracts would be used, and tagged certain areas to be managed keeping specific resource values in mind. It brought forward for further consideration for leasing an estimated 10-13 billion tons of publicly-owned coal, about 1.5 billion of which was expected to be strip mineable, including about one billion tons within the Preference Right Lease Application areas (except where they conflicted with potential wilderness areas).

The plan called for specially-managed "areas of critical environmental concern" in several locations. Some of these special management areas were for scientific (paleontological) resources, and others were designated for archeological reasons. Perhaps most importantly, the plan called for an on-the-ground management effort in what BLM called the "Bisti Critical Management Area" . . . that incredibly conflicted portion of the overall planning unit that contained Chaco Canyon, Bisti, De-na-zin and Ah-shi-sle-pah areas, the presumed most important paleontological areas (including Fossil Forest) and the PRLAs. According to the plan, a Bisti Multiple Resource Management Center was to be established in the heart of the critical management area, to be staffed by BLM scientists and wilderness specialists, coal experts and archeologists.

And planning had revealed a way around the tough conflicts presented by the federal coal underlying the Chaco-Bisti region. Toward the end of the planning process, local BLM officials came to regard the publicly-owned coal in the Lee Ranch area north of Grants as the solution to the resource puzzle. If the coal in the Chaco-Bisti area was too conflicted, there was another major area from which federal coal could be leased—in any quantity conceivably needed—without fouling Indian lands, archeological concentrations, wilderness areas or the more important fossils locations.

Public coal under Floyd and Iona Lee's Ranch, outside the Chaco-Bisti area, had another major advantage. Santa Fe Industries already controlled sizeable tonnages of private coal there, and, with an in-house railroad company (Santa Fe Pacific Railway), they were sure they would be able to get coal from Lee Ranch to markets. Santa Fe Industries' announced intention to mine at Lee Ranch and its ability to provide transportation made the nearby public coal exceedingly attractive . . . especially if offering coal leases there would eliminate the need to offer leases in the tortuous Chaco-Bisti area.

All in all, despite its flaws, the land use plan was seen by many members of the public as a relatively honest attempt to reconcile competing land uses. If the plan seemed heavily biased toward coal leasing in the region, that was not unexpected. Many assumed from the beginning that the coal companies and the utility companies would call the shots, so the land use plan still at least seemed to recognize the value of the other non-mineral resources in the coal region.

In fact, many people in government and out were relieved that the process was all but completed by the time President Reagan set James Watt loose on the Department of Interior.

But if Watt and his assistant secretaries wanted to put control of as much of the coal lands as possible into corporate hands, regardless of what other public resources might be jeopardized, they faced another legal snag. That was the legal requirement that the public receive fair market value for the sale or lease of its minerals.

The Federal Coal Leasing Amendments Act of 1976 specifically requires that the federal government obtain "fair market value" for the public's coal offered for lease. The public is paid for its coal in two primary ways: first, the purchase of a lease by a coal company through a bonus bid, and second, through royalties on each ton of federal coal mined and sold. It is relatively easy to assure that the public gains fair market value through royalties on tonnage mined, but to obtain fair payment on the value of the lease itself, the government must know the quantity and quality of the public's coal within the proposed lease area. And that was the problem.

How could Assistant Secretary Carruthers justify dumping hundreds of millions of tons of publicly-owned coal into a lease offering if the federal agencies responsible for managing the minerals had no idea how much the coal was worth? How would the federal government know whether the companies were paying enough for the lease if they didn't know how much coal was there? And even if they did know how much coal was in a specific coal lease tract, how could they determine the value of it if some parts of the lease area were later found to be off-limits due to belated discovery of eagle nests, archeological sites or Navajo religious sites?

The issue came to a head publicly in March 1982, at a state-federal Regional Coal Team meeting held in Santa Fe, some six months after completion of land use planning for the Chaco-Bisti region.

According to the federal coal program as set forth late in the Carter Administration, state government officials were to play an important role in determining when and where federal coal deposits would be offered for lease in their states. The forum for that state participation was to be a "regional coal team" for each of the 12 federal coal regions. The governor of a state included in a federal coal region was to be a voting member of the Regional Coal Team, as would be the BLM State Director in that state. Each coal team would include as many ex-officio (non-voting) members as might be appropriate, such as representatives of the National Park Service, state fish and game bureaus, members of the Soil Conservation Service, and others.

The Regional Coal Team for the San Juan River Coal Region was first convened near the end of the BLM's land use planning. It included representatives of the governors of New Mexico and Colorado (the two states in the coal region), the BLM State Directors for those states, a BLM official from outside the coal region as chairman, plus a multitude of ex-officios, among them the Navajo Tribe. At the outset, the State of New Mexico's representative was even more pro-coal development than were the Carter Administration BLM members of the RCT. Standing in for New Mexico Governor Bruce King was his Secretary for Energy and Minerals, Larry Kehoe, who consistently favored more coal offered for lease with less concern for the environment and for non-mineral resources on the public lands. The pro-mining stance of the state government representative was not remarkable, since New Mexico has had a long dependence on the extractive industries as a source of government revenues in a state otherwise extraordinarily poor.

At the Santa Fe meeting of the San Juan River Regional Coal Team March 10, 1982, the Resource Conservation Division of the U.S. Geological Survey made its presentation on mineral resource data known about the lands BLM had identified in its land use plan for further consideration for leasing. The USGS specialists systematically demonstrated that coal reserve data gaps in much of the region would make it impossible to offer certain tracts for lease, since the agency could not assure that the U.S. Treasury would get fair market value for the minerals.

Amid the federal geologists' arguments that only tracts with adequate coal resource data could be leased, a Washington Office Interior official broke in to assert that the tracts could, after all, be offered for lease without knowing what they were worth; rough guesstimates were good enough. Thus overruled by Washington, the local geologists proceeded to delineate coal lease tracts for which the values were unknown, a procedure which they were certain was a violation of the 1976 Federal Coal Leasing Amendments Act.

But when the Geological Survey officials continued to insist that delineating leasing tracts without adequate information was improper, Carruthers intervened to quell the rebellion. Contacted by New Mexico Energy and Minerals Secretary Kehoe about USGS misgivings, Carruthers responded in a letter dated February 17, 1982, "Thank you for bringing to our attention the 'adequate information' problem Minerals Management Service [formerly USGS] staff have been referring to in the San Juan Basin. I couldn't agree with you more that this situation needs immediate attention. Our conversations with Assistant Secretary Miller and Acting Minerals Management Service Director (Perry) Pendley suggest that your descriptions of the problem and solution are entirely accurate. Minerals Management Service has, at the field level, often cited a lack of data; and although detailed information may not be available for some tracts, sufficient data is present to permit sound, professional estimates of reserves present in lease tracts. . . . We will see to it that progress is made on this issue."

The Interior official from Washington who had contradicted his field personnel at the Regional Coal Team meeting, Dick Wilson, was subsequently reassigned to the New Mexico BLM State Office in Santa Fe as Associate State Director for Minerals. At the time of the meeting, Wilson was the U.S. Geological Survey's deputy chief of the coal section for the Office of Energy Resources. He was one of many influential Washington-level Interior officials who wound up working in the coal program in New Mexico.

But the instructions for delineating lease tracts without adequate mineral data were not the only public evidence of a federal coal program going awry. Another of the program steps following coal-related land use planning was the setting of leasing targets. In this process, the Watt-Carruthers coal program was exposed as the fraud that it truly was.

The federal coal program that Watt and Carruthers inherited from the Carter Administration called for the leasing of publicly-owned coal to make up any shortfalls in the amount of coal expected to be needed at various future dates. The amount of public coal to be leased was to be predicated on how much coal was expected to be consumed at specific time periods in the future. As such, the program was supposed to be driven by the amount of coal that would likely be needed, not how much the coal companies would like to have as assets. Leasing was clearly intended to be for market demand, rather than corporate demand for reserves.

How this system was perverted in the San Juan River Coal Region constitutes one of the more interesting and scandalous parts of the Watt legacy. And how Interior officials were trapped by concerned citizens is conversely one of the most encouraging parts of the federal coal scandal.

Unfortunately for Watt and Assistant Secretary Carruthers, the federal coal program was laid out in clear, easy-to-follow steps open to public scrutiny. As set up by Congress and the Carter Adminstration, the idea was to assure availability of domestic energy resources so that the United States would not fall victim to overseas oil cartels for its energy needs. The Department of Energy outlined a step-by-step basis for determining how much the total national energy need would be in target years 1985, 1990, 2000, etc. Then it apportioned those energy demands to potential sources, factoring in production from nuclear plants, hydroelectric, natural gas, oil, solar and coal . . . with specific emphasis on coal as the fuel of preference in the immediate future. A computer model cranked out how much coal would be needed on a yearly basis nationwide for the target years, and then made projections where the coal would come from. If the total national coal production goal for 1990, for example, was in the 1.2 to 1.9 billion tons-a-year range, the program called for each of the 12 federally designated coal regions nationwide to provide its share to meet that demand.

The San Juan River Coal Region, for example, was expected to come up with 33.3 to 44.2 million tons of coal per year in 1985;

55.9 to 67.4 million a year in 1990; and 61 to 77.4 million a year in 1995.

Then the federal agencies involved, chiefly BLM and the U.S. Geological Survey, were supposed to determine whether the amount of coal already under lease in each region would be sufficient to meet the projected demand. If coal already under lease, or expected to be leased through non-governmental sources, was not adequate to meet the projected demand, then the Department of the Interior was to lease publicly-owned coal to cover the shortfall. Conversely, if the amount of coal already under lease in a coal region was sufficient to meet the projected demand, there was to be no additional federal coal leasing.

And the method for determining whether there would be a regional shortfall of coal production was also explicit . . . too explicit for Watt and the "free marketeers". The relationship between the "regional production goals" and the "regional leasing targets" was clearly established in the federal coal management regulations, 43 CFR 3420.3. The regulations state that in deriving the regional leasing target from the Department of Energy's production goals, the Department of the Interior must evaluate expected and potential production from all non-federal coal holdings (including Indian tribal lands), outstanding federal leases, and the level of market competition in the coal region.

Expected production from existing coal leases from all sources in the region were to be tallied up as the baseline from which to determine whether additional federal leases should be offered.

At the tail end of the Chaco-San Juan land use plan, BLM Farmington Office Geologist John San Filipo was assigned the additional task of analyzing that baseline of coal from the San Juan Basin that was expected to be in production to meet the Department of Energy (DOE) production goals for the various time periods. San Filipo's report included detailed calculations which demonstrated that the San Juan River Coal Region would be able to produce 27.9 million tons of coal a year in 1985; 55.4 million tons a year by 1990; 57.1 million tons annually in 1993; and 58.1 million tons a year in the target date 1995 . . . all of that could be produced from coal already available to the coal mining companies, without additional federal leasing.

What, then, did the baseline production mean for the need to lease more federal coal? The U.S. Department of Energy said the

San Juan region should be producing a medium range of 37.7 million tons annually by 1985 and San Filipo's data showed existing leases could produce 27.9 million tons yearly; DOE called for a medium range of 64.1 million a year in 1990 and San Filipo's study showed that 55.4 million yearly could be produced without additional federal leasing. Similarly, DOE wanted at least 61 million tons a year available in 1995 and San Filipo's data showed 58.1 million could be produced that year even without additional federal leases.

In other words, relatively little additional federal coal leasing would be needed to meet projected demand.

It should be pointed out that San Filipo was hardly trying to make things difficult for the coal companies that wanted more federal coal. On the contrary, San Filipo was decidedly pro-industry in his personal biases, and was the BLM land use planning team member most strongly favoring additional federal coal leasing in the Chaco-Bisti region. But the facts clearly showed that little additional leasing of public coal would be needed there to meet expected demands. In fact, San Filipo had presented as needful a prospect as he could. His coal production baseline report actually shows that the amount of coal that *might* be available in the target years was really substantially higher than the figures above. He notes that coal reserves available but "unreliable before 1995" amounted to 33.9 million tons a year in 1985; 75.1 million tons a year in 1990; 91.5 million tons annually in 1993; and 94.5 million tons in 1995.

Using those figures, far more coal was already under lease in the San Juan Basin than was expected to be needed. The projected high production level in 1995, for example, would be 77.4 million tons a year; San Filipo's tally for "available but unreliable" tonnages in that year amounted to 94.5 million tons a year.

In his most pessimistic analysis, the coal region could produce within a half-million ton a year of the low end of what might be needed in 1990, which would call for a very modest federal coal lease sale to make up the short fall. But including the coal reserves he deemed "unreliable before 1995" the amount of coal available without additional federal leasing would be 19.2 million tons a year *over* what was expected to be needed in 1990.

What that meant for Watt and Carruthers is that economics showed no need to turn control of additional public coal over to corporate hands. Needless to say, that was an unacceptable conclusion.

Already the conservative ideologues were abandoning the notion of leasing federal minerals based on market demand, and instead were grasping for some other basis for leasing which would give public minerals to industry. The slogan for that new basis was "lease for demand for reserves", or, lease to meet the companies' demands for speculative assets. Or, even more bluntly, cheat the public out of the real value of its mineral wealth, by throwing federal coal out for lease when there was little market demand for it.

The guiding philosophy had changed from leasing to serve the public interest to leasing to give industry control over public mineral wealth.

But the new philosophy ran counter to the legally established federal coal program.

The program, based on federal laws and duly-promulgated regulations, called for determining the amount of public coal to be leased by comparing the projected market need with the amount of coal already available. In the fall of 1981, BLM New Mexico State Director Bill Luscher sent a memo which included San Filipo's study and worksheets to the BLM Colorado State Director, a fellow member of the San Juan River Regional Coal Team (RCT), saying: "The baseline will be used as the starting point for the calculation of the regional leasing target and for identifying environmental impacts associated with new competitive leasing. Please review these calculations, both with your staff and with the State of Colorado. If possible, I suggest that this be accomplished prior to the upcoming RCT meeting. . . ."

What happened instead was the abandonment of the San Filipo baseline production study, and the substitution of another blatantly corrupt study which suggested that much more public coal needed to be leased. The substitute report, developed through the pro-industry state government's Energy and Minerals Division, purported to show much lower production from existing leases, and inexplicably excluded production from some leases, even those issued by Interior. The exclusions in the substitute study clearly violated the federal regulations in 43 CFR 3420.3, in that it did not count all the production expected from existing federal leases in New Mexico, completely eliminated production from leases in southern Colorado which was part of the coal region, and did not include production from leases on the Navajo Reservation, also part of the designated federal coal region.

Yet BLM officials quickly and unquestioningly tossed aside the San Filipo baseline report and adopted the substitute which purported to show a greater need for leasing of public coal in the San Juan Basin. On December 2, 1981, the San Juan RCT made its recommendation for a coal leasing target to Watt and Carruthers: offer for lease 800 million to 1.5 billion tons of federal coal. It was an incredible sum, totally unsupportable by the legal process for determining the amount of coal to be offered for lease. In fact, the 1.5 billion tons level would have encompassed nearly all of the unleased, strip mineable federal coal in the San Juan Basin not already encumbered by the Preference Right Lease Application process.

The RCT's drastically inflated leasing target recommendation hit BLM field level officials and USGS geologists like a ton of coal. BLM specialists who had developed the land use plan knew that they had woefully inadequate data about surface conflicts to offer that much coal for lease. USGS officials knew they would never be able to comply with their legal mandate to determine fair market value of all that coal within the tight timeframe set for the first competitive lease sale, then set for September 1983.

The field level Interior officials were still in a state of near shock when, a month later, they learned that not only had Carruthers accepted the coal team's phony production baseline and the bogus coal leasing target, but he had hiked it even higher on his own. Carruthers set the preliminary leasing target at 1.2 to 1.5 billion tons, raising the low end of the target range by 400 million tons.

An executive summary used by Carruthers to support increasing the San Juan coal leasing target even higher includes the following rationale: "Ten companies initially expressed interest in leasing a total 2.563 billion tons of coal through the formal expression of interest process. Subsequently Chaco Energy Company formally withdrew its expression of interest in 900 million tons, bringing the total to 1.663 billion tons. The State of New Mexico has expressed its opposition to a leasing level greater than the 1.5 billion tons identified as the maximum feasible target in the RCT's report."

The January 6, 1982 document goes on to note: "In the RCT's report the ability for USGS to provide adequate data beyond 1.0 billion tons was presented as a constraining factor. Subsequent to the report the USGS has notified the BLM that adequate data would not be a limiting factor."

But if BLM State Director Bill Luscher was prepared to pretend the substitute baseline study was genuine, and that he had been convinced to cast his coal team vote in favor of offering up to 1.5 billion tons for competitive bidding (on top of the estimated 2.3 billion tons that he expected to go to the coal companies through Preference Right Leases), the public was not.

The federal coal program still in effect included a public hearing on the setting of regional coal leasing targets. About two months after the fraudulent leasing target was approved by the state-federal coal team, a public hearing on the matter was held at Albuquerque's Holiday Inn on February 23, 1982. In the course of the hearing, members of the public exposed the fraud in a manner so tellingly that the target was eventually cut in half.

Collaborating with environmental activists, mathematician Dave Marcus ripped the RCT's flawed coal lease target calculations to shreds.

"The target for new federal leasing in our region (1.2 to 1.5 billion tons of leasing in 1983) was set by Garrey Carruthers, DOI Assistant Secretary for Land and Water Resources, in his memo of mid-January 1981, 'San Juan Coal Region Preliminary Leasing Target'. This target is calculated based on DOE Final Coal Production Goals for our region which, after having been revised upward during the Carter-Reagan interregnum, were set at from 54.5 to 58.9 million tons per year by 1990, and adopted by DOE. Both goals and targets have been heavily fudged in the direction of massive leasing. If Carruthers, the RCT, and DOE had done the calculations in an unbiased way, the result would have shown that no new leasing is necessary for the San Juan River Region."

Marcus then traced through the mathematical equations used by Carruthers' office to arrive at the exaggerated leasing target. In proceding to tear apart Carruthers' fraudulent calculations, Marcus noted, "The baseline used in the Carruthers calculation seems to be the result of a mistake and/or swindle by the Regional Coal Team or its representatives. The 41 million ton figure is the result of an estimate by Larry Kehoe of the Coal Team made shortly before the Regional Coal Team meeting of December 2, 1981, and is itself the sum of two very reasonable figures—20 million tons/year for existing 1981 production, plus 21 million tons for PRLA production (that is, 40 percent of 2 billion tons of PRLA reserves developed in mines of a 30-year lifetime with 80 percent recovery factor). However, this 41 million ton baseline totally leaves out expansion in production due to undeveloped existing non-PRLA federal leases, and expansion due to development of state, private and Indian coal. This expansion is likely to be considerable; in fact, the baseline calculated for the Coal Team by BLM (San Filipo) includes about 25 million tons of such expansion.

"This BLM baseline, derived from a mine-by-mine survey by a knowledgeable geologist, gave a total of 56.4 million tons/year projected production from our region without any new federal leasing. Furthermore, this BLM baseline only includes 10.75 million tons/year from PRLAs in 1990—only 20-26 percent of potential PRLA production. . . . The 56.4 million ton baseline was duly presented to the Coal Team at its September 2, 1981 meeting, and was never publicly rejected by them. Why it was not used by the Coal Team in making their leasing target recommendations, or by Carruthers in setting the targets, we do not know."

Marcus concluded: "Sufficient coal has been leased in the San Juan Basin to more than satisfy any reasonable level of demand. According to the intent behind our present federal coal leasing program—which was to avoid overleasing and speculation, comply with the National Environmental Policy Act, and secure the public a "fair return" for its mineral resources—no new coal should be leased in such a situation."

If Marcus had them dead to rights, Committee on Coal member Mimi Lopez dug in to expose the deliberateness of the deceit. The following statements are taken from the hearing transcript:

Ms Lopez: At the Regional Coal Team meeting in December when the leasing target was decided upon by the RCT, the target was 800 million to 1.5 billion tons. After that meeting the State BLM Director sent a memo to the Director of the BLM in Washington transmitting the information. In that letter he said, "this recommendation was concurred in by all members present." That clearly states that the state BLM concurred since they were present. Why did the state BLM ultimately recommend a different leasing target [increasing the target from 800 million-1.5 billion up to 1.2-1.5 billion]?

Mr. Armstrong (Hearing Officer): Continue reading your questions please.

Ms Lopez: I would like an answer to this.

Member of the Hearing Panel: I wasn't present. What happened there was that Gene Day [N.M. BLM state office coordinator for the coal program in the San Juan Basin] went to Washington and talked with the department people about the leasing targets and that's where the decision was made. . . . There was a lot of discussion about forcing leasing targets, but then the recommendation of the State [of New Mexico] was that we go no higher than 1.5. As a result of those discussions they decided to go with the upper end of the range.

Ms Lopez: I have a couple of questions to ask about the baseline figure of 41 million tons [the fraudulent baseline conclusion]. Does that include Colorado coal?

Panel Member: The baseline figure was outlined in the last meeting and is based on non-competitive coal and current production.

Ms Lopez: That would include southern Colorado? What I didn't know was that Mr. Kehoe [NM Secretary for Energy and Minerals] was only looking at New Mexico production or if current Colorado production was also included.

Panel Member: I don't know if he did or not.

Ms Lopez: My next question is also in regards to the baseline. The original memo with Mr. San Filipo's figures based on a mine-by mine analysis gives a baseline of 55.4 [million tons a year] for 1990. You are now using a baseline of 41 as opposed to Mr. San Filipo's 55.4. Is there the same kind of documentation to support your use of 41 that was available from Mr. San Filipo? Did you develop a document comparable to that? If not, what kind of documentation do you have to support that baseline?

Panel Member: That was from the state computer file.

Ms Lopez: I assume that the point of view in this Executive Summary and the Department of Justice report talks about more market-oriented leasing policy as the primary objective to enhance competition and if this should be a coal development or government intervention. What it's saying is that by leasing a whole lot more coal than is actually needed to meet the demand, this is going to make more competition in the leasing process. Is that a correct assumption of what the thinking is?

Panel Member: As recalled, they were emphasizing two things: coal companies being allowed to enter the market, and that the federal government had some sort of monopoly of coal in the West, because of their great holdings of reserves, and this was one of the things they were looking at in terms of those two factors. . . .

Ms Lopez: It would seem on the basis of logic that if you lease more coal than there is a demand for, that would bring down the competitive leasing prices—leases would go for lower.

Panel Member: That is possible.

Ms Lopez: If that were the case, then it would seem that would mean the federal government, and the State, because the State gets 50 percent of the lease money that the federal government receives, would get less revenue than they might if they leased less. I have trouble justifying that with the current federal position on the economics in this country with the emphasis that the present Administration is putting on the urgent need to reduce the federal deficit. . . . If they're trying to reduce the federal deficit, then the federal government would have an absolute obligation to maximize its revenues in any way it could. It would seem that this particular philosophy of leasing such huge amounts would be contradictory to that goal for the federal government maximizing its revenues."

Away from public eyes and ears, BLM staffers in the Albuquerque District Office were amazed at Carruthers' blatant violations of the procedures which were supposed to guide the federal coal program.

Pondering over Carruthers' decision for a San Juan coal leasing target of up to 1.5 billion tons, BLM geologists went over the wording he had used in his memo as his justification: "A target of 500 to 700 million tons (offered for competitive lease in 1983) would satisfy a one-to-one relationship of leasing to production" and the other assertion that "A relatively small fraction of production from the PRLAs is included in the baseline used to calculate the 500 to 700 million tons one-to-one target". The BLM district geologist shook his head and exclaimed, "Beats the shit out of me. We don't have a baseline that would support a 500-700 million ton leasing target."

A month before the public hearing on the leasing target, Bob Armstrong, the New Mexico BLM State Office official who presided over it, told other BLM staffers, "Everybody has a problem with it (the coal leasing target calculations). It was sent down from Washington that way. I had problems with it the first time I saw it. But it's word-for-word out of Carruthers' letter."

The BLM State Office official continued: "Once we sent our RCT recommended leasing levels to Washington, they did some mumbo-jumbo over it up there, and this is what came out."

A few days later, Armstrong tried again to explain what Carruthers had tried to do in the numbers sham. "Carruthers' Preliminary Coal Leasing Target of 1.2 to 1.5 billion tons is based on a level of 500-700 million tons being one-to-one, or assuming that tons of coal leased equaled the same tons of coal produced." And the 500-700 million ton figure is based on a revision of San Filipo's baseline data, he said, adding that the "revision" took place November 11, 1981 in a meeting between NM Energy and Minerals Secretary Larry Kehoe, BLM's Gene Day and USGS officials. At the meeting, Kehoe had argued that San Filipo's estimate of 1990 coal production from the San Juan Basin, 55.4 million tons, was too high, that some mines would not be producing at the level San Filipo estimated. Although it was pointed out that San Filipo had simply used the mining company's own estimates (the preferred method of projecting), Kehoe insisted and the baseline figure be adjusted down to only 41 million tons a year being produced in

1990. Then with that lower projected production, calculations were made to demonstrate that 500-700 million tons of federal coal would need to be leased in 1983. But, just to make sure there was no shortfall of producible coal, Carruthers doubled the already inflated 500-700 million tons to bring the San Juan Basin leasing target up to 1.2 to 1.5 billion tons, Armstrong explained.

BLM specialists and managers were stunned that Carruthers would try something so blatant. A BLM minerals specialist lamented to BLM Albuquerque Assistant District Manager Mat Millenbach, "That 1.5 billion tons figure . . . our credibility is already shot on that to begin with."

On February 4, 1982, Assistant District Manager Millenbach met with state government geologist Louie Martinez, of Kehoe's Energy and Minerals Department, to learn what had really happened to produce such an unsupportable, inflated leasing target. Martinez admitted that the baseline was pushed down from 55.4 million tons/year to 41 million for purely political reasons.

Millenbach expressed disgust at the compromised procedures and later confronted BLM State Office's Gene Day about the deception. At Millenbach's insistence, the two worked out a recalculation of the leasing target that was at least more defensible, although the corrected work did not become the official version of how much coal was needed.

By the end of February, Millenbach was resigned to the fact that the coal program in New Mexico was hopelessly warped. "I've sort of lost touch with the coal effort now. It's getting so irrational that I've lost interest in it. There's nothing I can do about it anymore. You have to understand that this whole question has moved beyond management issues and into political issues."

The BLM manager closest to the coal issues, Farmington Area Manager Bob Calkins, was similarly distraught. Over dinner with other BLMers during the second week of January 1982, Calkins expressed fears that the coal program in his Resource Area would cost him his job. "I have nightmares about how they're going to have my ass. After I've been telling them about all the problems with mining this coal and them not listening, they're finally going to wake up and say, 'Why you dumb shit, why didn't you tell us about this!' "

District Manager Applegate replied; "I know it. You know, they still don't understand, they don't want to face up to the fact that it'll be a long, long time before they ever get any coal out of here. That's just not the way they want to see it." Applegate cursed BLM New Mexico Associate State Director Monte Jordan, formerly head of the BLM coal program back in Washington, for being too timid to relay the reality of resource conflicts in the San Juan Basin back to Carruthers and other Interior chiefs in Washington.

What Watt and Carruthers wanted was to end public control over the coal resource and hand that control over to industry. If the other publicly-owned resources—wilderness, fossils, archeological sites—and the survival of subsistence-level human beings got in the way, their importance was to be downplayed or denied. If federal regulations implementing Congress's laws were obstacles to that goal, then the regulations had to be bent, revised or ignored. If civil servants refused to bend the regulations and insisted on obeying the laws, they were to be harassed, transferred, or otherwise neutralized.

In the San Juan coal region, Carruthers conspired to dump essentially all of the commercially valuable public coal onto the market with minimal regard to resource conflicts, and with little or no regard for paying the public what its coal was worth.

By trying to force a federal coal leasing target of 1.5 billion tons (in addition to the 2.3 billion intended to be leased through PRLAs) into an already soft coal market, Carruthers would have aided and abetted the deliberate loss of more than $50 million from the potential coal lease revenues for his home state, and another $50 million from the U.S. Treasury.

There can be no doubt about his intentions. A very similar process was at work in Interior's Powder River Coal Region in Wyoming and Montana. Interior's coal leasing actions there dumped 1.6 billion tons of public coal onto the market in 1982, resulting in the public getting gypped out of $100 million or more. The Powder River Coal lease sale scandal triggered a complete shutdown on the federal coal program by Congress. But more important than documenting the loss of $100 million through resource dumping, investigations of the scandal revealed that the loss of revenue was no accident, that high Interior officials had deliberately rigged the process to turn over public coal at minimal price—that the officials had, in fact, leaked the secret "minimum acceptable bid" to prospective bidders.

Circumstances of the scandal are documented in a 1983 General Accounting Office report which found: 1) the Powder River sale was not competitive, as required; 2) the federal government did not receive fair market value for the public coal leased; and 3) a release of confidential pricing information was made to companies before the lease occurred.

A congressional report in 1983, by the Survey and Investigations staff of the House Appropriations Committee, found that the procedures used in the Powder River coal lease sale gave public coal resources to the industry "for next to nothing", and noted: "The Powder River Basin sale highlights the mismanagement of the coal leasing program. Such large-scale leasing under poor economic conditions destroys the market by flooding it with leased coal. It temporarily reduces fair market value, and allows the industry to acquire coal at 'fire sale' prices."

Carruthers later attempted to defend this process before a congressional investigating committee.

The 1983 Surveys and Investigations report gives this explanation of how the scandal occurred. "In late 1981, the MMS [Minerals Management Service] field office at Casper Wyoming (MMS Casper) received concurrence from headquarters (MMS/Reston) on the methodology and appraisal format to be followed in estimating the fair market value of the April 1982 Powder River coal lease tracts. This format and method was consistent with the Uniform Appraisal Standards. MMS/Casper spent 4,000 man-hours at a cost of about $60,000 to prepare the estimate of fair market value. On February 26, 1982, MMS/Casper advised MMS/Reston of the estimated fair market value for the Powder River Basin tracts to be included in the March 25, 1982 sale announcement.

"Some time between March 10 and 15, 1982, after the estimates of fair market value (minimum acceptable bids—MAB's) were received in the Department, these estimates of fair market value allegedly were 'leaked' to unauthorized individuals, e.g. coal industry officials. This 'leak' and the subsequent unsupportable reduction in the 'leaked' values have been called 'scandalous' by many government and industry officials. Several Interior officials believed that the sale should have been postponed. The then Deputy Assistant Secretary for Land and Water, however, reportedly had made a personal decision which he felt was irreversible."

That deputy assistant secretary, directly under Carruthers, was David C. Russell, generally credited with developing the conservative Heritage Foundation's coal policy.

The report continues, ". . . the Investigative Staff inquired why they have not requested the Office of Inspector General (OIG) to investigate the 'leak'. The former Deputy Assistant Secretary, [Russell] who was the acknowledged expert for the coal program, advised that he had not heard of the leak until he had read a letter dated March 26, 1982, from Casper, Wyoming, stating that the minimum acceptable bid values may have been compromised; and he pointed out that the date was definitely after he directed that the minimum acceptable bids be reduced."

The leak of confidential minimum bid data was later confirmed by a coal industry attorney who said he had been given the secret information by Russell himself. *Energy Daily* magazine reported that Brent Kunz, attorney for Texas Energy Services of Wyoming, said he received the inside information from Russell shortly before the ill-fated coal lease sale in 1982. Kunz reportedly told federal investigators that he took both Russell and MMS's William (Perry) Pendley out for a $500 dinner the day after they altered the bidding procedures which reduced the price companies would have to pay for federal coal in the coming lease sale.

The report says that approval for the last-minute switch in procedures for the April 1982 Powder River sale came in the form of a memo from then-Under Secretary of Interior Donald Hodel.

The report's summary includes the following warning: "In spite of the current reduced demand for coal, the depressed near-term future needs, excess capacity, undeveloped leases, and unresolved preference right lease applications, Interior continues to plan for three regional coal lease sales in the near future, with coal offerings exceeding 6 billion tons."

The next one would have been in the San Juan River Coal Region.

CHAPTER 8

CHANGING THE REGULATIONS & HIDING FROM THE PUBLIC

The last-minute change in lease sale procedures for the scandalous Powder River coal offering in April 1982 was only one of a wide range of adulterations in the federal coal program. Those changes in bidding procedures and fair market value determinations for the Powder River coal lease sale resulted in a loss to the public of $60-132 million: but that was just the beginning. The overall package of changes instituted by Watt and his lieutenants was meant to turn over billions more tons of public coal to private interests without paying the public what its property was worth. And, with the ideologues' new strategy, the public would be prevented from ever knowing what had happened.

Efforts by high Interior officials to subvert the legally-constituted federal coal program and the congressional acts intended to guide it can be traced through the department's attempts to formally change the leasing process. In 1982-83, Watt's Interior went through the obligatory motions of proposing changes in the federal regulations relating to coal leasing, ostensibly to "eliminate excessive, burdensome, and counterproductive regulations, procedures and policies". These proposed regulation changes, dutifully published in the Federal Register for public notice and comment, covered such alterations as: eliminating leasing targets based on Department of Energy projections of consumer needs; making it more difficult for landowners to qualify for "surface owner consent" rights; eliminating protection for historical or archeological sites judged eligible for (but not yet named to) the National Register for Historic Places; eliminating the land use planning screen which would approve for coal leasing only those tracts with moderate to high mining potential; and numerous other policy guidance meant to allow industry more freedom to get whatever it wanted.

But these official regulation change proposals were only the tip of the iceberg. Even greater impacts were being imposed by internal memos, policy directives and verbal orders never meant to be seen or heard by the public or its watchdog organizations. These in-house changes in the coal program—coupled with budget manipulations to de-fund agency functions which industry found objectionable and involuntary transfers of personnel whose adherence to the law made company executives nervous—produced far deeper alterations than the more visible regulatory changes.

From the right-wing zealots' point of view the then-existing federal coal program was set up by anti-business liberals during the Carter Administration, and, now that Reagan was in power, their task was to undo much of that nonsense. Anything which seemed to hinder the coal industry, such as comprehensive land use planning, was a target for elimination or modification.

An essential part of their effort to "eliminate burdens" on the coal industry was curtailment of the public's right to know. Perhaps the ideologues wouldn't have gone so far as to assert openly that the public in general didn't have a right to know what Interior was doing, but they had no trouble in deciding that the "environmentalists" didn't have a right to know anything. The Reagan team at Interior already considered environmentalists to be the enemy, and it was clear to them that the enemy shouldn't be privy to strategy planning. Environmentalists, they were sure, were out to destroy America. Any good patriot would, therefore, do whatever was necessary to thwart environmentalists' influence.

It was true, of course, that "environmentalists" were among the elements of the public most interested in information about the federal coal program. When Watt determined that he was a prime target of the environmental community, his department prepared and implemented a multi-faceted effort to deny them access to information about the coal program. As part of that campaign, Watt set out to deliberately curtail public scrutiny of his department's actions, and to formally eliminate opportunities for public participation in coal-related decisions for use of the public land and its minerals.

In effect, they began a cover-up operation even before there was anything to cover up. They knew environmentalists would fight what they intended to do, so they set out almost immediately to shut off access to information about their coal program.

The coal regulations which Watt inherited when he came to Interior were the product of almost ten years of compromise by parties on all sides. After the federal coal program was shut down in 1971 due to congressionally perceived abuses (including loss of revenue to the U.S. Treasury), coal industry representatives, government officials, environmentalists and public interest groups hammered out new procedures for leasing the public's coal. Incorporating the land use planning required in the Federal Land Policy and Management Act, the Federal Coal Leasing Amendments Act and the Surface Mining Control and Reclamation Act, among others, the 1979 regulations supporting the federal coal program at that time were in large measure a consensus effort. It is significant that coal industry executives were sufficiently satisfied with the revised program that they apparently felt no necessity to challenge the 1979 regulations in court (aside from the minor objections filed in a National Coal Association and Texaco suit claiming that Interior must provide a substitute coal lease for lands subsequently disqualified because they were determined to be in an alluvial valley floor).

Although they may have been satisfied with the 1979 coal regulations, the coal executives were not fools. It was patently obvious that with Watt heading Interior, they could now get whatever they wanted, the public interest be damned.

Public scrutiny was built into the 1979 coal program; it was just as surely thrown out in the Watt revisions of 1982-83. In the

1979 coal program, there were numerous points in the process for formal public hearings and other forms of input. Before Watt, for example, the public was given two points at which to comment on the setting of leasing levels and the ranking of tracts to be offered for lease. The Watt regulatory changes in 1982 eliminated all of these channels for public participation, leaving only the mandatory public comment period after release of a draft environmental impact statement. The 1979 regulations also required distinct opportunities for public input on expected impacts to local communities prior to preparation of environmental impact statements, and on the federal agency's application of the Unsuitability Criteria during land use planning. These were also eliminated by Watt's rule changes.

But the major difference was internal pressures within the BLM bureaucracy to halt the flow information to environmentalists and others opposed to indiscriminate coal leasing. At the outset of the 1979 coal program, the public was considered the owner of the coal in question and therefore fully entitled to see how its property was being managed. Under the right-wing ideologues, the public was considered to have no business owning the coal in the first place, and should be prevented from thwarting their plan to hand it over to industry.

With the new philosophy, then, if a member of the public (other than a coal company executive) sought information about the coal program, the inquirer was suspect. Civil servants were expected to give as little information as possible, mislead the inquirer if necessary, and absolutely refrain from explaining how the parts of the complicated coal program fit together and what the results of the program might be. Watt and his team were dead set on parting federal coal from its owners, and it only made sense to keep the public in the dark about it.

But Interior officials readily acknowledged proposing the following regulation changes, among others:

- Start out the coal program in each region by calling for industry's "expression of interest" in specific areas, rather than letting land use planning make the first determinations as to where public coal might be sought. Industry's desire for assets was to direct the land use planning.

- Consider for lease any coal anywhere a company might wish, whether or not the coal there has good potential for mining. The change eliminated the 1979 land use planning screen which said that only federal coal deposits of moderate to high potential should be considered for leasing.

- Eliminate the goal of leasing public coal to meet government projections for future energy demand, and instead substitute the goal of leasing to meet the companies' demands for assets.

- Tonnages to be offered for lease in a given coal region would be set by the Secretary of the Interior within a broad range of leasing levels, rather than a specific level being set by the state-federal Regional Coal Teams.

- Unsuitability Criteria established through the Surface Mining Control and Reclamation Act would no longer be applied to existing leases or to Preference Right Lease Application (PRLA) areas during land use planning.

- Eliminate the automatic prohibition against leasing coal under archeological and historic sites eligible for inclusion on the National Register of Historic Places.

- Make it easier for a coal company to obtain a lease based on an asserted "emergency" situation, in which a mining company alleges it needs nearby federal coal to stay in operation.

- In determining whether landowners will have the right of "surface owner consent", the burden would fall to them to prove they are "qualified" under the terms of the law. They are assumed to be unqualified for surface owner consent, unless they can prove otherwise.

- Eliminate oral bidding in the auction of federal leases, using only the written bid system.

- Eliminate restrictions on potential lessees who own existing federal energy leases which they are not developing into mines. The "diligent development" terms of the Federal Coal Leasing Amendments Act would be relaxed, allowing leaseholders to horde and speculate on public coal they control.

Many other proposed changes were to have been implemented without benefit of formal regulation changes. It was these "changes by directive" which most worried federal civil servants responsible for carrying out the laws relating to federal coal development. As long as Watt's changes were formally made through the regulatory process, federal bureaucrats felt buffered to some degree. But when memos or telephone calls came down directing them to procede in a manner they knew to be contrary to laws and regulations then in effect, the civil servant faced hard choices. He was sworn to uphold the laws and regulations, but he was being directed to break or evade them. Complying with the errant directives could mean criminal charges against him in some cases, and failure to comply could mean a de-railed career. More often than not, the troubled bureaucrat sought desperately for a compromise, some way to justify bending the rules. The more cynical or upwardly mobile bureaucrat tended to blank out the contradictions and do what he was told.

Those with more conscience, or more daring, would try to "leak" the offending directive to the media or to public interest groups in the hope that somehow members of the public might be able to stop the illegality, if only they could understand.

Such leaks to the public about how its coal was being managed eventually resulted in a level of Washington Office paranoia rarely seen by career BLM officials. Anyone who talked to the media or to recognized "environmentalists" was suspect; everybody was out to get Watt. In Washington, as in the field offices, civil servants who tried to explain the Watt coal program to outsiders did so at significant risk. Routine informational newsletters from BLM field offices, originally intended to keep the public updated on the coal program in each region, were subjected to severe censorship.

Political considerations became enormously important in the day-to-day functioning of BLM. While trying desperately to quash public information about the coal program, high Interior officials set about manipulating the public participation program for their own ends. Citizen advisory committees for BLM activities had a long and mostly honorable history, but under Watt, the advisory committee system was perverted into an ideological pressure group intended to intimidate local BLM officials.

Federal laws called for multiple use advisory boards to be formed in each BLM district; the citizens' boards were to be composed of representatives of industry, recreational uses of the public lands, wildlife interests, environmental protection advocates, and representatives of other public land uses. Having publicly sought nominations from the general public and from specific interest groups, BLM District Managers previously had enjoyed a free hand in selecting nominees who they thought could provide good advice and could relay BLM plans back to interest groups. Under Watt, the citizen advisory committees were transformed into right-wing cells intended to indoctrinate and intimidate local BLM officials.

In a drastic change from previous procedures, Interior officials in Washington packed local district advisory councils around the West with grassroots ideologues. The politicizing of the district advisory councils was regarded as an ominous sign by many veteran BLM personnel. Normally, the citizen advisors chosen by the District Managers were routinely confirmed by Interior officials in Washington, but suddenly a citizen's allegiance to the conservative ideology became the primary (and often the only) criterion for appointment to the local boards. In the Albuquerque BLM district, for example, Carruthers intervened to appoint former State Republican Party Chairman Steve Davis, who had no apparent previous interest in, or knowledge of, public land issues. In New Mexico BLM's four districts, 19 of the 40 citizen advisors appointed in 1982 were selected not by the local BLM official who they were to advise, but by high Interior chiefs in Washington.

Although the Federal Advisory Committee Act requires that membership in such citizen boards be "fairly balanced in terms of points of view represented and the functions to be performed", Watt and his team of ideologues flauted the law with thoroughly partisan appointments.

Two additional regulatory changes had major effects in the San Juan River Coal Region, where resource conflicts were most glaring. First, the 1982 program changes eliminated most of the regulatory standards by which local BLM officials were to determine whether they had adequate data from the field to make land use decisions. BLM officials directly responsible for coal-related decisions in the Chaco-Bisti area had been worried for years that they would have to make decisions favoring coal development without knowing what other resources would be jeopardized. The 1982 regulations changes assured that would be the case. Instead of learning on the ground what the repercussions of coal leasing would be for a specific tract, the BLM District Manager would be told by Washington that he already had enough information to make decisions—in effect, no matter what else might conflict with coal, coal was most important. It didn't matter what else might be in the way of the strip mining because nothing was more important than the coal there.

Second, the regulatory changes eliminated the "threshold concept" of cumulative impacts. The 1979 coal program had recognized that while coal development might be acceptable and advisable in some areas, too much coal development there might be unacceptable. Under the old program, BLM officials were to make determinations as to whether cumulative impacts from coal leasing in a given region might be unacceptable. In the 1979 regulations, BLM was empowered to halt, suspend or establish special conditions for continued leasing if its analysis showed that a threshold level of cumulative impacts was being reached. Under the Watt regulations, it was impossible to have too much of a good thing.

Retention of this threshold concept was perhaps more important in the San Juan River Coal Region than in other federal regions. In an area already heavily impacted by uranium mining and milling, the additional impacts of coal leasing for strip mining could have been used to recognize cumulative impacts approaching disaster proportions. Analysis of adverse impacts on Indian lifestyles, reclamation and water quality and availability could have benefitted greatly from BLM use of the threshold concept; instead BLM officials were denied this planning tool and pressured to avoid making cumulative assessments which might be prejudicial to coal interests.

Overall, the coal program changes initiated by Watt and Assistant Secretary Carruthers had four major effects: 1) more publicly owned coal was pushed onto the market; 2) less attention was given to environmental or socio-economic considerations; 3) the public treasury would receive less than the true value of its mineral resource; and 4) coal company speculation in federal leases was encouraged.

The numerous changes in the earlier consensus coal program brought objections from several quarters. Naturally the organized environmental groups protested, as did less well-organized groups of cultural resource specialists, wildlife habitat advocates and others. All of this grassroots opposition would have had little effect, however, except that the governors of nine western coal-producing states also charged that Watt and his cronies had undermined the validity of the coal program.

The governors formally protested the Watt coal regulations changes, arguing that his policies were "eviscerating" the states' role in the Regional Coal Teams, and were making it nearly impossible to conduct federal coal leasing in a business-like manner. Their terminology deliberately baited the confrontational Secretary Watt, who met with the governors November 22, 1982, and agreed to 16 concessions modifying his proposed regulations.

But the concessions by no means eliminated the objections voiced by many environmental groups. The National Wildlife Federation hauled the Bureau of Land Management into court challenging the Powder River Coal lease sale and the procedures used for it, as did the Northern Cheyenne Tribe which contended that BLM's EIS for that lease sale was inadequate to evaluate effects on the tribal reservation. And the Natural Resources Defense Council and seven other groups specifically challenged in a separate suit that Watt's 1982 revisions to the coal program were illegal. This latter suit charged that in changing the rules, Interior violated the National Environmental Policy Act and various provisions of the Federal Coal Leasing Amendments Act, the Federal Land Policy and Management Act and the Surface Mining Control and Reclamation Act.

Asked to study the effects of the Watt regulatory changes, the U.S. Office of Technology Assessment (OTA) reported in 1984 that "we conclude that the recent policy changes very likely have raised the cost and difficulty of ensuring environmental compatibility, and have increased the risk of adverse environmental impacts should those tracts be developed.

"As a consequence, public confidence in the environmental soundness of the federal leasing program has decreased."

The 1984 OTA report found that "some aspects of the 1982 rule changes significantly increased the probability (i.e., risk) that environmentally sensitive tracts would be leased and eventually mined. . . ."

CHAPTER 9

LAND GRAB FOR A POWER PLANT

If the officially-abetted theft of the public's coal resource would eventually be thwarted by a congressional crackdown, the Navajo residents of New Mexico's coal region still faced imminent loss of their homelands in the Bisti region through a questionable land swap between BLM and Public Service Company of New Mexico (PNM). New Mexico wilderness advocates stood to gain a smoke-belching power plant adjacent to the proposed Bisti Wilderness Area.

While PNM and its subsidiary could ostensibly use all the coal they could get to feed the San Juan Generating Station southwest of Farmington, or to broker on the regional coal market to other utility companies, PNM's grand design called for shoveling much of this San Juan Basin coal into a new plant, the proposed New Mexico Generating Station (NMGS). From the outset, PNM was secretive and deceptive about its plans for a new power plant . . . perhaps simple pragmatism, since if its electric rate payers had known what it would do to their utility bills they would have rebelled even sooner.

How PNM developed its plans for NMGS, and its subterfuge in inducing local BLM officials to approve it, reflect unfavorably on high-ranking PNM officers. Manipulation of civil servants on behalf of NMGS was rampant almost from its inception, but reached a climax under the influence of James Watt and Garrey Carruthers.

Under ordinary circumstances, PNM probably would have decided on its own that building a power plant in the Bisti was a bad idea. Indeed, other company officials, including chiefs of departments, had argued for years that a new plant at that site was a mistake. But the plan for NMGS was tied too closely to PNM President Jerry Geist's ego to fail on its own merits, especially when he could count on the Watt-Carruthers team.

The company had its own specialists prepare numerous reports on a wide range of conditions which could affect selecting the Bisti as a power plant site, and when the reports came back urging caution, it seemed to matter little as long as political manipulation could reasonably be expected to overcome the obstacles. With Watt and Carruthers in charge at Interior, there seemed to be no hurdles that were too high.

One of the bigger obstacles was right-of-way acquisition for the power lines that were to carry electricity from the proposed Bisti plant to the utility's customers. While right-of-way matters can be excruciatingly difficult under the best of circumstances, the "checkerboard" land ownership pattern in the Chaco-Bisti region was foreseen as a gigantic headache. There was little privately-owned acreage to go over, but a massive hodge-podge of Indian, federal, state and tribal-trust lands that had to be acquired for powerline right-of-way. Alternating one-mile squares of land would frequently be owned or administered by different agencies. Crossing Indian lands has usually been so tough that many rights-of-way specialists do their best to avoid them at all costs. Yet the NMGS site required right-of-way over thousands of acres owned by, or administered for, the Navajo. Said one high-ranking PNM official: "It (Bisti) may be a great place to generate electricity, as long as you don't try to deliver it anywhere."

And the power line rights-of-way problems over checkerboard land ownership were only part of the dilemma: the company also needed right-of-way for roads, and more right-of-way for water lines to bring water for steam. To top it off, of course, PNM didn't even own the land where it wanted to build NMGS and couldn't simply "buy" it no matter how much it was prepared to spend. The land sought was BLM land (public land) and although the government might be anxious to cooperate with PNM, a plethora of federal laws and regulations would have to be navigated before the Bisti lands could be turned over to the utility company.

Besides, the law said the land could not be transferred out of public ownership unless it was in the public interest to do so. And there was the rub.

PNM could show that it was in the company's interests to get control over the Bisti lands (although later analysis would question whether it was in the electricity rate payers' interests, or even in PNM stockholders' interests), but trying to convince the public that NMGS was in the public interest was quite another matter. For starters, New Mexicans already had at their disposal far more electrical generating capacity than they were expected to need far into the future. And then there were the multitude of other public resources in the Bisti region that would be degraded by operating a power plant there.

If the power plant went in at Bisti, it would send smoke into the soon-to-be Bisti Wilderness Area; it would greatly increase the amount of industrial, off-road driving that would tear up the delicate fossil record lying in the surrounding terrain; it would bring vandals and casual collectors who would obliterate the scientific value of the fossils, and would loot the thousands of archeological sites in the area; it would eliminate Navajo access to sacred areas that would become coal stockpile mounds; it would monopolize the already scarce water supplies in the region, and pollute some of what little water remained due to industrial run-off; it would significantly contribute to the acid rain problem, the adverse impacts of which were only beginning to be understood in the arid plains. And it would virtually assure that thousands of acres of public rangelands, used by subsistence Navajo families, would be strip mined, despite highly questionable prospects for reclamation.

But PNM President Geist was committed to NMGS, and if there were problems, the utility under his leadership would demonstrate how a responsible company went about resolving them.

The outlines of the public land fraud that would have given the Bisti lands to PNM through BLM's Ute Mountain Exchange have already been suggested in earlier chapters. In the mid-1970s, when PNM began its plans for building the Bisti plant, utility executives approached BLM officials in the agency's Albuquerque District Office to learn what lands BLM might be willing to take in trade. PNM indicated it would be willing to buy private land that BLM wanted if BLM would then entertain a proposal to trade off the public land PNM wanted. PNM's planned acquisition of the Bisti lands took the form of a land swap because Department of the Interior procedures for approval of land exchanges are far easier than the process of buying such parcels outright.

To PNM's offer, the BLM Albuquerque District Manager indicated that the agency might be willing to swap some Bisti acreage for land that was then privately-owned adjacent to the BLM-managed Rio Grande Wild and Scenic River near Taos. Still, BLM made no commitment to accept the trade, and legally could not make such a commitment until a wide range of preliminary matters were dealt with . . . such as a clear determination that the trade would be in the public interest and that the lands gained by the government would be at least as valuable as the lands lost. But based on an understanding that BLM would entertain the possibility of trading lands, PNM moved to acquire the Ute Mountain tract BLM had identified as a potential asset.

BLM had expressed an interest in acquiring additional lands along the Rio Grande Gorge as early as the mid-1960s, as part of its strategy of consolidating and protecting the "wild river" portion of the Rio Grande, dedicated in 1968. The privately-held land around Ute Mountain, which included a portion of the gorge rim, was one such parcel. However, BLM documents from those early days indicate that it was really only the rim portion that was of interest. An October 10, 1973 memo from BLM's Robert Buffington to his New Mexico State Director reports: "I told (Mr. Charles Waldvogel, representative of a group that had recently purchased a portion of the Ute Mountain tract) that we were interested in acquiring that portion of the (Sangre de Cristo grant) which borders the Rio Grande. We are interested because this was a portion of the Rio Grande Wild River area. I said our interest in obtaining the rest of Ute Mountain would depend upon the land which the corporation would select if an exchange were to be consummated. I told him that our acquisition desires would be in the following priorities: (1) An outright purchase of a quarter-mile strip along the Rio Grande. This we could program under the Land & Water Conservation Fund; (2) a scenic easement along the same quarter-mile; (3) exchange for the entire Ute Mountain."

By January 1975, the Ute Mountain property, also known as Top O' The World Ranch, was owned by Shuford Mills, of North Carolina, which had retained the Muchmore Realtors in New Mexico to broker any future transactions. Also by that time, BLM in New Mexico had funds already available to purchase the rim portion it desired. A January 31, 1975 BLM telephone confirmation report notes: "I told him (Ernie Harper, associated with Muchmore) our purchase of the quarter-mile strip would be a real fast transaction if they had merchantible title, as we had $100,000 ready to apply toward the purchase."

But a year later, the rim strip had still not been acquired, and then-BLM Albuquerque District Manager Keith Miller noted in correspondence to parties potentially involved in the Ute Mountain transaction: "At the present time, the Bureau has funds to purchase the land or interest in the land. We would like to proceed with the purchase to acquire this strip of land. This effort will not preclude or hamper our effort to acquire by exchange or some other method the remaining portion of Ute Mountain. Even if we acquire the quarter-mile strip, we will still be very interested in obtaining Ute Mountain as it would be an important part of the Bureau's programs in the area." With the funds in-hand to obtain the critical rim strip, the local BLM official apparently sought to try for an even larger tract. In earlier letters, Miller had indicated BLM would consider trading public lands in San Juan, Rio Arriba, Santa Fe, Sandoval or Bernalillo counties to facilitate the exchange.

Then in January 1977, Public Service Company of New Mexico executive Robert Rountree, president of the subsidiary Public Service Land Company, notified BLM District Manager Miller that, "Public Service Land Company proposes to purchase that portion of the Top of the World Farm includable in the wild and scenic river area to offer in trade." The Rountree letter at that time spelled out the public's lands in the Bisti it wanted to get in exchange for Ute Mountain. PNM did buy the land, for a reported $2.3 million, on the understanding that BLM would consider trading Bisti lands for it.

The $100,000 earmarked for acquisition of the important quarter-mile strip along the gorge rim went unused, as BLM found itself negotiating with PNM for the entire Ute Mountain parcel.

When BLM veteran Paul Applegate assumed the position as BLM Albuquerque District Manager in 1977, replacing Miller, he inherited the "agreement" his predecessor had made with PNM to consider the Ute Mountain Exchange. Through political pressure and intimidation described earlier, Applegate eventually felt himself committed to do PNM's bidding, at least on a matter of such importance to Geist as trading off the coveted Bisti lands. When it became obvious in analyzing the proposed exchange that it would not be in the public interest, other BLM officials, including Applegate's assistant district manager, Mat Millenbach, wondered aloud why Applegate should feel so committed to going through with the exchange.

But if BLM officials like Millenbach, whose distinguished career included Washington office experience in similar lands transactions, had trouble justifying PNM's proposal, so did PNM's own consultants.

One of PNM's first NMGS fiascos involved a power plant siting study it commissioned by San Francisco-based Woodward & Clyde Consultants. In 1974, the consulting firm was hired by PNM and El Paso Electric Company (EPE) to assess potential locations in New Mexico and southwest Texas for a new power plant, and to recommend which seemed best according to the utility companies' criteria. Of course, one of the crucial steps for any consultant is to discover what it is the client wants to hear, but perhaps that communication was ineffective, because the consultant's report on the best sites for NMGS did not even include the Bisti location!

But on the second try, the consultants discovered that not only did the Bisti site make the new list of prospects, it even turned out to be the best choice.

According to Woodward & Clyde's first report, four broad objectives were to be used in determining where a new power plant might go. Those objectives were, in the order stated: "(1) To maximize public health and safety; (2) To minimize adverse environmental effects; (3) To minimize adverse social effects; and (4) To minimize economic costs." It sounded laudable and clean, but in fact, the first three objectives meant little. It was minimizing economic costs that led PNM to choose the Bisti site, certainly not any intent to minimize adverse social or environmental effects. At any rate, the various screening processes used by Woodward & Clyde to come up with candidate sites brought forward a total of 22 potential locations scattered around New Mexico and in Culberson, Texas. Sites were reported in Grant, Roosevelt, Socorro, Quay, Colfax, San Juan, San Miguel, Torrance and McKinley Counties in New Mexico, with McKinley County (in the San Juan coal region) accounting for 12 of the 22 candidates. Even so, the Bisti site as not among them.

The consultants' analysis stated: "Sensitivity analyses showed that when only the environmental factors were evaluated (i.e., when cost considerations were excluded), the candidate site area in Torrance County ranked highest, but when cost considerations were also included, the McKinley County candidate site areas ranked highest. Location of the site nearer available coal (coal transportation costs) accounted for much of the higher ranking for the McKinley County areas."

A BLM document entitled "NMGS Project Description Summary" explains how the Bisti site came to be selected even though it was not originally ranked within the top 22 candidate sites. "In 1977, PNM learned that lands under BLM management in the Bisti region may be available for exchange, and that the Top of the World Farms (owned jointly by PNM and EPE) property may be acceptable for such an exchange, subject to BLM's land exchange policies and procedures. In 1976-77, PNM reached agreements with several mining companies in the Bisti region to have an option to purchase their wastewater, which could be used for a power plant.

"These developments reduced PNM's uncertainties about land and water availability in the Bisti region, and offered PNM another potentially feasible siting option in northwestern New Mexico. However, the Bisti region had not been included as a candidate site area based on the screening process because of two screening criteria: (1) areas containing potential oil and gas reserves were avoided; and (2) areas beyond 25 miles from potential sources of water were not studied further [Bisti is approximately 35 miles from the San Juan River]. Neither of these two screening criteria was of a "go/no go" type (as is, for example, the criterion to avoid siting in national parks); it was simply considered reasonable to apply them during screening in order to reduce the remaining geographic area into a manageable size for further study. Since new information showed the Bisti region was a feasible candidate site area, it was considered appropriate to relax the original criteria and include the Bisti region as a candidate site area. . . . Using the previous ranking process, the 22 candidate site areas and the Bisti site area were then ranked using updated cost and different cooling system scenarios. The three highest-ranking candidate areas were Bisti, Torrance and McKinley-22, with Bisti ranking highest. . . . PNM selected Bisti as its primary site for the New Mexico Generating Station (NMGS)."

The matter was settled, then, despite the early credibility gap: the new plant would go in at the Bisti site, assuming BLM agreed to the Ute Mountain Exchange.

The next step, in 1980, was for BLM to conduct an "environmental assessment" of the land exchange: what would the social, economic, environmental impacts be if the federal government agreed to swap? Would the land exchange be in the public interest? Having twisted its consultant, PNM proceeded to twist the BLM.

In federal procedures, an environmental assessment is a "mini-environmental impact statement", an initial determination of whether the proposed action under review might have such impacts as to constitute a "significant federal action", which would require a full-blown EIS. Under the influence of PNM and higher Interior officials, the local Albuquerque BLM office was persuaded to try to approve the Ute Mountain Exchange proposal with the level of analysis in the lesser "environmental assessment".

But how could BLM contend that the land trade would not have "significant impacts" when the lands traded away would be used for a power plant? Simple. BLM specialists analyzing the exchange for the environmental assessment were told to assume they didn't know what PNM intended to do with the Bisti land it would acquire. It was to be viewed as a paper transaction . . . what impacts would there be from two parties signing deeds over to the other?

Over protests by local BLM staffers who regarded such a treatment as deceitful at best, the political directives from the BLM State Office in Santa Fe won the day. BLM's analysis would pretend that it didn't know the Bisti lands would be used for a coal-fired power plant.

Even so, BLM staffers' analysis pointed to serious problems with the land exchange. For one thing, there was no public demand for BLM acquisition of the Ute Mountain tract in the Taos area, and there was substantial public opposition to trading away the Bisti lands. In fact, citizen groups in the Taos area, who would presumably have been the prime beneficiaries of BLM's acquisition of Ute Mountain, were adamantly opposed to the trade, based on its implications for the Chaco-Bisti region.

Besides, the public resources that would be lost in the Bisti far outweighed resources that would be acquired with Ute Mountain. The "mountain" was, in fact, little more than a bump on the horizon, with minimal scenic value except that it overlooked the Rio Grande Gorge, and with no water . . . no babbling brooks, streams, springs, and it had little forested parts. The Bisti land that would be lost, on the other hand, had Navajo sacred areas, major fossil locations, archeological sites, and the stark, scenic beauty that had fascinated visitors in increasing numbers in recent years.

But what the Ute Mountain tract did have, and the reason BLM had identified it for possible acquisition in the first place, was that quarter-mile portion of the rim of the Rio Grande Gorge. BLM's interest in the tract had been to preserve the rim from commercial or residential development that would detract from the wilderness experience within the gorge. In essence, BLM had said it was willing to consider acquiring the property to protect its scenic character.

Even that reason for acquiring Ute Mountain for the public ceased to exist in March 1980, when BLM purchased a scenic easement along the gorge rim. As far as PNM was concerned, this snafu occurred against its better judgment. It was in the waning days of the Department of Interior's fiscal year 1979, when the BLM Albuquerque District received a call from Washington urging field level officials to identify scenic easements they would like to obtain. Washington was calling many field offices with the same proposal since the bureau had been given funds by Congress to acquire such easements and if the money was not spent by the end of the fiscal year, it would be turned back unused. Turning back money is low priority for most governmental agencies, since it suggests that the agency hadn't needed it in the first place and would likely jeopardize congressional response to future requests.

Hurriedly, Albuquerque BLM searched for any existing paperwork already done on the need for scenic easements, and the prime prospect turned out to the the gorge rim. Moving expeditiously, BLM was able to convince PNM to sell the scenic easement for $160,000 ($60,000 more than would have been necessary if BLM had followed through with its intention to acquire the strip in 1977).

Initially PNM objected, of course, fearing BLM would renege on the proposed Ute Mountain Exchange. Rather than secure the easement through condemnation, which had been discussed by BLM staffers, District Manager Applegate assured PNM executives that BLM was still interested in the land swap and would continue to process the exchange.

The BLM Albuquerque District realty specialist who guided acquisition of the scenic easement expressed her reservations about making commitments to PNM to make the land exchange. In her memo to the files, July 27, 1979, LaJoan Metz cautioned, "I personally feel that we should not commit ourselves to PNM by telling them that we will exchange under FLPMA (the 1976 Federal Land Policy and Management Act) at a later date without a written opinion from the Solicitor; however, I also feel that if we can strongly justify fee acquisition that we could also name the River Act in our exchange and this would probably cover us. The justification for acquiring in fee (full title) would have to be rather strong since we already have all the rights that we need, but we could probably justify it by saying that we are leaving PNM with an uneconomic remnant and that a scenic easement along the river could cause administrative problems."

The federal realty specialist also noted: "We also discussed the thought that the State Director should not be put into a position where it is committed to make the over all exchange."

Ostensibly, BLM had made no decision that it would approve the Bisti-Ute Mountain land trade at that point, because none of the preliminary findings of equal value or public benefit had been made. Furthermore the Chaco-San Juan land use plan which was to consider the land exchange also had yet to be completed. In reality, however, District Manager Applegate appears to have made a personal commitment to PNM to approve the trade.

Two years later, April 30, 1984, Applegate admitted in discussions with his staff that "PNM agreed to the scenic easement on the understanding that we'd go ahead and take title to the land. The only reason we didn't do it before is we didn't have it covered under an environmental impact statement, and it was too controversial."

Rather than eliminating the need for the Ute Mountain Exchange, then, the scenic easement acquisition actually cemented its approval . . . despite the violation of law that occurred when BLM decided to approve the trade without first completing the required environmental impact statement, determination of public interest, and assessments of equal worth.

Thus compromised, BLM was to be on shaky ground in completing its land use plan, in conducting its environmental assessment, and in its acceptance of a subsequent environmental impact statement on the NMGS proposal. The land use plan completed in the fall of 1981 revealed that the Ute Mountain exchange was inadvisable and inconsistent with other land management responsibilities; yet Applegate had already committed to PNM to "take title to the (Ute Mountain) land." The compromised Ute Mountain environmental assessment completed that fall painted as favorable a picture of the exchange as possible, including the absurd pretension that BLM did not know PNM would use the Bisti lands for a power plant.

Was acquiring Ute Mountain so critical to the public interest that it was necessary to violate the spirit and letter of the National Environmental Policy Act, warp the congressionally-mandated land use planning process and circumvent the department's land transactions procedures? Was Applegate so convinced of the value of the lands PNM wanted to trade that he would make such predeterminations?

In fact, Applegate had never even set foot on Ute Mountain at that time, according to BLM officials in the Taos office which administered that area. As late as February 27, 1982, Applegate admitted he had never been on Ute Mountain to see what it had to offer.

Yet BLM information officers were told to pull out all the stops to show how great an acquisition Ute Mountain would be for the public . . . and to downplay the losses that would occur in the Bisti area. When the BLM Albuquerque District Information Officer requested that the Taos BLM office send down for publicity purposes all their best photographs of the Ute Mountain prize, the staffer's response was: "There ain't nothing there." Nevertheless, the Taos BLM recreation specialist (whose program would supposedly benefit most from acquiring the land from PNM) was instructed to take photographs of the most attractive aspects of the mountain and send them to the district office for a major publicity effort. When the photos came in, they were distance shots, showing a bare hill a mile or more away, with virtually no distinguishing characteristics.

Angered by the results, the district office contacted the Taos recreation specialist to complain. But the response was: "Listen, that's all there is."

"Why didn't you get closer and shoot some nice craggy cliffs or a creek or something?" the information officer demanded.

"Hey, the closer you get, the less there is there," the Taos specialist advised.

But that was only a minor problem; at least the public didn't know what it wasn't getting. BLM bravely contended that the land trade would hugely benefit the public. The real problems came when BLM and PNM tried to foist a bogus environmental impact statement off on the public which was beginning to wise up to the corrupt deal which had been cut to let PNM build the generating station on land it would get from BLM.

Despite all this, the BLM New Mexico State Director Bill Luscher was prepared to make his decision to trade away the Bisti lands within days after publication of the final environmental assessment on the Ute Mountain Exchange, in September 1981. A decision document, which was to accompany publication of the assessment, gave the State Director's approval. But release of the report was delayed while a substitute decision document was prepared. Dated November 27, 1981, it said: "As a result of activities in the San Juan Basin, some of which relate to this proposed exchange, I have decided to defer any decision on this proposal."

The difference was not a change of heart on whether the land should be traded, but was instead the bombshell that the Bisti lands PNM wanted had been selected by the Navajo Nation for acquisition under terms of Congress' Navajo-Hopi Indian Settlement Act Amendment of 1980.

The Navajos' selection of the lands PNM wanted for its power plant and company town was a crisis which BLM officials had feared for some time. An amendment to the original act in 1974 specified that the Navajo Nation was to select the 35,000 acres to which it was entitled from those public (BLM) lands within 18 miles of the eastern boundary of the existing tribal trust Navajo Reservation, and the lands selected had to be contiguous to that reservation. Presumably the tribal government would want to choose some of BLM's better grazing lands since they would be relocating rural Navajo families accustomed to a pastoral, subsistence lifestyle. Actually, the tribe's choices were relatively limited; BLM didn't have too much acreage that was good grazing land contiguous to and within 18 miles of the existing reservation.

But the real clincher for selecting the Bisti site coveted by PNM was that Navajo Tribal Chairman Peter McDonald was running hard for reelection. One of the most troublesome political issues he faced as the election approached was the strong sentiment against uprooting the Navajo families from the disputed Navajo-Hopi Joint Use Area. If McDonald didn't go along with the highly unpopular relocation he would find himself in contempt of Congress; if he did go along, he might well lose the election. But there was a way out: he could select lands for relocation that he knew would never be acceptable to the federal government.

If McDonald did not want to move Navajo families from the Joint Use Area, his best choice for land selection was the Bisti lands desired by PNM, because he could expect his choice to be thwarted by the Department of the Interior—at least until after the election. On the other hand, if he had to relocate the Navajo families, his best choice was still the Bisti lands, because they contained some of BLM's best rangeland meeting the congressional criteria.

Rather than notify Interior precisely which acreage the Tribe wanted, McDonald instead relayed the Tribal Council's resolution stating that the selection would be made from within the Paragon Ranch, a 55,000 acre tract controlled by PNM's land management subsidiary, Paragon Resources, primarily through leased public rangeland. Stating that its congressionally-authorized 35,000 acres would come from within the 55,000 acre Paragon Ranch, McDonald requested the Department of the Interior to "withdraw" the land from the general pool of public lands and in effect to reserve it for the tribe's final selection.

The announcement upset many an applecart within Interior. Not only was McDonald jeopardizing PNM's long-planned scheme to take over the Bisti for the power plant, but he also claimed his selection would give the tribe the rights to the minerals under the lands chosen . . . that the coal there would no longer the federal coal, but would belong to the Navajo Tribe.

Working quickly to counter the tribe's move, Assistant Interior Secretary Carruthers tried to block McDonald's selection, saying that his request for a land withdrawal (to reserve land) was not sufficiently specific . . . that Interior had to know which specific 35,000 acres the Navajo wanted, rather than the notification that the lands to be chosen would come from PNM's Paragon Ranch in the Bisti area. And then Carruthers double-crossed the Navajo.

While rejecting McDonald's request for a land withdrawal to aid the Navajo-Hopi Indian Settlement Act selection, Carruthers notified PNM of the attempted withdrawal, and urged PNM and the BLM New Mexico State Office to initiate their own request for a land withdrawal to aid the Ute Mountain Exchange.

The underhandedness of Carruthers' action prompted BLM's local Field Solicitor to react in horror. The Tribe, he said, would have no trouble convincing a judge that Carruthers had acted in bad faith, especially since the Department of the Interior is charged by law as having an overriding trust responsibility for Indian nations.

Furthermore, the wording of the land withdrawal request to aid PNM's land exchange makes it clear that Carruthers' aim was to subvert congressional intent. The land withdrawal document approved by Carruthers states, "Our request for a temporary withdrawal stems primarily from our concern that additional mining claims may be filed on the public lands and that the Indians may select from these lands as part of the Navajo-Hopi Settlement (Public Law 93-531)."

And that was not the only admission that Carruthers was deliberatedly attempting to thwart Congress's mandate by turning over the coveted land to PNM. Within days of BLM's request for withdrawal of the Bisti lands to benefit the Ute Mountain Exchange, BLM Associate State Director Larry Woodard told a large audience at an Albuquerque public hearing that the lands were being withdrawn for PNM so that the Navajo wouldn't get it. On March 4, 1982, at a public meeting for the New Mexico Generating Station EIS, Woodard admitted, "We have received a withdrawal this week for purposes of aiding the Ute Mountain Exchange. We did this so the Navajo Tribe would not be able to select those particular lands."

Interior's attempt to subvert the congressionally-authorized Navajo selection is recorded in a March 5, 1982 letter from the chairman of the Navajo & Hopi Indian Relocation Commission, Hawley Atkinson, to Secretary Watt. "Since last summer the Commission, the Navajo Tribe and the Bureau of Land Management have been reviewing and discussing potential lands for selection by the Navajo Tribe in New Mexico. The Navajo Tribal Council passed a resolution directing its officers to make a selection of 35,000 acres of public lands within the Paragon Resources Ranch in New Mexico pursuant to the Settlement Act. This was communicated to BLM personnel and on October 23, 1981, the Commission sent you a telegram requesting withdrawal of public lands within the Paragon Resources Ranch pending final selection by the Navajo Tribe. That request was denied by letter of November 18, 1981 from the Acting Director of Bureau of Land Management. The explanation given was that he did not agree that an emergency existed which would justify withdrawal or other segregation [of the Bisti lands] at that time.

"We are now advised that the Assistant Secretary for Lands and Natural Resources [Carruthers] has recently granted a similar request for withdrawal submitted by New Mexico Public Service Company for certain public lands within and adjacent to the Paragon Resources Ranch. This was done without any communication with the Commission or the Navajo Tribe concerning the intention of the Department to do this. In fact, the Commission and the Navajo Tribe were led to believe that no action would be taken concerning public lands within the Paragon Resources Ranch prior to submission by the Navajo Tribe of its selection under the Settlement Act. We are not aware of any emergency or other justification which has occurred since November 18, 1981, which would justify the withdrawal or other segregation of these public lands on behalf of New Mexico Public Service Company."

When officials in the BLM Albuquerque office learned that the Navajo Tribe was sending an attorney to research the office's files on the Ute Mountain Exchange, the Carruthers document approving the land withdrawal in favor of PNM was removed and hidden away. After several hours work, the tribe's attorney called the local BLM public affairs officer to say the files seemed to be incomplete, that the official decision document on the withdrawal was missing. Privately, records clerks told the public affairs officer that some documents had been removed recently by a realty specialist involved in the withdrawal action. When the specialist was confronted, he admitted he had deliberately removed the decision document and other potentially damaging memos "because I thought they might be embarrassing."

It was a clear violation of the Freedom of Information Act. At the public affairs officer's insistence, the documents were restored to the file and provided to the tribe's attorney. But when the violation was reported to District Manager Applegate, it was the public affairs officer, rather than the realty specialist, who was censured.

Riding out the storm of protest from the Navajo Tribal government and the environmentalists who saw the Navajo selection as a way to halt construction of the power plant, BLM held firm and proceeded to the next step in handing the Bisti lands over to PNM: a full-blown environmental impact statement on the New Mexico Generating Station.

It was clear the public would not accept the first-level analysis provided in a BLM "environmental assessment" on the Ute Mountain Exchange as being adequate to approve the power plant. Enough procedural problems were evident that PNM itself began to push for a full EIS. With this lead from PNM, of course, BLM was willing to oblige.

Since the outcome of the power plant EIS would be critical to PNM's grand design, arrangement were made for PNM to control the EIS writing process. In a departure from normal procedures, it was decided that the EIS would be handled as a "Non-Bureau Energy Initiative" (NBEI) document. NBEI environmental statements are paid for by the business proposing an action involving commitment of federal lands. In theory, a company eager to press on with its proposal and not wait for normal federal budget funding to allow production of an EIS can put up the money itself so that people can be hired to prepare the report; frequently a non-governmental, third-party contractor is hired to do the environmental document which is then only supervised by BLM, rather than being prepared in its entirety by the agency. A BLM NBEI team working out of the Santa Fe State Office was to oversee development of the NMGS EIS by an outside contractor paid with PNM funds.

If the process seemed peculiar on the surface, anyone looking for evidence of collusion found more than they expected when it was learned that the outside contractor would be none other than Woodward & Clyde Consultants, of San Francisco, the same company PNM had hired to do its power plant siting study. And if the siting study has been embarrassingly compromised when the consultant failed to come up with the answer PNM executives wanted, the EIS became a major scandal.

An NBEI team already existed at BLM New Mexico State Office when the proposal was made that the NMGS EIS would be a "non-bureau energy initiative" effort. The team, composed of a variety of specialists, had been formed in 1979, and had worked mostly on other PNM projects, such as powerline rights of way over public land. For the NMGS project, the team was beefed up and given a new team leader, Leslie Cone.

The legitimacy of the required EIS was called into question from its inception. Doubts were expressed about the "independence" of the document based on the fact it was being done by Woodward & Clyde (whose future lucrative consulting contracts with PNM might be jeopardized if the EIS conclusions turned out unfavorable). Fears of a compromised process were quickly borne out when the BLM-generated guidelines for environmental analysis were warped to assure that projected environmental damage from the power plant was downplayed or ignored. For example, the NMGS EIS was to assess the environmental damage resulting from BLM approval of rights of ways across public land, while ignoring the damage from operating the power plant itself. And the analysis was to assume that the Bisti lands were already traded into private ownership, rather than belonging to the public.

Another example: it was decided to assume that acid rain was not known to be caused by coal-fired power plant emissions.

Another example: it was to be assumed that water for running the steam generators could be acquired by the utility company (even though water is extremely scarce in the region) and that the company's acquisition of water rights would not be prejudicial to others seeking water.

Another example: it was to be assumed that building a power plant in this region was in the national interest; that there was a need for the electricity that would be produced—even though it had been demonstrated that additional power was not needed. In fact, PNM had already produced its own revised forecasts showing a drastic reduction in need for electricity, but insisted that BLM use old projections giving the erroneous impression that the power would be needed in the immediate future.

Internally, BLMers rankled at the blatantly pro-industry bias that guided the NMGS EIS. For those whose sense of public service and just enforcement of the laws governing natural resources was offended, there were internal review processes for attempting to correct such impending abuses of the public trust. But the official insistence upon a corrupted environmental analysis created many casualties among lower level civil servants.

In a 16-page critique of Woodward & Clyde's preliminary draft EIS, the BLM specialists in the Santa Fe office blasted the document, charging again and again that it was put together as a justification for approving the power plant, rather than to seriously assess its impacts. The State Office Division of Resources' comments charged: "In general, the document seems to be a justification written for the proposed action. There is no true analysis of 'no action' . . . there is no presentation of 'no action'. Not only will the public be confused (or angered), but the range of analysis that results is less than complete." Elsewhere in their comments, the BLM specialists note: "Many parts read as a justification document to support pre-conceived ideas. There is very little impact analysis."

The in-house critique quotes a federal judge's admonition that an EIS is supposed to be objective: "'Objectivity is required of federal agencies, particularly with respect to evaluation of environmental impacts, and this objectivity should be equally applicable to a federal agency with respect to all environmentally related activities . . . [including] the preparation of environmental statements'. Sierra Club v. Froehlke." The author then noted, "It appears to me that this PDEIS [preliminary draft environmental impact statement] is a justification statement for the proposed action. One method to insure that a project will not have any significant impacts is to set the level of significance just above the level of expected impacts. It appears that this was done for this project."

In private conversations, BLM specialists were even less charitable toward the blatantly corrupted EIS process as guided by the NBEI team and PNM's consultant, Woodward & Clyde. "These are not petty things . . . this is what's going to bury the whole thing," said a member of the NBEI team who confided that team members were under orders to make the power plant assessment seem acceptable. Said a member of the BLM State Office Planning and Environmental Assessment Division: "It is no exaggeration to say that this is the worst draft EIS I have ever seen."

The draft EIS's easy dismissal of adverse impacts upon the Navajo residents in the vicinity of the proposed power plant fit into the pattern established in the BLM land use planning and in environmental analyses for PRLAs. While some in BLM suspected that racism played a part in this insistent disregard of Indian concerns, the truth of the racism charge became evident in the course of public meetings intended to solicit comment on the draft document. During the long journeys to and from these public meetings in the Navajo areas, off-hand comments by NBEI team leader Leslie Cone revealed the telltale attitude of racism. A BLM woman who had previously worked with Navajos on the reservation reported the following conversation with Cone. "Do you like Navajos?" Cone asked. The fellow BLMer responded that she did, generally. To which Cone, a single woman, further inquired, "Well, would you date one?"

It was not just the Navajo and a few sympathetic BLMers and angry environmentalists who criticized the prostituted NMGS process. Officials of sister agencies, notably the Bureau of Indian Affairs, were equally persistent in trying to correct the corrupt EIS. It seemed clear to BIA officials that BLM had already decided to give the Bisti lands to PNM for its power plant, regardless of what adverse impacts might be shown in a legitimate EIS. Such a premature decision is, of course, contrary to law: federal officials are bound to refrain from making decisions until they have the benefit of a comprehensive EIS, according to the National Environmental Policy Act.

BLM New Mexico State Director Bill Luscher and Associate State Director Larry Woodard inadvertently provided proof that the agency was proceeding illegally in a January 13, 1982 memo to Albuquerque District Manager Applegate, instructing the latter to issue rights-of-way for pipelines to serve the proposed power plant. The State Office's NBEI team was still months away from completing a highly controversial EIS for the project, yet the BLM State Director told its Albuquerque District officials to give PNM the rights-of-way it needed for the power plant.

The damning memo, entitled "Ute Mountain Exchange", and apparently drafted by BLM Associate State Director Woodard for Luscher's signature, was also routed to Washington and Farmington BLM offices. Referring to a meeting that top BLM officials in New Mexico had held with PNM representatives earlier that month, the memo states: "We advised PNM to submit their application for the well sites and pipelines [for NMGS] to FRAH [Farmington Resource Area Headquarters] and that we would proceed to issue the R/W [right of way]. The R/W had been withdrawn earlier at our request as being premature. However, in light of a new water policy, we should issue the R/W subject to PNM getting authority from the State Engineer to drill the wells." This paragraph was seen by other BLM officials and by persons outside the agency as a tacit admission that the EIS process still going on at that time was irrelevant; that the decision to approve the Ute Mountain Exchange and the power plant were already made. For those who had already recognized the EIS as a farce, the memo simply provided the proof.

The Luscher memo goes on to instruct the BLM Albuquerque District Manager as follows: "With the selected lands [public lands in the Bisti sought by PNM] now tentatively agreed upon, you should take the lead to draft a Record of Decision and Notice of Realty Action." A Record of Decision is the formal approval document, and a Notice of Realty Action is the official public notice that a realty transaction is being taken; the two documents constitute final approval by the agency.

All pretense that BLM was conducting an impartial analysis of PNM's proposed NMGS collapsed with the memo. BLM officials in Farmington and Albuquerque were chagrined that their efforts on the EIS process were so thoroughly discredited by the admission on paper that a decision had already been reached.

For months the Bureau of Indian Affairs' Jim Analla had argued with BLM officials about the subverted NMGS EIS process. Analla, BIA chief of the Environmental Quality Section, based in the Navajo capital, Window Rock, had for more than a year worked with BLM as part of a multi-agency steering committee for the San Juan Basin projects. One of those meetings fell on January 13, 1982, the day of the Luscher memo. Analla asked BLM New Mexico Indian Coordinator Bill Brady whether BLM was already in the process of approving the Ute Mountain Exchange despite the fact that the NMGS EIS was far from complete at the time. Brady responded that BLM was not getting ready to approve the land exchange. Analla passed a note to Brady, saying, "That's a lie. Yesterday Uram said you were."

In fact, Bob Uram, the Department of the Interior's Field Solicitor, had for months been trying to stall a premature decision on the land exchange. Uram knew that such approval steps were insupportable in law and certain to lock BLM (and PNM) into lengthy court battles.

For reasons of personal ego if no other, Uram wanted the federal coal program and its associated projects to go smoothly if possible. Prior to his transfer to Santa Fe as an attorney for Interior, he had been intimately involved in structuring the federal coal program in Washington. It was a matter of personal pride, and a belief in "the system" that caused him to steer it through the many possible snags of field level implementation. He was the legal counsel for BLM New Mexico's coal-related San Juan Basin Action Plan which combined the procedures for the PRLAs, the Ute Mountain Exchange, the proposed competitive coal leasing and the New Mexico Generating Station.

Analla's concerns were made official at the end of March, when the head of the BIA for the Navajo Area, Don Dodge, sent a scathing letter to BLM officials charging a premature decision on Ute Mountain Exchange, irregularities in coal leasing procedures, and a host of other wrongdoing. The letter bears a marginal note from then Associate State Director Woodard: "Bullshit".

According to Uram, he advised State Director Luscher almost monthly not to take any steps which constituted approval for the Ute Mountain Exchange or NMGS. But in January 1982, BLM officials were so nearly pushed into such violations by pressures from PNM and Interior officials in Washington that Uram felt it necessary to draft a memo from the inter-agency workgroup for the San Juan Basin Action Plan urging the State Director not to approve the land exchange. At the January 13 meeting Analla referred to, the following memo was written and incorporated into the minutes: "When it issued the Final EA [environmental assessment] on the Ute Mountain Exchange, the Bureau said it was deferring a decision on whether to complete the exchange. The Workgroup understands that the Bureau is now considering taking final action in the near future to complete the exchange and take a separate but related action to grant PNM rights-of-way to a well field. The Workgroup is very concerned that these actions, if taken, have a high potential to disrupt and delay the orderly process now underway to resolve the numerous actions pending in the San Juan Basin.

One specific concern is the effect of these actions on the general credibility of the Bureau in this process. At a minimum, the Workgroup believes that prior to taking these actions, the Bureau must ensure that the public and all interested parties understand why the actions are being taken. The Workgroup recommends that strong consideration be given to not proceeding with these actions at this time, unless a general consensus can be reached that they are proper."

That memo, listed as Enclosure 6 in the minutes of the San Juan Basin Action Plan Workgroup Meeting of January 13, 1982, is referred to in the coverletter as a "Draft Statement of Concern".

Two days later, January 15, 1982, when State Director Bill Luscher attended a public meeting in Farmington on Watt's changes in the federal coal program, half a dozen BLM staffers, including District Manager Paul Applegate, Public Affairs Officer Jeff Radford, Farmington Area Manager Bob Calkins, San Juan Basin Project Coordinator Gene Day and Bisti team leader Rich Watts, urged Luscher not to take any steps which would lead to approval of the Ute Mountain Exchange. Luscher backtracked, saying his instructions on the right-of-way approval for PNM were intended only to clear up last-minute tasks which might hold up approval of the Ute Mountain Exchange *should he wish to do so.* "I only wanted us to get ready to approve," Luscher told his underlings. "I come to find out that I couldn't approve it yet, even if I wanted to. There is still work to be done on it [the exchange] that we've let slip, like the cultural resource clearances. I'm not saying that I've approved it; I haven't, and couldn't even if I wanted to. But I'm not saying I might not approve it two weeks from now."

Luscher told Applegate to have his staff prepare two opposite decision documents, if that would make him feel better; one document approving the Ute Mountain Exchange and one disapproving it.

Environmental activists had also gotten wind of the State Director's January 13 "decision" to approve the land exchange. On February 3, Alison Monroe, of Southwest Research and Information Center, visited BLM offices in Albuquerque and pressed Associate District Manager Millenbach on the matter. Millenbach told her that it would be contrary to law for the State Director to direct the Albuquerque office to initiate the approval process at this stage. "There's lots of internal disagreement over that, as you can imagine." Millenbach told Monroe that he had responded to Luscher's directive on the rights-of-way with a memo of his own saying the Albuquerque District Office would proceed with steps leading to the approval of the rights-of-way, but would not approve them yet.

On February 17, after Albuquerque District Planning and Environmental Assessment Chief Rich Fagan had reported at a regular Monday morning staff meeting that the decision document approving the exchange would be ready by the end of the week, Radford told him, "I still think the Ute Mountain Exchange will go down as one of the worst decisions yet." Fagan replied: "I do, too. I think everyone agrees on that."

The next day, Millenbach received a call from BLM Associate State Director Woodard, urging him to find out who is "leaking documents" to the environmentalists. Millenbach reported that Woodard told him, "You know, I think we've got a little Watergate going here."

On April 20, a BLM official from Colorado, attending a meeting of the San Juan River Regional Coal Team as a voting member, also was concerned about the right-of-way approvals for NMGS, because they might encumber possible coal lease tracts. Colorado BLM official Ken Smith asked Field Solicitor Uram whether the rights-of-way for NMGS had been approved, and Uram responded: "We've decided to grant them, but we're not telling anybody." State Director Luscher was standing right beside Uram and overheard the comment, but passed up the opportunity to contradict Uram's answer.

Environmentalists leaped to attack Luscher and the January 13 document. Sierra Club Attorney John Tiwald reprimanded the BLM State Director, saying, "Your actions and those of your agency demonstrate a premature disposition toward development of the NMGS in violation of the letter and spirit of NEPA [the National Environmental Policy Act]." Quoting the Luscher memo, Tiwald charged, "These actions on your part, as demonstrated by this January 13 memorandum, constitute a blatant disregard for, and violation of, NEPA.

"The case law abundantly demonstrates that to meet the requirements of NEPA the proposed use of the exchange land must be adequately considered. Furthermore, BLM must assess whether the exchange is in the public interest, as required by FLPMA Section 1716(a). We have seen no evidence of such assessment on BLM's part. Proceeding with the Ute Mountain Exchange at this time would therefore violate both NEPA and FLPMA." Tiwald's letter quoted federal regulations: "Environmental impact statements shall serve as the means of assessing the environmental impact of proposed agency actions, rather than justifying decisions already made," citing Council on Environmental Quality Regulations 1502.2(g).

He also took Luscher to task for deliberately undermining the Navajos' right to select the Bisti lands for relocating families. "Your actions in this matter constitute a gross breach of propriety."

Luscher's reply to Tiwald pleads that the January 13 memo had been misunderstood, and that no decisions had been made.

Under heavy pressure from PNM, Watt and Carruthers, BLM was poised for months to come, ready to trade away the Bisti lands as soon as it became expedient. In fact, it never became expedient, since the Navajos' legal maneuverings kept the State Director from approving the land exchange. Even after the NMGS EIS was completed in November, 1983, when Luscher could legally have approved it, the transaction remained inextricably snarled.

A year later, BLM was still desperately fighting for cultural resource clearances on the land PNM wanted for its power plant.

PNM, with the aid of Watt and Carruthers, continued to use the Ute Mountain Exchange as a threat against the Navajo Tribe as it negotiated for the Bisti lands, for the minerals under them—and for a piece of the action on the New Mexico Generating Station should it eventually come out that PNM did, in fact, have the clout to locate a power plant there.

But PNM's grand design for the Chaco-Bisti region was already unraveling. A series of setbacks shook the utility executives' confidence that they could control events: as public interest was generated over the NMGS EIS, somehow a copy of the suppressed Woodward & Clyde power plant siting study fell into the hands of environmentalists, suggesting that in fact the Bisti site had not been a first choice; utility expert Dave Marcus had blown a gaping hole in PNM's assertion that electricity from NMGS was needed any time in the near future; Marcus and Alison Monroe had also exposed the fraudulent federal coal leasing target which was to have dumped a billion tons of cheap coal onto the market; the NBEI EIS process had been shown as the farce that it was; the Navajo Tribe had selected the Bisti site that PNM wanted for

NMGS; the Sierra Club had launched an "Unsuitability Petition" with the State of New Mexico over Sunbelt Mining Company's plan to mine 600 acres of State-owned land adjacent to the Bisti Wilderness Study Area; environmentally-oriented residents in the Taos area had argued consistently against the Ute Mountain Exchange even though they presumably would have been the beneficiaries of the land swap; the Regional Director of the National Park Service had formally requested that "the New Mexico Generating Station not be built at the Bisti location", due to potentially "grave consequences on Chaco Culture National Historic Park"; the Star Lake Railroad, which was to haul mined Chaco-Bisti coal to the power plant, was still tied up in court by legal aid attorneys for local Navajo opponents; and someone within BLM, or more likely numerous people, were leaking sensitive, legally questionable BLM directives to environmentalists. To make matters worse, the indomitable James Watt was beginning to fall from grace in Washington circles due to his gaffes and combative style.

With a defensive mentality, PNM executives went through an internal shakeup. Security became an obsession. Investigators were hired to gather intelligence on company opponents.

By early May, 1982, State Police investigators were reportedly spying on environmentalists at the request of executives with PNM's mining subsidiary, Sunbelt Mining Company. On or about May 10, Rich Watts, of the BLM Farmington Office, was visited by Officer Roger Payne, of the New Mexico State Police Intelligence Division, who sought information about environmentalists who had been critical of PNM at Regional Coal Team meetings. The names of Alison Monroe (Southwest Research and Information Center), Dave Glowka and Jonathan Teague (Sierra Club) and Mimi Lopez (American Indian Environmental Council), were mentioned. The investigator wanted to know what kinds of things these people had written to BLM about proposed coal strip mining, and what they had said at public meetings. The officer said police were concerned about potential sabotage at Sunbelt Mining Company's newly opened Gateway Mine, adjacent to the Bisti Wilderness Study Area.

It was later learned that the undercover investigator had attended BLM public meetings in Farmington posing as a news photographer. He photographed at least one of the environmentalists critical of strip mining, and added this to police dossiers.

When the environmentalists named learned they apparently had been targeted by police investigators, they were shocked. The BLM staffer who had informed them they were under investigation was reprimanded by superiors. An editorial in the *Albuquerque Journal* blasted the spying as a practice unbefitting a democratic society, but BLM officials generally saw the spying as an acceptable consequence of public participation. State Director Luscher said he felt PNM and the State Police were justified. BLM Attorney Uram urged Luscher to issue a news release deploring the State Police investigations, and encouraging public participation. Uram argued that the targeted environmentalists had grounds for a lawsuit against the police. Luscher declined the news release option, but instructed his public affairs officer to draft up such a release, just in case.

In the Albuquerque BLM office, District Manager Applegate was also supportive of the police investigation of citizens who criticized government plans. Said Applegate: "There has been vandalism up there, on oil and gas rigs. They (company officials) have to maintain a full time "drip crew" to find damaged pipelines and things. Besides, you know, I don't know that you could really call it spying. They were just there to observe, and you know, the environmentalists come to these meetings for the same purpose. . . . This sort of thing does go on. Did you know what happened up in the Taos area where the Forest Service wanted to spray for spruce budworms? They (environmentalists) chained themselves to the planes and had the forest filled with naked people! So it's not like these things don't occur. The police have got to keep an eye on that sort of thing."

Applegate later endorsed the spying in conversation with State Office officials: "As far as I'm concerned, they were just doing their job." He recounted the "naked people in the forest" story to stop budworm spraying, to which the State Office personnel responded that the Forest Service should have sprayed Agent Orange, or "pure DDT".

A month later, in the early morning hours of July 28, 1982, one of the primary targets of the State Police investigation, Alison Monroe, staff scientist for Southwest Research and Information

Center, was assaulted in her bed as she slept. At 3 a.m., Monroe was awakened by a blunt object bashed into her head. The intruder, a white male, had slipped in through a bedroom window with the sole objective of administering a severe beating. There was no attempt at robbery, no attempted rape . . . just a thorough bludgeoning of her head. After repeated blows, the assailant escaped through the window and fled. Police found no clues, made no arrests. Monroe's face was bruised and pulpy for weeks; she was treated for concussion and severe contusions. The physician suggested the weapon had been a blunt object, possibly a board.

PNM's influence eroded even more toward the end of 1982 as the democratic process began to work its will. In the fall of 1982, a liberal Democrat, Toney Anaya, won the governorship in New Mexico, and a former legal aid attorney, Peterson Zah, won election as Navajo Tribal Chairman.

It would not be long before Watt was forced from office, and before the federal coal scandal loomed as the one major issue which might cost President Reagan his reelection.

CHAPTER 10

GATEWAY MINE: DESTRUCTION TO MAKE A POINT

The Bisti region is a strange, erie place. The most scenic parts of the more than 70,000 acres of badlands are devoid of nearly all vegetation.

Over millions of years, erosion has crafted a setting that would have frustrated a Disney special-effects expert. The ground is crusted and baked; the white and grey hills have horizontal ribbons of black, orange and red, displaying the remnants of soil layers of bygone eras. Startling earthen spires capped with flat rocks protrude from the surface where other multi-colored domes seem to bubble up. Natural pillars, in groups or singly, stand as if they were sentinels petrified eons ago, now motionless, wrinkled and weathered in the blistering desert sun. Bisti terrain has been compared to a landscape on the moon, or the surface of another planet. The Creator indulged in flights of fancy when putting together this special piece of earth.

The stark beauty and strange, unnatural appearing geologic formations have attracted humans' attention for thousands of years, yet little evidence exists of their visits. Instead, the wandering tourist now sees fossilized dinosaur bones, teeth of long-vanished oceanic fish, petrified tree stumps and the logs which fell from them 60 million years ago.

Although well-known to the Navajo who live in the region, outsiders who visited the area tended to keep its existence as a secret, one of the many special places off the beaten path that you feared to tell too many people about. But more and more people did learn of the Bisti region, especially when the entire northwestern corner of New Mexico came under heavy exploration for oil, gas and coal. By the 1960s, with coal mining interests moving into the area, naturalists, rockhounders, sightseers and paleontologists began to regard the area as one which ought to be spared from coal strip mining.

Very little of the land in the Bisti is privately owned; most of it is used by Navajo either as tribal land, federal land or acreage owned by the State of New Mexico. Coal lies under the landscape at varying depths, and in fact, it is the coal and near-coal layers in the geologic strata that contribute the dark stripes. Natural combustion of coal under certain rocks created the dramatic red and orange colors. Coal companies began applying for federal leases in the Bisti in the late 1950s. Two federal coal leases were issued to Public Service Company of New Mexico's coal mining subsidiary on August 1, 1961.

Sooner or later, most of the landscape probably would have been stripped away by miners, were it not for two pieces of congressional legislation. One was the Wilderness Act of 1964, and the other was the Federal Land Policy and Management Act of 1976. Among many other provisions, the latter act required the Bureau of Land Management to inventory all of its public land holdings to determine which acreage, if any, might be suitable for inclusion in the National Wilderness Preservation System.

When the Albuquerque District Bureau of Land Management began its survey for wilderness characteristics, the Bisti, or at least of portion of it, was already being tagged by environmentalists and wilderness advocates. A dirt road running roughly along the eastern boundary of the Navajo Reservation cut through the badland area about 30 miles south of Farmington. To the west of the road was amazingly colorful terrain of blacks, yellows, oranges and reds, but it was Reservation land, rather than BLM land, and therefore not eligible for federal wilderness consideration. To the east lay several thousand acres of spectacularly scenic geologic toadstools, spires, pinnacles and domes. Most of the land the east of the road was either state land or federal land, and the BLM portions met the criterion for potential wilderness designation by being remote and roadless. Vehicles had ventured into the badlands countless times in the past, to be sure, but any such trails had not been bladed through by graders and the tracks themselves were regularly obliterated by the powerful forces of erosion which gave the region its special character.

As the miles of badlands stretched farther to the east of this most scenic area, man-made encroachments became more common, with powerlines, roads, residences, and other elements which generally rendered some areas unsuitable for wilderness designation. It was no accident that these badlands were in public ownership; ranchers using the Homestead Act wanted land they could live off of, not just look at. With almost no vegetation, the badlands were among the last choices any rancher would make.

In their assessments for wilderness characteristics, BLM staffers in 1979 delineated about 3,900 acres of public land which became known as the Bisti Wilderness Study Area (WSA). Two more portions of the long stretch of badlands farther to the east were also designated as BLM wilderness study areas: the De-na-zin area and the Ah-shi-sle-pah area. Part of the BLM wilderness inventory process was to gauge the amount of public support that existed for each of the potential federal wilderness areas, and those three areas of the Bisti region seemed to have overwhelming backing, perhaps precisely because they had already been targeted for strip mining.

Bisti WSA had two federal coal leases on it, obtained by Public Service Coal Company. The 6,563-acre As-shi-sle-pah WSA was virtually covered with Preference Right Lease Applications, while part of the 18,554-acre De-na-zin WSA also was claimed for mining through the PRLA process. By the time the BLM wilderness inventory was completed for the Chaco-Bisti region, Public Service Company of New Mexico (PNM) was already preparing to relinquish its coal leases in the Bisti WSA for federal coal of equal value elsewhere in the region. PNM and its coal mining entity were trying to pull out of the two Bisti leases after their mine plan for that area ran into trouble from the Office of Surface Mining which questioned its reclamation potential. With the support of the Rio Grande Chapter of the Sierra Club and the Wilderness Society, PNM executives had U.S. Senator Pete Domenici introduce a bill in Congress which authorized the desired coal lease exchange. It breezed through both houses of Congress in the fall of 1980, becoming Public Law 96-475 on October 19, 1980. That act all but assured that at least a 3,900-acre piece of the Bisti region would be preserved.

But having agreed to "save the Bisti", PNM and mining executives were in no mood to back away when environmentalists pushed to preserve other areas of the Bisti region. It was clear to BLM, to reclamation experts, and to members of the public, that mining in the Bisti entailed special problems. Some people were seriously questioning whether the entire region was suitable for strip mining. Having given up two existing federal leases in the Bisti WSA, utility executives apparently felt the need to drive home the point that coal mining would take place in the Bisti region in any event. PNM's coal subsidiary announced plans to file a mining plan for an estimated ten million tons of state-owned coal under land that was surrounded on three sides by the federal Bisti WSA.

That 600 acres of Bisti was chosen as the place where industry would challenge the preservationists and assert its right to mine the region. The tract had been leased for coal from the State Land Office since 1961. Dubbed "The Gateway Mine" by Sunbelt Mining Company, PNM's subsidiary, the state land contained the same rich coal beds and the same spectacular scenic and scientific qualities as the much larger Bisti WSA on its northern, eastern and southern boundaries. In its land use planning exercise in 1979-81, BLM officials had identified that section of state land as desirable for acquisition to buffer and augment the Bisti WSA. But BLM's interest in obtaining the land through a swap with the State of New Mexico dimmed quickly when Ronald Reagan won the presidency and assigned James Watt to oversee the Department of the Interior.

Suddenly it looked as though even the Bisti WSA would be lost to strip miners. Under Watt, the suitability of the 3,900-acre

Bisti WSA as federal wilderness was thrown into doubt because the tract did not meet the size criterion established for the BLM wilderness review process. Guidelines called for wilderness study areas to be a minimum of 5,000 acres to offer the kind of seclusion that was deemed necessary for a federal wilderness area. When the survey was taken by BLM in 1979, local officials won the support of their superiors in arguing that although the Bisti area was less than 5,000 acres, it still provided the degree of isolation called for, due to its topography and remoteness.

The Rio Grande Chapter of the Sierra Club organized a "Save the Bisti" rally in late fall 1981, to show its resolve to stand against plans to strip mine the area. About 200 people turned out for the rally in the wilderness, a bitter cold camp-out on a Halloween weekend. The event not only served to forge an alliance to protect the area, it led to the recruitment of two major public figures into the environmentalists' corner. As a direct result of organizing for the Bisti Rally, Georgia O'Keeffe, perhaps America's greatest living artist and a resident of northwestern New Mexico, gave substantial monetary contributions to the preservation effort. She also wrote to BLM officials urging them not to permit destruction of the area she loved and had used as subjects for her highly-prized landscape paintings.

Likewise, the rally kicked off the involvement of film star Robert Redford, whose ranch in Utah served as headquarters for his environmental activities in the Southwest. Redford told Sierra Club activists that while he could not donate funds for the preservation campaign, he would be willing to appear in and narrate public service announcements calling attention to the strip mining threat to the Bisti. Redford's message was taped and aired frequently across the Southwest in 1982.

In March 1982, the local Sierra Club had the money and public visibility to launch a challenge to PNM's plans to open the Gateway Mine in the Bisti. Led by its San Juan Basin Task Force (mainly consisting of Dave Glowka, Jonathan Teague, Ron and Kay Grotbeck and Attorney John Tiwald), the Sierra Club chapter filed an "Unsuitability Petition" with the State of New Mexico, charging that the Gateway Mine should be stopped.

The Surface Mining Control and Reclamation Act passed by Congress in 1977 included provisions for any individual or group to petition to have certain areas declared unsuitable for strip mining. A formal agreement between the U.S. Office of Surface Mining and the State of New Mexico made the State's Mining and Minerals Division the appropriate agency with which to lodge an "Unsuitability Petition". However, state government in New Mexico had a long history of calculated permissiveness toward the mining industry. So pro-industry were state officials that in 1981 when they were called upon to comment on BLM's land use decision to save at least a portion of the Bisti, they could not bring themselves to admit the area had any scenic quality worth retaining. According to officials in the N.M. Mining and Minerals Division: "The Bisti badlands, along with the other many numerous badlands of the San Juan Basin, are a major source of natural pollution of the streams and of the atmosphere. Strip mining of the areas, followed by reclamation to produce range land, will decrease this natural pollution."

Little wonder, then, that the state agency rejected the Sierra Club's petition. The group's arguments had cited lack of evidence that the lands could be reclaimed adequately, particularly for recreational and scenic values, and potential disturbances to the adjacent BLM Bisti WSA from blasting and other industrial activities.

Bolstered by widespread public support, as well as by a sizeable and growing war chest, the Sierra Club appealed to the N.M. Coal Surface Mining Commission. On November 3, 1982, the appeal was denied; the next day, the group's attorney announced their intention to appeal to the Santa Fe District Court.

The Sierra Club argued before the appeals boards and before the media that PNM and its subsidiary, Sunbelt Mining Company, had no real need for the coal in the state lease adjacent to the Bisti WSA, but were determined to strip away the surface at Gateway just to prove a point.

Sunbelt Mining Company officials asserted that coal from Gateway was critical to the operation of PNM's San Juan Power Plant west of Farmington. It was said to be the only coal available for the PNM subsidiary to fulfill its contracts to supply coal for the power plant. According to a company spokesman: "Sunbelt must have the Gateway coal reserves to replace the depleting De-na-zin Mine. These reserves are essential to Sunbelt for fulfilling existing coal delivery agreements and for remaining viable as an employer and operating entity. It should be noted that Gateway represents the only coal reserves available to Sunbelt that have been approved through the mine-permitting process and that are available in the timeframe in which Sunbelt needs them."

The company's arguments were more than adequate to convince the state agencies hearing the Sierra Club's petition and appeals. Sunbelt Mining Company began erecting a heavy-duty chain-link fence around the section of state land in September 1982 and announced they would be shipping coal from the Gateway Mine by the end of the year. A huge, surface-stripping dragline was delivered to the site, with its long crane arm pointing east across the Bisti region. When the stripping began, Sierra Club members and others were on hand to document the destruction. PNM had, in fact, made its point.

But an analysis of PNM's coal usage does not bear out the assertion that coal from Gateway was urgently needed, as claimed. A factsheet on Gateway Mine prepared by Sunbelt itself in 1982 provides evidence that the purported urgency was more a ruse than an physical reality. The company's factsheet said: "The San Juan Mine [immediately adjacent to PNM's San Juan power plant] does not have sufficient coal resources to supply the San Juan Generating Station over the station's economically productive life. Thus, the San Juan Mine requires supplemental coal supplies, and Sunbelt's production helps to fill that need. Purchasing supplemental coal now helps to average down the total price paid for fuel over the life of the station. The alternative is to deplete all lower-cost, on-site coal reserves and then pay much higher prices for fuel later when all coal must be transported to the station from off-site mining operations." The statement is an admission, then, that mining coal from the Bisti region was seen as a way to stretch out the supply of cheaper, mine-mouth coal that existed next to the San Juan Generating Station.

Even so, PNM's subsidiary already had the De-na-zin Mine in operation two miles south of Gateway. If there was some pressing economic reason to haul Bisti-area coal to the San Juan power plant, why couldn't the fuel be trucked from the De-na-zin Mine? Sunbelt officials lamely contended that they had underestimated the amount of coal in the De-na-zin Mine and that it would soon be depleted, leaving Gateway as the only alternative. In fact, the De-na-zin Mine was still producing coal when the Gateway Mine opened in 1982; as late as 1986, coal from De-na-zin was still being hauled to the San Juan power plant.

The mine history at Gateway is also evidence that the destruction which took place there was motivated more by politics than by economics. Sunbelt's mining of the "urgently needed" Gateway coal actually occurred at a snail's pace. Two years after the stripping started, Sunbelt had only delivered about a million tons of coal from Gateway. By mid-1984, the slow pace had begun to present problems for BLM's plans to manage the adjacent Bisti WSA as a federal wilderness area. At a May 2, 1984 meeting of BLM officials, State Office San Juan Basin Coordinator Gene Day noted bleakly, "Originally they were to have mined much faster. They are not nearly as far along as Sunbelt expected. There's supposedly ten million tons in the whole thing (the State coal lease), and maybe nine million is still left under the undisturbed area."

BLM Albuquerque District Manager Paul Applegate commented, "They told us they'd have it all mined out by 1988. Now they're talking about stretching it out . . . that could create some problems for us once it's (Bisti WSA) a wilderness area, from the dust and the blasting." Applegate had counted on the mining activity at Gateway being finished by the time the BLM Bisti Wilderness Area was managed as such.

In retrospect, it seems clear that the real purpose of the Gateway Mine was to demonstrate that PNM and Sunbelt Mining had the power to tear up the damn land if they wanted to.

But to the dismay of mining and utility executives, the general public was growing evermore attracted to the fascinating Bisti. The colorful, tourist-oriented placemat printed for McDonald's restaurants in New Mexico in 1983 depicted the "Bisti Badlands" along with Carlsbad Caverns and other top attractions. Cartooned on the placemat is a dinosaur skeleton emerging from the Bisti sands.

CHAPTER 11

DEMOCRACY AT WORK

James Watt's excesses played an important role in the election of one of New Mexico's most liberal governors in the fall of 1982. Although Democrat Toney Anaya had a large populist following derived from his "protect the little guy" posture during his stint as New Mexico's Attorney General 1974 to 1978, he couldn't count on strong party support in his gubernatorial bid in 1982, because as the State's chief prosecutor he had launched an aggressive campaign against corruption by several high officials in his own party. But what he lacked in effort by party regulars, his campaign was able to make up through enthusiastic, organized environmental activists working on his behalf statewide.

Perhaps the leading environmental issue that caused hundreds of activists to work for his election was the blatantly corrupt federal coal program being played out in the state. Opposition to Watt and Carruthers transcended party lines in New Mexico and created common ground for many divergent organizations that had previously found little reason to cooperate. In a state where environmentalists tended to polarize over the nuclear power issue, coal and its obvious potential for environmental degradation provided an issue on which all could unite. For example, the Sierra Club in New Mexico drew a substantial portion of its membership from the well-educated and relatively affluent scientists and technicians who worked at the Los Alamos and Sandia National Laboratories. While Los Alamos scientists had long provided leadership for the New Mexico Clean Air and Water Coalition, with a number of successful challenges against power plant smokestack pollution, Sandia Laboratories had several staffers in leadership positions in the Rio Grande Sierra Club and in the New Mexico Wildlife Federation. These groups had little in common with other environmental groups that worked against nuclear power (and the then-powerful uranium industry), but they were quick to join forces over the coal issue.

Together, they played a decisive role in bringing the combative Anaya to power as governor.

At the same time, the Navajo Nation was in the throes of an election which would return the pro-development Peter McDonald as tribal chairman, or would bring to power a scrappy legal aid attorney, Peterson Zah, whose team had won wide respect protecting Navajo families from the destructive impacts of coal and uranium mining . . . activities McDonald had pushed through as chairman.

Watt had been directing the Department of the Interior for more than a year when those electoral campaigns geared up. The abrasive, confrontational secretary and his mean-spirited policies constituted an easy issue to rally the voters. The coal issue became a campaign centerpiece for both Anaya and Zah because it had a high level of public awareness, organized groups involved in fighting it, and a widely recognized "public villain" (Watt) as a foil. Watt had aroused environmentalists and wilderness advocates with his anti-wilderness rhetoric; he had angered clean air advocates with his wide-eyed blindness to pollution; he had picked up opposition from wildlife groups that repeatedly saw him caricatured in the national and local media as an enemy of wildlife; he shocked the sizeable community of archeologists and persons interested in cultural resources with his attempts to change federal regulations to diminish congressionally-mandated protection for archeological sites; Navajo families who saw themselves pitted against large-scale industrial exploitation of their homelands knew that Watt was the champion of such exploiters.

PNM's Interior-supported plan for the San Juan Basin had mobilized substantial opposition in the northern half of the state, which is easily the most populous region (including Albuquerque, Santa Fe, Farmington, Gallup, Taos and other communities along the Rio Grande, San Juan and Chama Rivers). Politically-effective groups in Albuquerque, Santa Fe and Taos took up the coal-related issues and involved thousands of voters who looked to Toney Anaya as the fighter who could stop the abuses on public land. Environmental groups in those areas had coalesced under an umbrella organization known as Committee on Coal, which monitored the federal coal program as perhaps no other federal activity had ever been scrutinized locally before. Many members of the Committee on Coal were more knowledgeable about federal regulations than were the civil servants themselves . . . just as corporate interests routinely are. Tracking the federal coal program was relatively easy, and when the activists spotted irregularities (of which there were many while Watt and Carruthers were circumventing laws to abet PNM's plans) membership bulletins, press conferences and statements at public hearings exposed the improprieties with astounding success.

The Sierra Club's "Unsuitability Petition" on the proposed Gateway Mine had kept the Bisti issue hot throughout 1982, as the candidates geared up for the November election.

As any politician would, Anaya recognized the environmentalists' growing strength and respectability. He familiarized himself not only with the basic issues, but learned how he might be able to affect the outcome of the coal program if he became governor. In fact, the federal coal program as developed during the Carter Administration (and still nominally the program under Reagan) called for a relatively high-profile involvement of state governors, through the BLM's state-federal Regional Coal Teams. In his campaigning, candidate Anaya announced what his first steps would be to combat Watt after he won the election.

For their part, members of the Committee on Coal made an easy transition from "public participation" in BLM's coal program to activism in electoral politics. In reality, facing Watt's intransigence and disregard for federal laws and regulations, the environmentalists and Indian rights advocates saw little hope for influencing the course of events without shifting into electoral politics. Having been invited to participate in BLM's coal leasing process during the Carter Administration, they soon learned that the Reagan team was dismayed that the public might be watching the coal program. Early on, the Committee on Coal set a strategy to help elect candidates that might try to straighten out the misguided coal program. They organized for Anaya and against his opposition in the primary, and then organized successful telephone campaigns and other grassroots efforts to see that Anaya won the governorship. They also targeted incumbent U.S. Senator Republican Harrison Schmitt and went all-out for his Democratic challenger, Jeff Bingaman.

Nor did the environmentalists ignore implications of the race for State Commissioner of Public Lands. The State Land Office controlled the nine million acres of land and minerals owned by the State of New Mexico. For years, voters had paid little attention to the race for land commissioner, and the office had become the secretive domain of public officials who worked hand-in-glove with energy mineral interests. At least that was the case before PNM's Sunbelt Mining Company sought a mine permit for the coal lease it held on the 600 acres of State land that jutted into the highly-controversial BLM Bisti Wilderness Study Area. The Gateway Mine suddenly thrust the office of the State Land Commissioner into the public spotlight right before the elections. Jim Baca, a former newsman, was serving as State Liquor Director when he ran for land commissioner. Riding a public mandate to reform the state's corrupt liquor licensing system, Baca had gained much esteem by carrying out the clean-up effort which many had regarded as all but impossible. In his campaign to head the State Land Office, Baca quickly picked up on the Gateway Mine issue and asserted that had he been commissioner, he would never have leased the State section of Bisti land for coal strip mining.

Hoping for a clean sweep in the November 1982 elections, the environmental activists brought their enthusiastic campaigning efforts to Baca's challenge of the old regime at the State Land Office.

And the "green vote" counted. Several political observers gave credit to the environmental activists for the toppling of Senator Schmitt and for victories by Anaya and Baca. An analysis by a key green vote organizer, Erv Kreischer, of the New Mexico Wildlife Federation, pointed out that much of the electoral success was a product of two consultants from the Wilderness Society office in Washington, working with Lynda Taylor at Southwest Research and Information Center and Kay Grotbeck for the Rio Grande Sierra Club. The mobilization of environmentalists for Anaya (and Bingaman in the senatorial race) came from the vast mailing lists of the Sierra Club and the Wildlife Federation, Kreischer explained.

In the Navajo election campaign, Peter McDonald had a serious challenge from Peterson Zah, and a hard-hitting campaign in which the incumbent was characterized as a corrupt dictator. McDonald, an engineer by profession, was the best-known Indian leader in the United States, but it was widely believed that corporate lawyers in Phoenix actually called the shots during his administration. McDonald had run up heavy political losses by supporting uranium mining developments and by forcing local Navajo families to accept coal strip mining operations. He had set in motion his own grand design for industrialization of the eastern portion of the Navajo Reservation, bordering the Chaco-Bisti region, and dealt harshly with the grassroots opposition he encountered.

Less than a year before he stood for reelection, the muckraking *Mother Jones* magazine did a coverstory, "tomahawk job" on McDonald, recounting old allegations of corruption and collusion with corporate despoilers. The magazine article in January 1982 carried the following sub-heading: "Is Peter McDonald the Moses of the Navajo Nation, or Is He an Energy Baron Out For Himself and a Few Loyal Cronies?"

It looked as though McDonald's 12-year hold on the Navajo Tribal chairmanship was coming to a close. His opponent, director of the DNA—Peoples' Legal Services Corporation in Window Rock, was more charismatic, had the wits of an attorney, and enjoyed a reputation as defender of the common man. (By contrast, McDonald's image was that of a corporate executive whose concern for the bottom line led him to disregard human costs.) While McDonald dressed in pinstripe suits, Zah wore jeans and a leather jacket; the latter had labored with hammer and nails to build his legal aid headquarters—in a traditional Navajo hogan style—while McDonald worked out of the U.S. government-built, bureaucratic-style office complex that seemed more an appendage of the Bureau of Indian Affairs offices than the seat of government for America's largest Indian nation.

Zah picked up important endorsements, too. The U.S. Bureau of Indian Affairs director for the Navajo Nation, Donald Dodge, made a public statement of support for Zah in late July 1982. The endorsement clearly demonstrated to Navajo voters that McDonald's support was seriously waning. The day after his endorsement of Zah, Dodge was transferred to North Dakota by high Interior officials who cited "an important mission" as the reason for the reassignment. No suggestion was made that Dodge's endorsement might be a violation of the federal Hatch Act (which prevents civil servants from engaging in partisan politics), because the act only deals with "partisan" elections. Navajo elections are nonpartisan.

A critical issue for McDonald was his handling of the forced relocation of Navajo subsistence ranchers and their families away from the controversial Navajo-Hopi Joint Use Area in Arizona. Any Navajo politician's participation in forced relocation of Navajos from their "traditional lands" was sure to carry a massive electoral liability. McDonald was on the horns of a dilemma. Congress had repeatedly declared that the Joint Use Area be partitioned, giving Hopi Indians the northern portion and the Navajo the southern part. The congressional decision meant thousands of Navajo families would be uprooted and sent to new, distant lands which were to be made available from BLM lands in New Mexico and elsewhere in Arizona. McDonald had stalled as long as he could, unwilling to be seen as a traitor who compelled his people to give up their land to the rival Hopis, but he faced the real threat of a contempt of Congress charge unless he made a selection of BLM lands onto which the Navajos from the Joint Use Area would be relocated.

He saw his chance for political salvation by selecting the BLM lands in the Bisti area that he knew were sought by PNM for its New Mexico Generating Station. He did so, and thus infuriated PNM, Watt and Carruthers. But the maneuver was not enough to prevent his defeat at the polls. As soon as the new Zah Administration was fully briefed on the federal coal program in the off-reservation area in New Mexico, the tribe attempted to assert a greater role on the state-federal Regional Coal Team for the San Juan Basin. Although the tribe previously had been invited to attend these meetings as an official observer, or ex officio member, Zah requested that the tribe be accorded full voting rights on the coal team. At the first request, the Navajo's demand was declared impossible on the spot by the BLM chairman of the panel. When the tribe insisted at subsequent meetings, the BLM officials referred the question to Interior in Washington, which sent back the same reply: regulations for regional coal teams stated clearly that only representatives of state governors were to be given voting power; an exception would have to be made to the rules in order to have the Navajo Tribe so represented, and Interior was unwilling to make that exception.

Environmentalists working to preserve the Chaco-Bisti region, and Navajo residents of the coal region saw the Zah-Anaya electoral victories as the one-two punch which just might turn the tide against the Watt-Carruthers headlong rush to make the San Juan Basin into a coal and utility company bonanza. In fact, the two successful candidates arranged an early meeting to celebrate their victories and explore common goals.

Within days of his victory, Anaya demanded that BLM officials in Santa Fe postpone an official comment period on the BLM-PNM power plant EIS and a companion draft of an environmental impact statement for federal coal leasing in the San Juan Basin. Anaya and Zah insisted on the extension beyond the February 7, 1983, comment deadline because they would have just barely been sworn in, and therefore would be unable to set up a review team prior to the Interior-imposed deadline.

While the previous New Mexico governor, Democrat Bruce King, had been highly permissive of Watt's blatantly pro-development policies, Anaya took up the coal issue for his anti-Watt banner as his administration began to define itself. Political commentators were quick to assess the kinds of people the new governor was relying on and it was not hard to detect a decidedly pro-environmentalist cast. As one of his chief staff assistants, he named Sally Rodgers, founder of the Environmental Clearinghouse in Santa Fe and long a lobbyist for environmental causes. Anaya named Brant Calkin, former National Sierra Club president, as Under Secretary of the Department of Natural Resources. He named a former DNA Legal Services attorney in the Chaco region, Paul Biderman (also formerly with the NM Attorney General's Office), as Secretary of Energy and Minerals. He tapped

Denise Fort, formerly an attorney for Southwest Research and Information Center, as Secretary for Finance and Administration.

Industry representatives rocked on their heels. Never had a governor of New Mexico placed so much power in the hands of "the enemy". With his appointments and pronouncements, Anaya was being labeled by the national media as "the most liberal governor in America". And Anaya himself lost no time in labeling himself as the nation's only Hispanic governor.

It was clear from the start that Anaya wasn't going to "play ball" with the Reagan Administration, and particularly not with the evermore unpopular James Watt and his lieutenant from New Mexico, Garrey Carruthers.

Suddenly the Committee on Coal, and other environmentalists, had access to people with power in Santa Fe, the state capital. The activists were almost stunned to discover that when they talked about issues that troubled them, people in state government listened. The governor's top assistants eagerly solicited position papers, advice and insights from members of the Committee on Coal. News analysts went so far as to suggest that environmentalists at Southwest Research and Information Center controlled the Governor's Office. It was certainly true that high state officials soon adopted Committee on Coal positions on a reduction of federal coal leasing targets; on preservation of the Bisti, De-na-zin and Ah-shi-sle-pah as BLM wilderness areas; on the inadvisability of PNM's New Mexico Generating Station; on the Navajo Tribe's right to participate as a voting member on the BLM regional coal team; on the need for strict application of federal regulations meant to protect fragile lands from strip mining; on protection for fossil sites and archeological sites; and on greater respect and attention being paid to Navajo lifestyles in the coal region.

By early April 1983, the new Anaya team had responded to BLM's draft San Juan Basin EISs: Anaya's coverletter for his staffs' comments asserted that the BLM documents were totally inadequate, should be thoroughly rewritten and re-issued in draft again, and that BLM should halt PNM's Bisti power plant project. When the Navajo Tribe's comments came in, a host of legal issues were raised while citing the EISs treatment of socio-economic impacts to Navajos as woefully inadequate.

Other persons commenting were even less pleased. Dave Marcus, hired by the San Francisco-based Environmental Defense

Fund to analyze the coal leasing EIS, again ripped apart the BLM's assumptions of need for additional federal coal leasing. Alison Monroe, hired by the Committee on Coal to respond to the draft, took issue with just about everything in the document. That they found so much wrong with the draft EIS came as no surprise to its preparers: the document was overseen in great detail by Washington-level Interior officials, with guidance coming direct from Garrey Carruthers. The multitude of warped assumptions, outright fabrications, deceits, downplaying of adverse impacts and deliberate slanting of presentation to favor massive coal leasing in the Chaco-Bisti region were very much at Carruthers' insistence.

It was rare that Washington officials became so intimately involved in the preparation of EIS documents at the BLM district office and resource area level. But for Carruthers, if not for Watt, these deliberate attempts at subverting the requirements of the National Environmental Policy Act were imperatives. EIS review specialists from Washington were dispatched to Albuquerque and Farmington to convince the EIS writers to tone down parts of the report which suggested adverse impacts, to re-word and obfuscate descriptions of environmental, social and economic damage—which the EIS writers had already tried to make as tame as possible as a result of repeated instructions from Carruthers. For example, in dealing with the critical issue of post-mining reclamation, a Washington office envoy had come to the Albuquerque District on February 16, 1982 to persuade the EIS writers to send out the draft EIS saying reclamation potential was good, rather than poor as the internal, preliminary draft stated. The Washington official argued that since the coal-bearing lands' vegetative productivity was so low to begin with, the EIS should state that reclamation prospects are good since very little revegetation would have to be established before achieving the previous level of ground cover.

That argument had already been thoroughly considered by the EIS writers, who had discarded it as totally insupportable. The problem was that earlier reports by a Department of the Interior sister agency, the U.S. Geological Survey, had already concluded that the lands had "low reclamation potential". The Washington official was told that to take the stance that reclamation prospects were good would be to contradict the best scientific evidence which BLM itself had requested and which had been provided by a sister Interior agency. The visiting critic reluctantly agreed that the draft would have to say that reclamation potential was low. But it was by no means the first nor the last attempt made to downplay the Chaco-Bisti lands' potential to recover from the strip mining that Carruthers' policies encouraged.

Among the many other distortions in the draft coal EIS prepared under Carruthers' guidance was the assertion that the public attitude toward coal mining in most of the proposed tracts was positive, or favorable. In fact, the exact opposite was true. Time and again, in hearing after hearing, and letter after letter, the overwhelming public reaction to Interior's coal leasing proposal was strongly opposed. Letters and comments sent to BLM during land use planning, during comment periods on the PRLAs, and during Regional Coal Team hearings on leasing targets, made it abundantly clear that the proposal was highly unpopular. And state elections had just installed candidates who had taken hard lines against Watt's programs. The town of Farmington, the largest (and largely Anglo) city in the coal region, was the only portion of the state where significant support had been voiced for coal leasing, as might be expected. But hundreds of individual Navajos living over the coal had expressed strong opposition, as had dozens of formal resolutions adopted by the Navajo Chapters in the area, statements of opposition by the Navajo Tribal Council, and hundreds of letters from "average citizens" rejecting the BLM plan. When the Albuquerque District public participation specialist noticed the draft EIS reference to a positive public attitude toward coal mining, he called the EIS writers in Farmington for an explanation. First, the BLM's Navajo liaison officer, Danny Charlie, agreed that the assertion seemed patently wrong. He could not explain how that statement had found its way into print. Later the same day, EIS team leader Rich Watts called to inquire what the problem was. Watts said he considered the public attitude to be favorable in San Juan County (of which Farmington is the county seat). But the evidence clearly did not support such a conclusion. The voice of the general public in New Mexico, and surely within the coal region itself, was overwhelmingly opposed. Watts responded that perhaps the EIS could be clarified on that point.

In fact, BLM District Manager Applegate had admitted the high level of opposition for some time. On January 21, 1983, Applegate told staffers: "The public says they're against the power plant. Bullshit! They're against the coal mining. But I'm under different orders."

When the *Washington Post* carried an article in early April on Governor Anaya's attack on the San Juan Basin coal EIS, the war between the already-embattled Watt and Anaya intensified. And increasingly BLM officials in New Mexico were pulled into the fray as pawns. Albuquerque District personnel were caught in the middle, with Carruthers directing deceit and falsifications in the official documents while environmentalists, state officials and others were having a field day exposing the deceptions. After Applegate and other local BLM officials returned from briefing Carruthers on the wretched reception his impact statement was receiving, EIS Coordinator Mary Zuschlag told them: "They really nailed us to the wall. I don't know how we can answer those points (in a final EIS) because they're all right. Dave Marcus' main points are on the leasing target, and he's absolutely right.

"The only way we can respond is to say that we did it that way because of politics, but we don't want to say that."

Her immediate supervisor, Rich Fagan, the Albuquerque District Office's chief of planning and environmental coordination, concurred: "They've (the environmentalists ripping apart the bogus coal EIS) got it all down cold. They know more about what we did and why we did it than we do ourselves. They've got it all right there, footnoted and annotated . . . when we met, what we decided, why, and who was there. I'm keeping a copy of it to use as a record of what we did," he added with a slight giggle.

And nailed they were. If the opposition had come only from the usual, obstructionist environmentalists, the BLM officials could probably have ridden out the storm of protest. But the political equation had changed dramatically with the state government and the Navajo Tribal government reinforcing the environmentalists' objections.

By early summer 1983, Watt, Carruthers and other proponents of massive coal leasing probably knew their little game was over. They were not only being raked over the coals by upstart Governor Anaya, but they were aware of the congressional investigations into the irregularities that had occurred in the April 1982 Powder River Coal lease sale in Wyoming. On January 19-20, 1983, Congressional Staffer James O'Kane, working for the Survey and Investigations Office of the House Appropriations Committee, paid a visit to the Albuquerque District BLM office, probing for evidence of Interior-instigated wrongdoing in the proposed San

Juan Basin coal lease sale. O'Kane explained that the Appropriations Committee chairman was concerned that Watt was giving away federal coal elsewhere around the West, as had happened in the Powder River Coal Region. His basic questions to BLM New Mexico officials were: 1) Will the government be getting fair market value for the coal it planned to offer for lease in the Chaco-Bisti region? and 2) Would the lease sales here be genuinely competitive? All six of the coal geologists from the Albuquerque Minerals Management Service (MMS) assured O'Kane that the Watt coal regulations and procedures would not produce fair market value for San Juan Basin coal.

Jim Fassett, of the MMS's minerals evaluation team, expressed concern over the ability of government geologists to be able to determine fair market value in the near future, due to the ongoing Watt-inspired reorganization of MMS through a merger with BLM. Said Fassett: "A cynical person would say the real reason for this reorganization is to prevent an adequate appraisal of the fair market value of federal coal."

When O'Kane asked his opinion of the Carruthers procedure to use coal company bids as the determining factor for establishing fair market value of public coal, as had happened in the Powder River coal sale, Fassett and other MMS officials argued that it was an entirely inappropriate method of setting fair market value. "Everybody knows that the coal companies will collude to bring down the bid levels if the government tries to use bid levels to establish fair market value. Of course, they'll collude," said Fassett. "They've even admitted it on the record."

With Congress investigating the coal program, and with state governors beginning to complain publicly about it, Watt's siege mentality went into full gear. From the ideologues' point of view there were enemies everywhere. People who complained about Watt's coal program and other questionable policies came under heavy suspicion: if people and organizations were against Watt, they were un-American, traitors, communist dupes.

And few people were making as much noise about Watt as the new governor of New Mexico, who had begun to cast himself as a national, rather than a state or regional political personality (possibly with an eye to the the national Democratic Party primaries which were to begin shortly). Washington-based columnist Bob Duke, writing for the *Albuquerque Tribune,* reported on May 2,

1983 that "Governor Toney Anaya is trying to rally the nation's governors against Interior Secretary James Watt's decision to lease federal coal reserves in New Mexico and other states to private firms at bargain prices. The New Mexico chief executive has sent letters to his fellow governors urging them to stand firm against Watt's 'giveaway' plan, and if the majority respond favorably, it will enhance his image as a governor who not only airs his grievances, but acts. Anaya, already recognized in the National Governors Conference as the foremost champion of Hispanic rights, is determined to thwart Watt's coal leasing policies."

The article noted that Anaya had "fired the opening shot against Watt" on April 8 when he had asked BLM to delay a proposal for a huge coal lease sale in the San Juan Basin and to reject PNM's plan to construct a power plant in the Bisti region. The article quoted an Anaya spokesman explaining the governor's tough stance: "The governor not only considers Watt's leasing policy a giveaway program which would reap windfall profits for private companies, but contends it would cost the state mineral royalties. It's a terrible program." The columnist concludes his piece by observing: "Seventeen days after Anaya challenged the New Mexico portion of the leasing plan, *The Washington Post* ran a front-page story saying an eight-month House Appropriations Committee study had concluded that Watt was leasing federal coal reserves to industry at 'fire sale' prices, permitting private firms to harvest windfall profits at the expense of the federal treasury."

But it was clear that Watt's coal program—especially in New Mexico—was really Garrey Carruthers' program. On a day-to-day basis, Carruthers monitored the San Juan Basin coal effort, and fired off directives on a regular basis to assure that his wishes were implemented. By early 1983, it had become clear to many New Mexicans, particularly those in New Mexico offices of the Bureau of Land Management, that Carruthers wanted to be governor of New Mexico himself.

In a quick visit to New Mexico, James Watt boosted Carruthers' candidacy, musing before the media how nice it would be if the assistant secretary were to become governor of New Mexico.

A key element of the Reagan Administration's basic philosophy of government was the federalist principle: the national government had taken too much power and it should be de-centralized back to the states. It is certainly a laudable principle, and one which citizens of any partisan persuasion might support enthusiastically. But that is what made Anaya such an annoyance. Federalism was the right idea . . . but not when a state was governed by an anti-Watt liberal like Anaya. Federalism made sense only if a state were led by right-wingers, or at least, governors who "played ball" by conservative rules.

Federalism, in short, made sense if somebody like Carruthers was governor, but not someone like Anaya.

Carruthers' political ambitions for a return to New Mexico as the state's governor soon became the driving motivation for much of what the Department of the Interior did in New Mexico. Agencies of the federal government, particularly the Bureau of Land Management, were directed by Carruthers in such a way that results favored his intended bid for the governorship. During 1983 and 1984, Carruthers' perversion of the federal civil service to serve his own political ambitions reached outrageous levels.

Not only was public information about BLM activities, particularly the federal coal program, routinely manipulated and suppressed, but increasingly BLM budgets were being diverted to efforts which would give Carruthers a platform. Information about events which might reflect negatively on Carruthers were suppressed; although a high level of public information dissemination about the federal coal program had been an important cornerstone of the program in New Mexico, by early 1983, nearly all information to be released had to be cleared through the BLM State Director who kept a watchful eye for what might be prejudicial to Carruthers' interests. When BLM public affairs officers at the State Office in Santa Fe and at the Albuquerque District Office sent out news releases, or responded to news inquiries in ways which were later found to have infuriated Carruthers, they came under heavy reprimand. On June 10, 1983, State BLM Public Affairs Officer, John Gumert, was stripped of his job at Carruthers' insistence. The firing came just a few weeks after Gumert, a registered Republican, had refused to arrange a political rally for Carruthers at taxpayer expense.

That incident offers a clear insight into the mentality that pervaded the ideological world in which Watt and Carruthers worked on a daily basis.

As part of his campaign to cover up irregularities at Interior through public relations maneuvers, Carruthers hired a Las Cruces television reporter, Selma Sierra, as his personal public relations operative. (Las Cruces was Carruthers' "hometown", in that it was here that he had worked as State Republican Party Chairman 1977-79 while a faculty member at New Mexico State University.) At a starting salary of $30,000 a year as Carruthers' administrative aide, Sierra served chiefly as image maker for Carruthers' expected run for office. But in the summer of 1983, seeing his boss, Watt, losing influence, Carruthers was growing desperate to secure his own political future back in New Mexico. In another of a long string of personal appearances in New Mexico designed to create favorable exposure for him, Carruthers was to fly in on June 14 for routine ceremonies.

As usual, BLM personnel in New Mexico were to assure that favorable public exposure for Carruthers was maximized. But in this case, Carruthers and his aide, Selma Sierra, crossed the boundary of propriety and legality. In making arrangements for Carruthers' visit, Sierra telephoned from Washington to the BLM Public Affairs Office in Santa Fe asking that a luncheon rally for Carruthers be arranged in Santa Fe between the morning and afternoon ceremonies on June 14.

Gumert, who took the call from Sierra, recalled that it was supposed to be a Chamber of Commerce-type of luncheon for Carruthers, and that Sierra wanted it held at a large facility like Santa Fe's Sweeney Convention Center. And she wanted Gumert to handle ticket sales to the event.

Gumert backed away quickly. The suggestion that BLM personnel would sell tickets to a luncheon intended to promote Carruthers' prospects for a gubernatorial bid was outlandish. Gumert told Sierra that he could not do such a thing; that it would be improper. He recalled that Sierra apparently did not understand what the impropriety might be, and was annoyed that Gumert found the idea objectionable.

Gumert reported the Carruthers-Sierra request to BLM Associate State Director Monte Jordan, who concurred with Gumert's refusal. But Sierra called back to Gumert the following day to insist that the luncheon be set up and that BLM personnel sell tickets for the event. Gumert's continued refusal undoubtedly played a role in his being dismissed at Carruthers' insistence shortly thereafter.

With Gumert gone, rumors ran fast in BLM New Mexico offices that he would be replaced by none other than Selma Sierra, so that she could direct Carruthers' pre-campaign more closely, totally controlling information about his role in Interior which might be favorable or unfavorable to his electoral chances. But selection of Gumert's replacement was delayed and Sierra's appointment to the position was eventually thwarted by that bane of all right-wing ideologues—the federal regulations. Sierra, it seemed, could not meet the qualifications for the job, and civil service procedures tend to be strict regarding job placements. With Sierra out of contention, the Santa Fe BLM public affairs position was eventually given to Sally Wisely, who had worked in that office for four years.

During Carruthers' nearly four years as Assistant Secretary of Interior, he made more than 20 field tours to New Mexico at taxpayer expense, and almost invariably the trips were used to promote his candidacy for governor. In the preceding 20 years, previous Assistant Secretaries for Land and Water were reported to have visited New Mexico only twice.

But Carruthers' political manipulations of what was supposed to be professional land management by BLM in New Mexico was by no means limited to arranging ceremonies and suppressing unfavorable information. Through directives, promotions, demotions, transfers, and budget shifts away from activities Carruthers and Watt disliked because of the troubles they caused for industry, BLM New Mexico ceased to be a professional land managing agency dedicated to serving the public interest and enforcing federal laws. BLM was politicized as never before in its history. BLM veterans of nearly 30 years experience, serving under more than a half-dozen previous administrations, Republican and Democratic, concurred that the agency had never been so corrupted by political influence as it was under Watt and Carruthers.

BLM New Mexico Associate State Director Monte Jordan complained at one point, "You won't believe how sensitive Carruthers is to stuff. There are all kinds of things that he jumps down our throats about because he thinks they'll have implications for his political chances here. We've known for over a year that he was going to run for governor." Asked whether Carruthers realized it was unfair to pressure the BLM State Office that way, Jordan responded, "I'm sure he does, but that doesn't mean it'll stop."

BLM personnel who more easily accepted the political perversions found promotions and new influence, while those who opposed the directives for compromising the public interest were systematically shunted into dead-end positions, or forced to resign. The team leader for the thoroughly corrupted New Mexico Generating Station EIS, for example, was rewarded with a coveted promotion into management, reassigned as an Area Manager in California.

The following assessment by another civil servant who found it easier and smarter to play Carruthers' game, and had just been awarded a major promotion, illustrates what was happening within the bureaucracy in New Mexico:

"The longer I hang around this outfit, the more I realize the less I know, and the less I'm supposed to know. If you just look back, you learn that the people who questioned decisions, or who made judgments about what was illegal or immoral are no longer here. If you try to fight for what you think is right, you get demoted, or get a directed re-assignment (transfer), or otherwise get pushed out. . . . It took me a long time to figure it out, but what I'm here for is to make as much money as I can and get promoted. What you have to do is do whatever you're told and not question whether it's right. If I'm told to do something that I know will screw up the results, I'll do it anyway. Experience shows that if you go ahead and do it, you'll be promoted and out of there by the time the shit hits the fan."

The following troubled statement was made by a Washington-level BLM official: "Our office has got to try to satisfy Carruthers and the law at the same time. And quite often, that's just not possible."

CHAPTER 12

CRACKDOWN AT INTERIOR

At Interior headquarters, opposition to James Watt was viewed as tantamount to treason; by mid-1983, large portions of the nation, Congress, and certainly the media, were already traitors.

The more people he offended, by his policies, permissive regulatory changes, and foot-in-mouth pronouncements, the more of a liability Watt became as President Reagan approached the end of his first term. The president's conservative revolution had been started, but a second Reagan term would be imperative to actually implement the programs that had been formulated. As the anti-Watt momentum spread across the West and across the nation, the Washington offices of the Department of the Interior grew all the more blinded by paranoia and self-interest. The Public Affairs Office at BLM headquarters in Washington was under strict orders not to say anything at all to the *Washington Post, The New York*

Times, and other media with national clout. If a reporter, or a private citizen, sought information about activities within the Department of the Interior, they were suspect; they were out to get Watt.

Columnist Jack Anderson lit into Watt early on, warning, "When he's not thinking of ways to use up the nation's natural resources in time for the Second Coming, he's scheming to keep Congress and the public from knowing anything about what's going on in the Executive Branch of the government. And I mean anything." Anderson told of Watt's attempts to keep members of Congress from learning about Interior policies as revealed in certain documents, which Anderson later obtained and found to be totally innocuous.

"Why, then, did Watt defy Congress over this bag of marshmallows? The reason may be more sinister than ridiculous," Anderson explained. "Watt's legislative counsel at Interior is Theodore Garrish, who was one of Richard Nixon's attorneys in the unsuccessful effort to keep the incriminating Watergate tapes from the special prosecutor. With Garrish's advice, Watt seems to have been trying to win the kind of executive coverup fight that Nixon lost."

Certainly there was a massive national movement to dump Watt. Environmental groups, wildlife clubs (and not just a few businessmen who saw the secretary's atrocious behavior as a long-term liability) demanded that the errant zealot be stopped. Members of Reagan's own party were quietly urging the president to cut Watt loose rather than jeopardize his reelection prospects. If many of the president's programs were popular with the electorate, the secretary and his programs decidedly were not. And as if Watt's abrasive personality were not enough trouble, his department was under investigation for the federal coal lease scandal in the Powder River Basin. If the president continued to support Watt, and the accusations against Interior were proved true, Reagan might well lose what would otherwise be an almost surefire second term.

In August 1982, the governors of nine western states, including New Mexico, had taken Watt to task over his coal leasing policies. Under the letterhead of the governor of Wyoming, the top state officials cautioned, "We are concerned that new policies regarding fair market value for federal coal leases, relaxation of diligent development requirements, potential excessive leasing of federal coal, together with reductions in royalty rates, may lead to a loss of mineral leasing revenues to the federal government and to the states which share in those revenues.

"The Department's policies appear to be the product of a misconception that the Department can ignore the marketplace in making its coal leasing decisions. We believe the marketplace must work, and the only way it can is if the federal government takes a businesslike approach to coal leasing."

If it seems strange that nine western governors of public land states admonished the exceedingly pro-business Watt for not taking a businesslike approach to coal leasing, and chastened him for not allowing the marketplace to influence federal decision-making, the answer to this paradox is simple. Watt and his lieutenants had no intention of maximizing mineral leasing revenues to the public; they intended to assist coal companies in looting the public's mineral wealth.

Aside from the grass roots opposition to Watt, the first major threat to his regime at Interior came when congressional committees, primarily in the Democratic-controlled House of Representatives, initiated probes of alleged wrongdoing, first in Interior's handling of oil and gas royalties, and then in the coal program.

In April, 1983, the Surveys and Investigations Staff of the House Appropriations Committee released its report on "The Coal Leasing Program of U.S. Department of the Interior", a 121-page document which uncovered Interior's complicity in giving away public coal in the Powder River lease sale, and demonstrated how the administration had deliberately and consistently tried to circumvent the laws and regulations meant to protect the public—and the public Treasury—in the management of its coal reserves.

The congressional report asserted:

"The April 1982 Powder River Basin sale highlights the mismanagement of the coal leasing program. In spite of poor economic conditions, a very soft coal market, and the potential lack of bidding competition, the Department persisted in 'holding the largest coal sale in history'. Such large-scale leasing under poor economic conditions distorts the market by flooding it with leased coal. It temporarily reduces fair market value and allows the industry to acquire coal at 'fire sale' prices. In the Powder River Basin sale, Department officials augmented the depression of fair market value by arbitrarily reducing by one-half the fair market value appraisals for the Powder River Basin. Interior officials were unable to furnish any workpapers, calculations, or other documents which supported their presale Powder River Basin appraisal or bid decisions."

The congressional investigators also reported that, "Because of Departmental edicts, which included unsupportable and undocumented manipulation, unrealistic assumptions on the maintenance tracts, and an unjustifiable 50/50 split in the estimate of fair market value for maintenance tracts, the Investigative Staff has estimated that the Government received about $60 million less than fair market value for seven of the Powder River Basin tracts."

A General Accounting Office (GAO) report released a month later estimated that the lost revenue amounted to $100 million, rather than a mere $60 million.

But the Investigations Staff referred to other evaluations provided through the federal Office of Technology Assessment (OTA), which had "also expressed serious doubts that fair market value was received from the Powder River sale." OTA stated that for about half of the tracts offered, no attempt was made at a fair market value calculation.

"An analysis, prepared by another consultant, charged that there is overwhelming evidence that the federal government has failed to receive fair market value for the vast majority of leases. The report concluded by stating that the Powder River lease sale was a microcosm of the constant failure by the Department to obtain fair market value for coal. The consultant stated that even a conservative estimate of fair market value for five of the Wyoming lease tracts would have brought in an additional $131 million either at the time of the sale, or at a later date when the market was stronger."

The House Appropriations Committee staff warned of ongoing attempts by Interior to give away the public's coal at substantially less than its full value. "In spite of the current reduced demand for coal, the depressed near-term future needs, excess capacity, undeveloped leases, and unresolved preference right lease applications, Interior continues to plan for three regional coal lease sales in the near future [one of them in New Mexico's San Juan Basin], with coal offerings exceeding 6 billion tons. These plans are supported by recent [Watt] procedural changes which allow leasing targets to be derived based on demand for reserves rather than demand for production. Supporters of leasing for reserves applaud the concept as a move that brings the federal coal leasing program more in line with the marketplace. Opponents denounce it as a distortion of the marketplace, flooding it with coal, depressing prices below their long run competitive level, and preventing the federal government from receiving fair market value for its natural resources."

The document also probed the effects of the "leak" of confidential information on the minimum acceptable bid to industry representatives, a criminal investigation about which was under way. The investigators revealed in their April 1983 report, "Shortly after the Minerals Management Service/Casper [Wyoming office] forwarded the minimum acceptable bid on February 26, 1982, and before the elimination of the minimal acceptable bids on March 19, 1982, the bids fell into the hands of unauthorized individuals from industry. The 'leak' has received substantial publicity and is the subject of an ongoing review by the General Accounting Office. The 'leak' and the subsequent unsupportable reduction of the minimum acceptable bids has been called 'scandalous' by many cognizant officials in and out of government. One high Interior official remarked that the Powder River Basin sale was either dishonest or the height of stupidity, and both situations are unacceptable."

On May 4, 1983, a House Appropriations subcommittee, following the lead of Rep. Sidney Yates (D-Illinois), voted to prohibit any additional federal coal leasing during the remainder of that fiscal year, or "until the accusations against Watt are answered." The vote, of course, would not really be binding on Interior until the proposal was approved by the full committee and both houses of Congress. But it was the decisive first step that would eventually lead to a full moratorium on federal coal leasing.

On May 11, the General Accounting Office (GAO) released its own "Analysis of the Powder River Basin Federal Coal Lease Sale: Economic Valuation Improvements and Legislative Changes Needed". The GAO report concluded that the prices the public received for its coal leases in the 1982 lease sale were "roughly $100 million less than GAO's revised estimates of fair market value."

The Comptroller General's report suggested that Interior cancel those Powder River coal leases for which fair market value was not paid, and further recommended a halt in the federal coal program until deficiencies in fair market value determination were corrected.

The GAO's brief probe into the alleged "leak" of the confidential minimum acceptable bid produced nothing conclusive. But the document does note that "One Minerals Management Service official said a coal company representative contacted him on Mar. 25, and knew two MABs 'down to three decimal points'."

Subsequently, an attorney representing a coal company admitted to the media that he had been told the confidential minimum acceptable bid by Carruthers' deputy assistant secretary, David Russell.

In New Mexico, newly elected Congressmen Bill Richardson (House) and Jeff Bingaman (Senate) participated in a congressional field hearing in Santa Fe on the federal coal program. On May 21, 1983, an impressive array of opposition to Watt's coal program turned out to testify before the field hearing conducted by Congressman James Weaver, an Oregon Democrat.

Governor Toney Anaya was among the first speakers to address the field hearing, and he attacked aggressively, charging that Watt and his federal coal managers intended to cheat New Mexicans out of their mineral wealth. He called the coal program "Watt's giveaway program", and dubbed it "Watt's Folly".

"I can't knowingly turn over our state's natural resources to Watt's Folly," the fiery governor said. "I intend to insure that New Mexico gets top dollar for its coal resources. It is not irrational to fear a repeat of the Powder River firesale in New Mexico."

Anaya estimated that New Mexicans would be robbed of somewhere between $47 million and $79 million if Watt and Carruthers proceeded with their intended San Juan Basin coal lease sale. He went on to cite federal coal tonnages already under lease, saying it was enough to meet the nation's need until the year 2100. "Watt calls for long-range planning, but this is ridiculous," he remarked.

The governor concluded by asserting, "Secretary Watt is hellbent on getting all of our natural resources into industry hands as quick as he can. I think he has been charged with getting rid of our natural resources now, because they're afraid they may not have another four years to do it."

Representing the Navajo Tribe, Louis Denetsosie spoke: "The wholesale giveaway of coal is nothing new to the Navajo people. For years, the Secretary of Interior has given away our oil and gas, coal and water at rock bottom prices, and now it's happening to the American people."

When BLM State Director Bill Luscher was called to speak, Congressman Weaver began an interrogation.

Weaver: How much federal coal were you originally planning to lease?

Luscher: 1.2 to 1.5 billion tons.

Weaver: How much is presently under lease?

Luscher: Four hundred million tons are already leased and undeveloped.

Weaver: How long would that last?

Luscher: In excess of 30-40 years, assuming present levels of production.

Weaver: Then what's the rush to lease this coal? Can you explain that?

Luscher: No, I can't. But the decision has not been made to lease it. But we have been directed by policy from Washington. . . .

Weaver: Will most of your leases be "maintenance tracts" [intended to keep an existing mine in operation] or competitive?

Luscher: Most of them would be competitive.

Weaver: Do you anticipate getting competitive leasing, given the present state of the coal market? As you know, few of the Powder River lease tracts had more than one bidder. I'm asking you for some foresight. Do you think these tracts here will receive competitive bids?

Luscher: It is safe to say we would probably have very few [tracts] that would have more than one bid. . . . There's a good chance that on some tracts, there'd only be one bid.

About the same time back in Washington, congressional committees were flexing muscles for a coal leasing moratorium. But Interior officials said they had the full backing of the president and they intended to maintain the policies under attack. *Public Lands News*, a Washington-based newsletter, quoted an unnamed Interior official on May 26, 1983 as saying, "We're definitely hanging tough. Not just on the Powder River sale, but on future sales. There's no talk of compromise."

On May 25, the House voted to drop any funding for Interior's coal program for the remainder of the fiscal year, and the Republican-controlled Senate narrowly defeated a similar moratorium, by a 51-48 vote.

Congressmen, state officials and moderate Republicans called for an independent investigation of federal coal leasing. Forced into such a corner, Watt appointed a blue-ribbon panel to analyze the coal program, specifically to determine whether the U.S. Treasury had received fair market value for the coal it had leased at the ill-starred Powder River coal lease sale in 1982. Professor David Linowes, a University of Illinois expert in public policy analysis and political economy, had been called in earlier during Watt's tenure to review the federal oil and gas royalty procedures which had erupted in scandal in 1981. President Reagan had appointed the first "Linowes Commission" to investigate allegations of mismanagement and fraud in royalty collection from mineral leases on federal and Indian land. That report had been submitted in January 1982.

The new Linowes Commission, actually named The Commission on Fair Market Value Policy, was created July 30, 1983. It moved quickly to expand its limited scope, to look at the federal coal program generally. Assisted by its own staff and Interior officials, the group got an earful when it conducted hearings in Washington and in Denver. The more outspoken field level officials, such as Jim Fassett of New Mexico's Interior offices, laid the cards on the table and raised serious doubts about the legality of the coal program Watt, Carruthers and other high Interior officials were implementing.

Watt, in the meantime, was quickly losing support at the White House, at least from Nancy Reagan. When the secretary made a decision to ban the Beach Boys from performing at the Washington Monument for Fourth of July celebrations, because the group attracted the wrong kind of crowd, a howl went up over the embattled secretary's latest indiscretion. The First Lady complained that Watt's intolerance and warped sense of who constituted good citizens had indeed gone too far. She reportedly told Watt that she liked the Beach Boys, and didn't consider herself to be "the wrong crowd". Watt retracted his ban, of course, and days later was publicly chided by the president with a jesting presentation of a plaster foot with a bullet hole shot through it. The president was, finally, making a public statement that perhaps his loyal Secretary of the Interior did occasionally go too far. Watt would be relieved of his duties within six months.

But for Carruthers, the battle over coal in the San Juan Basin was still raging. If Governor Anaya, the surprisingly powerful environmentalists and the Navajo Tribe demanded a major overhaul of the Bisti power plant EIS and the regional coal EIS, at least it was another opportunity to make the strip mining proposal seem more acceptable. The obvious deficiencies, such as incomplete archeological surveys on the lands proposed for strip mining, were to be "dealt with", even to the extent of mounting a crash project to do new cultural resource clearances in time to reference them in the second draft of the coal EIS.

Although Carruthers had been directing the Albuquerque District BLM EIS writers, the errors and deficiencies which had been exposed during the official comment period were now, naturally, blamed on the BLM staff at the lowest level. When it was acknowledged that the archeological clearances hadn't been done, the BLM staffers in the Albuquerque District were scolded—despite the fact that they and their predecessors had been pleading for years to be allowed to do the work because they knew federal laws and regulations required it.

Associate District Manager Mat Millenbach defended his personnel against a continual barrage of attacks from Washington, through the BLM New Mexico State Office. As Millenbach reminded the Santa Fe Office's Gene Day: "These people are not responsible for that decision (to do all of the required clearances at mine plan stage, after the lands were already leased to the coal companies). That decision was made years ago by your office. Our people tried to tell you, and Washington too, that, but it was decided in your office to do it the way we did it. The State Office has known all along how we were doing it."

And District Manager Applegate was stuck with the responsibility of cleaning up the mess. Back from a frantic, troubleshooting trip to Farmington July 22, 1983, Applegate told staffers: "They (Washington and Santa Fe) are now trying to set it up so that I sit down with a pencil and make it (the coal EIS and the NMGS EIS) all right. They're setting me up to be the fall guy. You know, when this cultural resource clearance thing came up, I told them there'd be other problems, too, lots of them. And you know what? I was right. Now they want an ethnographic survey done on the Navajo! God!"

(One of the first BLM staffers to suggest that the coal program would need an ethnographic study was Carol Thompson in 1979-80. Because she insisted this was important, she was intimidated, given poor performance ratings and eventually was forced to leave the bureau. As for the lack of cultural resource clearances that caused so much recrimination in 1983 when the coal EIS was published, the BLM Albuquerque District archeologist, Randy Morrison, had written memo after memo insisting that this be done—five or more years earlier. His persistence only earned him disrespect from his superiors, and a "directed reassignment" intended to force him out of BLM.)

While Applegate was under heavy pressure to make legitimate corrections and additions to the coal EIS, there were also mounting internal demands that the potential adverse impacts from strip mining in the San Juan Basin be covered up. Under instructions from his superiors, Applegate again attempted to make the EIS writers tone down the cautions about post-mining reclamation and other potentially serious problems. "And over all, as you're starting out (with the re-write of the coal EIS), try to be more positive . . . put in more about the positive impacts," he instructed his EIS team on August 8, 1983.

He specifically objected to a statement in the EIS's third chapter: "forced relocation of 35 Navajo families . . . will result in increased mental illness. . . ."

"But it's true, Paul," responded Mary Zuschlag, district office coordinator for the EIS, "that *is* what has happened."

Applegate shot back, "That may be true, but do you have to say it?"

BLM staffers in the Albuquerque District grew increasingly exasperated over Watt's policies and antics. Members of the general public were apparently growing even more restive. By July, the U.S. Senator from New Mexico, Republican Pete Domenici, was calling for Watt's resignation, asserting that the abrasive secretary had become too great a liability for the president to carry into his reelection bid.

Finally, on October 9, 1983, the Sunday before the federal Columbus Day holiday, James Watt resigned. Within days, Reagan's Number One troubleshooter, William Clark, was tapped to fill in behind Watt.

But Watt wasn't the only Interior official to get the axe at about that same time: the dismissal of Interior Field Solicitor Bob Uram gave evidence that the Reagan Administration's arch-conservative ideologues had by no means been chastened by the illegalities being revealed in the coal scandal or by James Watt's other excesses. Uram, one of Interior's most knowledgeable and influential authorities on the federal coal program as it had been developed under the Carter Administration, had been guiding BLM New Mexico officials for three years through the complex coal leasing process. In Washington during the late 1970s, Uram had been one of the chief architects of the federal coal leasing program, translating the various federal laws on coal leasing into what was hoped to be a workable program. For Uram, the San Juan Basin was to have been the "test of fire" for his creation. But because he stood firm against James Watt's perversions of the regulations and laws, and because his thorough knowledge of the coal program allowed him to suggest possible compromises which were unacceptable to Watt and his lieutenants, Uram was given a directed reassignment from Santa Fe to Atlanta in the fall of 1983 . . . removing him completely from the federal coal program.

After a brief challenge to the transfer, Uram resigned from Interior. In his final days with the department's legal section, a colleague asked why Interior would risk jeopardizing the sensitive San Juan Basin coal lease sale at that juncture by transferring the person most familiar with how to make the process work. "Why wouldn't they wait until after the San Juan coal lease sale?" Uram was asked. "Don't they realize that you are the only one who knows all the legal vagaries of the Generating Station EIS, and the coal EIS?"

Uram responded: "Do you think they really care whether any federal coal gets leased in the San Juan Basin? They (the ultraconservative Heritage Foundation ideologues who he accused of arranging his firing) could care less. They're really only interested in their long-term objective, which is to destroy the government."

"Destroy the government. . . ." Uram's words stunned the two BLM people standing with him. Granted, such an analysis coming from a person who had recently been virtually fired could easily be disregarded as bitterness over a politically de-railed career. But there was something about his charge that rang too true to be dismissed as the anger of a "disgruntled employee". If the chief function of government—any government, municipal, state or federal—is to regulate for public health, safety, welfare and security, and this highly-ideological administration was dedicated to dismantling, destroying the government's regulatory power, then weren't "they" in fact destroying the government? If—by chicanery, intimidation, questionable regulatory and procedural changes, and by deliberate failure to adequately fund governmental departments charged with monitoring and regulating industry—if the government is rendered incapable of performing its functions, then aren't those politicians responsible for destroying the government?

Perhaps it isn't treason if it is the government itself that is destroying the government. Perhaps . . . but only if the citizens in a democratic nation realize that is the government's real agenda.

In the San Juan Basin, there was little indication that Reagan, Watt, Clark or Carruthers were concerned about democracy. Or, for that matter, concerned about protecting the public interest. With the re-written second draft of the San Juan River Regional Coal Environmental Impact Statement ready to be re-issued for public comment as required by law, Carruthers continued his attempts to thwart the will of the people.

At first, Carruthers sent word to New Mexico BLM offices that there would be no public hearings scheduled for the revised EIS, even though he must have known that such hearings were required by law. It was his political ambition, rather than the law, which had to be satisfied, and with the federal coal program in so much trouble across the West and in the halls of Congress, Carruthers preferred that BLM slip the EIS past the public without it becoming a focal point.

At the insistence of lower level BLM officials, Carruthers finally agreed to a single hearing for the EIS comment period . . .

and he dictated that it be held in Farmington, where public support for his massive coal leasing program was most likely to be heard. From the beginning, it had been people from Albuquerque, Santa Fe, Taos and in the Navajo areas who had been most critical of the leasing proposals, and mostly people related to the oil, gas and coal extractive industries in Farmington who had favored the administration's plan to dump almost three billion tons of public coal onto a soft market.

Even so, only one-third of the people who testified at the Farmington hearing on the re-issued coal EIS that November favored additional coal leasing in the San Juan Basin. *Gallup Independent* Reporter Dave Carlson, who specialized in energy developments in northwestern New Mexico, covered the hearing and offered the following observations to a BLM official afterward:

"I know why Interior made the decision to hold the only hearing in Farmington—because that was where they had the most positive response at the last hearing (on the first draft of the coal EIS). But even so, by my count, only seven out of 22 people who spoke at the hearing were in favor of the (leasing) proposal, and even some of those weren't totally in favor.

"So at some point, you have to ask whether there is any point in opposing it, if the government is going to do what it wants. This is supposed to be a democracy, but is the government going to do what the people want, or is it going to be a 'Big Brother' kind of thing?

"I'm sure it sounds naive, but isn't this supposed to be a democracy?"

With Watt gone and the president's confidant, William Clark, trying to hush the growing scandal, the Linowes Commission continued its work. Governor Anaya appeared before the commission in Denver and noted: "I realize that 'Watt-isms' may be somewhat outdated these days now that Mr. Watt has resigned his post as Secretary of the Interior over comments he made about this commission. However, I must underscore that I am extremely disappointed in Secretary-designate Clark's statements—statements I hope he retracts—that he intends to continue the policies and programs Mr. Watt initiated and implemented.

"New Mexico has, through our involvement in the new federal coal leasing program, tried very hard to deal with former Secretary Watt and his staff in good faith. We have consistently maintained a reasonable approach to a coal leasing program within our state, and for the West. However, Mr. Watt and many of his lieutenants did not act in good faith, and thus we are here today to discuss some of the problems. . . ."

Anaya continued: "Even the Federal Trade Commission, an agency charged with protecting competition in industry in this country, stated that to allow industry to control the rate at which coal lands have been leased did not and would not assure the competition for individual leases which is a prerequisite for the receipt of fair market value. They noted that by selling coal leases in reaction to industry demand, the Interior Department had allowed industry to secure a position from which it could take advantage of anticipated price increases. Sound familiar? Those statements aren't recent. They were developed and published in 1975 by the FTC. Even so, they are most pertinent to what has been going on since new leases were let under Watt's coal leasing program."

The New Mexico governor also laid out the fraud that had been perpetrated in his state regarding the federal coal leasing targets. "We, in New Mexico, have been greatly concerned over the determination of leasing levels since, in general, the levels picked by former Secretary Watt and his staff bore no relationship to demand or markets for coal. . . . Last year, the (Regional Coal Team) board met three times to discuss ways in which the department of the Interior calculates how much coal should be leased in individual federal lease sales. The board made a determination that certain ways being considered be given priority over others which were noted as arbitrary, unsupported, statistical manipulations. The board felt that these other types of manipulations would have the perverse effect of driving up the amount of leasing beyond any reasonable levels when forecasted coal production is depressed and, conversely, forcing less leasing when forecasted production is high."

Anaya also made a direct accusation that Assistant Secretary Carruthers was responsible for raising the proposed leasing levels in the Fort Union and San Juan River coal regions.

"Past practices of the Department of the Interior reaffirm the need to solidify the regional coal team's central role in the leasing process. For example, the original recommendation of a leasing target made by the Fort Union Regional Coal Team set the regional leasing target at 400 to 800 million tons. In a letter signed by Assistant Secretary Garrey Carruthers, dated August 24, 1981, the Department overrode the team recommendation. In that letter, the department designated a preliminary leasing target of .8 to 1.2 billion tons, and included an alternative of 1.2 to 1.5 billion tons in the regional coal leasing impact statement.

"Mr. Carruthers was also responsible for raising the preliminary leasing target recommended by the San Juan Regional Coal Team from a range of .8 to 1.2 million tons to a range of 1.2 to 1.5 billion tons. You may be interested in knowing that, as a result of our opposition to that figure, now Interior has had to back off a bit, and is supporting the lowest end of our initial range, 800 million tons."

On November 4, less than a month after Watt's ignominious departure, Congress imposed a full moratorium on coal lease sales, to remain in effect at least 90 days after submission of the Linowes Commission report.

But while Congress, the Office of Technology Assessment and the Linowes Commission were causing a shutdown of the federal coal program in Washington, the BLM continued to march along in New Mexico as if nothing had changed. The moratorium on coal leasing was interpreted strictly to mean that there should be no leasing, but any processing for upcoming leasing, including the two billion ton Preference Right Lease Applications, could continue. Much interpretation and re-interpretation occurred in the New Mexico State Office as to whether continued work on the PRLAs constituted a breach of the congressionally mandated moratorium. Since the PRLAs were the big prize in the San Juan Basin anyway, there was heavy pressure from Washington to continue the critical assessments of fair market value in the application areas. When some geologists in the Albuquerque District BLM office questioned the legality of their continued work on the PRLAs, the response they got from their supervisors in the State Office was largely gobbledy-gook, easily seen as an attempt to evade the issue. Months later, when a memo finally came down to the District Office on the significance of the moratorium, it still waffled.

With Interior under investigation by Congress and the Department of Justice, field level BLM officials sought in vain for any indications that superiors in Washington admitted their guilt and intended to reform. But Watt's departure brought little or no change in policy or direction. The new secretary, Clark, was simply less abrasive, less confrontational, more careful, and more public relations oriented. It seemed clear that while President Reagan and Clark, his former National Security Advisor, recognized the potential political trouble that could arise from the stench at Interior, they had no real disagreement with Watt's policies and procedures. From his confirmation hearings in the Senate to his policy directives, it was abundantly clear that Clark's role was to keep the lid on Interior until the president's reelection . . . a presumption verified when, less than two months after the election, Clark said he intended to leave Interior.

It was true that a few Interior officials implicated in the Powder River coal lease scandal were fired, notably William (Perry) Pendley and David Russell in the fall of 1983, but Carruthers' position was strengthened even though he, too, was involved in similar abuses, and steadfastly defended the practices and policies which the General Accounting Office, the Office of Technology Assessment, the House Appropriations Committee, and later the Linowes Commission, determined to be contrary to the public interest. And if anything, Carruthers' cover-ups, deceits and distortions increased dramatically in New Mexico after Watt's dismissal.

Interior stubbornly supported the original Watt concept of leasing to meet a company's desires for reserves, rather than to meet the public's need for energy, and it was equally clear that the "new" regime still intended to conduct massive coal leasing in a depressed market.

Field level BLM officials had an opportunity to evaluate the intention of Washington's ideologues at Interior in the fall of 1983, just as William Clark was undergoing confirmation hearings on his appointment to replace Watt who had been ousted less than a month earlier. BLM public affairs officers from around the West had been called to Washington for an annual conference. The real purpose of the meeting, it turned out, was to recruit BLM public affairs officers to the Reagan reelection effort. Led by Lynn Engdahl, special assistant to BLM Director Robert Burford, the overriding message of the conference was the role that BLM would—and would not—play in the election which was then one year away. "Whether you like it or not, you are politicians," warned Engdahl, "You can't work for an agency like BLM and not be political."

Director Burford reinforced that message during a brief appearance at the conference. "You must get involved in politics at the local and national level. We need an intelligence gathering apparatus."

Both men indicated by their tone and terms that they understood that the federal civil service is by law non-partisan; that it is illegal for federal officials to order civil servants to participate in political campaigns. Yet that is precisely what they demanded. Burford and Engdahl made it clear that they expected their field level public affairs officials to actively support the president's re-election campaign, by informing the higher up, political appointees in the administration about potential election campaign trouble areas, by withholding information from the public and the media which might jeopardize the campaign, and by planting news releases intended to mislead the public as to the administration's true policies and objectives.

Even more revealing of the corruption which remained after Watt's departure was discussion at the public affairs conference regarding BLM's continued policy of suppressing information, particularly regarding the federal coal program. While admitting that Interior had become obsessively opposed to disclosure of information to the media and to the public, Engdahl said the agency would continue to crack down on civil servants who leaked information about BLM programs and policies to the public. It was clear that the political appointees still running Interior believed the public had no right to know what they were doing, and they were determined to stop the flow of information reaching the public about the agency's activities. Apparently few things angered top Interior officials more than having their internal policy directives fall into the hands of environmentalists or unsympathetic reporters.

Engdahl told the convened public affairs officers that the problem of leaked directives would soon be cured by installing throughout BLM desk top computer-conferencing terminals so that instructions could be sent electronically. "That way there's no paper trail," he said smugly, no physical document which could be used to expose what the administration's was actually doing.

If it seemed like the same old game plan, perhaps that should not have been surprising; Carruthers, after all, was given even more direct responsibilities over the coal program. In an internal reorganization, Carruthers became Assistant Secretary for Lands and Minerals (rather than for Lands and Water). He had in no way recanted the wrongdoing of his previous years under Watt.

In the San Juan Basin, Carruthers had been forced into reducing the proposed leasing level, from 1.2-1.5 billion down to 800-900 million tons, but that still constituted massive leasing in a depressed market, especially considering the near-certainty that at least another half-billion tons of coal would be leased through the pending Preference Right Lease Applications in New Mexico.

Interior still intended to give away the public's mineral resources to private companies as cheaply as possible and with minimal consideration of adverse environmental and socio-economic impacts.

In fact, nine months after Watt's departure, Carruthers made the following remarks at an annual convention of the Wyoming Mining Association: "When a restaurant comes under new management, usually the only things that really change are the prices and the specials. So instead of fried chicken, it might be country fried chicken or something like that. That's also the case at the Interior Department. Since coming under new management, the only things which have changed are the specials."

Carruthers' remarks are even more astounding in that they were made five months after the Linowes Commission had issued its report, citing colossal mismanagement in the Watt regime's coal program.

In a March 1984 interview with Jim Lehrer, of the MacNeil/Lehrer NewsHour, the chairman of the blue-ribbon commission, David Linowes, said the coal program was seriously mismanaged and disruptive.

Lehrer: How bad was the mismanagement, sir?

Linowes: Well, we found the management very disruptive, occasioned by considerable controversy and changes in direction, quick changes in direction; unresponsive to the needs of consumers, to the needs of the coal-mining states, and to the needs of the nation itself for stability so that it could engage in long-term economic and environmental planning. . . .

Lehrer: And the result of this haphazard state of affairs was what? I mean, who's gotten hurt, if anybody? Why should we care?

Linowes: Well, naturally, the consumer got hurt. . . .

In its 36 recommendations, the Linowes Commission addressed procedures for arriving at federal coal leasing levels, selecting tracts, conducting lease sales, mineral appraisals, and many other issues arising during their probe. The commission made it clear that a multitude of irregularities had indeed occurred under Watt's direction.

The commission advised that the federal government should neither seek to raise the coal lease price above the competitive market level by limiting the amount of coal that federal policies make available, nor should it lease so much coal as to flood a depressed market.

It recommended that the amount of coal leased should ensure that the federal government receives a fair return consistent with the achievement of other public policy objectives, such as promoting efficient land use and environmental planning and conserving appropriate amounts of coal for the future.

The Linowes Commission also urged rapid completion of the processing of the remaining Preference Right Lease Applications, preferably within two years, so that future competitive leasing could be conducted with greater predictability and consistency.

It recommended that provisions for surface owner consent be retained as part of the federal coal program, although perhaps with some "cap" on the amount of money a surface owner could demand in exchange for permission to mine. The recommendations also urged continuation of the "diligent development" conditions which require coal lease holders to actually mine the resource instead of simply "banking" the lease as an asset, or holding it for speculation.

The findings of the commission came as no surprise to high Interior officials, of course, because they had contributed "staff support" for the investigation and were kept informed of the direction the probe was taking. Nevertheless, Interior would have to officially respond to the commission's recommendations as a necessary step in getting the coal program moving again.

Clark formed a task force within Interior to formulate the response, and named Carruthers to head the team, apparently unaware of the extent to which Carruthers had been implicated in the coal scandal. Clark had promised the House Appropriations subcommittee on Interior that anyone associated with the 1982 Powder River coal lease sale would be barred from serving on the task force. In early March 1984, Clark announced that Carruthers would not, after all, oversee Interior's response to the Linowes Commission, and that the review task would be performed by an outside, independent group.

When the Department of the Interior responded to the commission's findings, they expressed agreement with nearly all the recommendations, indicating that, for the most part, they had never done things any differently.

Secretary Clark observed in his response to the Linowes Commission that "our review of the Department's proposed procedures, as well as the report of the Commission, convinces me that we may soon be able to proceed with a responsible program for leasing Federal coal resources. . . . The Department seeks only that use of Federal coal lands which reduces energy dependence while conserving total energy resources, and protecting the environment. As the Commission recognized, the continuation of a proper coal leasing program is in the national interest and essential to the national security.

"The proposed procedures (formulated by the Interior task force) incorporate almost all recommendations made by the Commission. They provide a comprehensive framework within which responsible decisions can be made regarding future coal lease sales. These proposed procedures would restructure the Department's planning process to permit decisions to be made with fuller information and closer to the times of sales."

Clark's cover letter to the official Interior response notes that investigations were continuing into alleged misconduct by Interior officials in the course of the Powder River coal lease sale. "I further asked the Deputy Under Secretary to review all questionable conduct by individual DOI employees including questionable investigations of such conduct. Because this review may require the collection and development of factual materials not now of record within the Department, it is not yet completed. . . . The results of our review of employee conduct should not affect or relate to proposed procedures for future sales."

Secretary Clark's reference to "questionable investigations" touched on the extensive cover-up which was under way inside Interior following public disclosure of the illegalities and improprieties in the federal coal program. Just as the American people had witnessed in the Nixon Administration "investigation" into the Watergate scandal, Watt, Carruthers and other top Interior officials had overseen an "un-vestigation", maneuvering to thwart any full disclosure of wrongdoing in their department.

Interior's internal investigation naturally showed that the department's top leadership had behaved properly, without violating the public trust. But they had trouble with the cover-up when it came to complicity in leaking the minimum acceptable bids prior to the 1982 Powder River coal lease sale.

When the Linowes Commission released a draft of its findings, the document did not include the evidence which was already available on the alleged leak of confidential information. Only the least damaging of three reports by Interior's Inspector General's Office were forwarded to the Linowes Commission, indicating that no evidence had been found of a leak prior to the 1982 lease sale. But the last two reports included statements by Cheyenne attorney Brent Kunz that Carruthers' former deputy assistant secretary, David Russell, had passed along confidential bid information to him a month before the sale. The last two reports also said the leak may have led to lobbying by energy industry representatives to have Interior lower the appraised values of several of the Powder River coal lease tracts.

Congressmen leading the attack on Watt's coal program, Edward Markey, of Massachusetts, and James Weaver, of Oregon, mounted a new offensive, charging that Interior officials helping the commission had deliberately covered up the damaging evidence. Congressional sources then provided to commissioners the Inspector General reports that had been withheld.

The Linowes commissioners publicly admonished the Inspector General's Office for failing to disclose the existence of the two missing reports.

Even with the two additional reports, Congressmen Markey and Weaver were dissatisfied with the effort made by the IG's office in investigating the leak, so they called for another probe by the General Accounting Office. On June 12, 1984, the GAO report did, indeed, find that the Inspector General's Office had been half-hearted at best in its earlier investigation of the leaked minimum acceptable bid data.

The GAO report asserted that the investigation by Inspector General Richard Mulberry "misled the Congress and the public" and that it had so many deficiencies that it was "incomplete and unreliable". The GAO said Mulberry's investigation failed to follow up well-founded reports of different leaks, and failed to put key witnesses under oath. The IG also was criticized for waiting more than a year to initiate an investigation into the allegations.

Representatives Markey and Weaver called for the resignation of Mulberry and his assistant, James Yohe. Said Markey: "By every measure of professional conduct they have failed the department and the American people."

Two months later, still under fire, Mulberry resigned as Interior's Inspector General.

By the fall of 1984, the federal coal scandal had brought down Secretary James Watt, Deputy Assistant Secretary David Russell, Deputy Assistant Secretary William (Perry) Pendley, and Interior's Inspector General Richard Mulberry. Assistant Secretary Garrey Carruthers was under investigation for complicity as well, and by mid-November 1984, he, too, was on his way out.

Indirectly, the fallout was even wider. Scores, if not hundreds, of lower level Interior officials had resigned or been forced out of their positions as a result of the blatant illegalities and sacrifice of the public interest. Sandra Blackstone, deputy director of the Bureau of Land Management for energy and minerals, left her post in the summer of 1983 when the coal program was being exposed as a corrupt con game. Similarly, Harold Doley, director of Interior's Minerals Management Services, resigned at that time, as did another of Carruthers' deputy assistant secretaries, fellow New Mexican Frank DuBois.

And there were other changes. The man who had been the field coordinator for the coal program in Powder River at the time of the scandal, Stan McKee, was transferred to the BLM's Farmington Area Office as Assistant Area Manager to supervise the coal program in northwestern New Mexico.

McKee became BLM Acting Area Manager for the Farmington Resource Area after Mat Millenbach was promoted out that slot to become the new BLM District Manager in Miles City, Montana, in March 1986.

When the political storm blew over, Interior would again be ready to push billions of tons of publicly-owned coal onto the market.

As might be expected, New Mexico BLM State Director Bill Luscher got a transfer to another state. He became BLM State Director in Oregon in July 1986. After having abetted the Watt-Carruthers travesty in the Chaco-Bisti, he would be long-gone when the public's coal was actually dumped into industry's eager hands.

CHAPTER 13

THE COAL PROGRAM ROLLS ON

While the disastrous coal program was falling apart, other interest groups were taking advantage of the crisis at Interior. Indians, environmentalists and wilderness advocates pushed their causes harder knowing they had a window of opportunity which might not be repeated later in Reagan's second term.

In New Mexico, the Sierra Club and other environmentalists seized the moment to advance their objective of congressional protection for the Bisti, De-na-zin and Ah-shi-sle-pah Wilderness Study Areas, as well as preservation of the BLM's Fossil Forest. Other groups urged that serious attention finally be given to the conflict between coal development and water in the exceedingly arid region, now that the coal program had been stalled. Similarly, taking advantage of the recriminations inside BLM regarding the inadequacy of the agency's archeological work in the San Juan Basin, members of the public interested in cultural resources and anthropology pressed again for new studies to determine just what would actually be jeopardized if Interior leased the thousands of acres in the Chaco-Bisti region it intended for strip mining.

And the Navajo Tribe finally began to make headway in its arguments with BLM for fairness to the Indians living over the federal coal.

During 1983-84, the Navajo and the Bureau of Indian Affairs grew increasingly more assertive the more high Interior officials were seen to be under pressure from Congress. BIA and tribal officials assigned to interface with BLM's coal planning activities had argued from the beginning that BLM was ignoring laws and responsibilities to the Navajo based on treaties, laws and regulations, but at the height of Watt's sway, these objections customarily had been waved off as irrelevant.

In the summer of 1983, as Interior's coal program ground to a halt, the Indians' representatives on inter-agency coordinating teams pressed for more concessions from BLM regarding stipulations to be placed on any coal leases coming out of the PRLA processing. BIA and the tribe had long held that the Navajo families living on public land over strippable coal in the PRLA areas should be regarded as surface owners, and therefore entitled to withhold their consent to the leasing, or to sell their consent to companies wishing to lease the coal deposits. If, however, the BLM were to push the families from their small subsistence ranches, they were to be compensated in the manner set forth in the Uniform Relocation Act, according to the tribe.

As always, the arguments boiled down to whether the Navajos in the coal region held legal or equitable rights to the lands they had occupied for generations.

But not all the Indians' objections were related to surface ownership; from the beginning the BIA and tribal representatives claimed that BLM had not, and did not intend to, comply with federal laws on cultural resource clearances, for example. While conceding that BLM held the responsibility for leasing of federal minerals under land administered by BIA, the latter agency insisted that it had responsibility for assuring that other resources on the surface, such as vegetation for grazing and Indian sacred areas, were safeguarded. Since it was clear, by BLM's own documents, that the Navajos would gain little or nothing from the leasing and mining of coal in the Indian areas, the BIA and tribal officials naturally sought assurances that BLM found obstructionist, especially given the heavily pro-development stance taken by Watt and Carruthers.

It was not uncommon for BLM's inter-agency coal coordinating meetings with BIA and tribal officials to degenerate into name-calling and threats.

By their reading of the laws and regulations, the Indians' representatives insisted on the following guarantees, among several other stipulations:

1) Prior to granting of permission to carry out any mining operation, the coal lease holder must undertake a Social Impact Assessment based on interviews and other primary data gathered specifically to address the impacts of the proposed mine. The BIA Navajo Area Director would have to approve the personnel conducting the assessment, as well as the methodology used and the report submitted.

2) The coal lease holder would have to comply with federal regulations and policies regarding the American Indian Religious Freedom Act, and must identify any and all places within the lease area that are considered "special" or sacred, or are otherwise respected by local people. Should the lease cover a Navajo plant gathering area or other sacred or respected areas, the lessee must contact local ceremonial practitioners and the Navajo Tribe to determine the extent of use of the areas by religious practitioners and the attitudes of the local people toward the areas. All plant gathering areas, and access to those areas, should be undisturbed unless the lessee first develops an alternative gathering area, through reseeding measures or otherwise, in the same vicinity.

3) The lease holder would have to use all reasonable efforts to educate its employees, officers, and anyone else doing business for the company in the lease area regarding the Navajo lifestyle, customs and values.

4) If the lease included occupied dwellings, a minimum of 300 feet would have to be left undisturbed around the boundaries of the occupied land, unless the lessee received written permission from the occupant or owner allowing coal mining activity within that buffer area. The lessee would have to provide for ingress and egress to the occupied land and sufficient domestic water to accommodate the occupant.

5) Lease holders must give preference in employment to Navajos and other local Indians in all positions for which they are qualified, and must abide by the Navajo Contracting Preference laws. The lessee would also have to establish on-the-job training programs to assist Navajos in improving their skills to obtain and hold jobs offered preferentially.

6) The lease holder must pay an overriding royalty of three percent of the total value of the coal produced from the leased area to the BIA Navajo Area Director, which would be allocated among the owners of the Indian allotments covered by leases in proportion to the surface acreage disturbed by mining activities.

7) If any Indian occupant agreed to be relocated out of a coal lease area, certain minimum requirements must be met, including: compensation for all buildings and other improvements on the land which would be destroyed by strip mining; occupants must be relocated on lands with equal animal grazing capacity and within the same Navajo chapter, or another chapter area of the relocatee's choice; and no family should be required to move unless the lease holder has demonstrated the availability of comparable replacement housing approved by the BIA and the Navajo Tribe. All costs for obtaining replacement housing, grazing areas and any necessary rights-of-way for relocatees must be borne by the lease holder.

8) During mining operations, a qualified archeologist must be present each time topsoil is removed to observe any archeological resources which might not have been identified during pre-mining surface inventory. If cultural resources are discovered during topsoil removal and stockpiling, the lease holder must immediately bring operations to a halt in the area. The BIA Navajo Area Director must be notified immediately to determine what further actions for data recovery may be necessary. The cost of such data recovery would be borne by the lease holder.

9) Before disturbing the surface of the lease, the lessee must develop a post-reclamation grazing management plan, approved by the BIA Navajo Area Director. The plan must be implemented for at least two consecutive years prior to release of the lease holder's bond, which in any event, would not be released until the effectiveness of the reclamation has been demonstrated through application of grazing on each reclaimed area. Revegetation on mined land would have to emphasize reestablishment of a variety of native plant species.

Needless to say, BLM officials were outraged by many of these demands, arguing that existing regulations would not permit them to agree to such lease stipulations. BLM raised strong objections to providing a buffer of 300 feet around occupied land, and to the notion that Indian occupants would be entitled to a three percent overriding royalty on the coal tonnage removed.

Months later the conflicts still raged, with BIA and the tribe asserting their positions more boldly. Among other points, they had insisted that PRLA leases include post-mining reclamation bonding for the lease holders which extended the bonded period much longer than is normal in other federal coal lease regions. Citing the uncertainties of reclaiming the land after strip mining, and BLM's own admissions that rehabilitation could take 20-30 years, the tribe demanded that any PRLA leases include the stipulation that the bond was to be held for 20 years. Such a demand was a minor bombshell for BLM: the companies would not want Navajos grazing (particularly over-grazing) on the revegetated lands until their bond had been released, and that meant BLM would have to find "substitute" grazing lands for displaced Navajo residents of the coal region for 20-30 years.

BLM's Applegate knew that would be nearly impossible. His concept for dealing with the thorny "Navajo relocation" problem was to rotate families off the land ahead of the mining draglines and onto the lands already reclaimed from mining; take them from the front of the mining operation and move them to the rear where the mining had already been done and reclamation performed. He had arrived at that plan after years of being stymied by the nagging question of where the Navajos would go in order to let the miners in, since he and everyone else knew that all potential grazing areas in the Chaco-Bisti region were already used by someone. Given the disruptions to such land-based peoples who were forced to move long distances from their homelands, and given the abject failures recorded at moving such pastoral folk into urban areas, Applegate faced the very real prospect that his decisions would in fact kill hundreds of local people—unless he could find a way to move them out of the way of the draglines while at the same time keeping them in their original areas. The way out for Applegate was to rotate Indians from in front of the mining onto the newly-reclaimed lands behind.

But that wouldn't work, he realized, if 20-30 years would have to pass from the time of mining to the time of grazing again on reclaimed land.

The dilemma continued unresolved.

The Indians' counter-offensive to gain some control over the federal government's coal leasing and mining program drew considerable support from the two newly-elected Democratic congressmen from New Mexico, Representative Bill Richardson and Senator Jeff Bingaman. Both had taken up the San Juan Basin coal conflicts as major issues in their electoral campaigns and, once in office, saw these as relatively easy, high visibility vehicles to demonstrate their concern and effectiveness. They lost no time in demanding that the Navajo Tribe be given voting rights on the San Juan River Regional Coal Team, and supported the Navajos' complaints against BLM's coal leasing environmental impact statement and plans for the Bisti power plant.

The local chapter of the Sierra Club had lost in its legal maneuver to halt strip mining in the Bisti's Gateway Mine. In March, 1982, the club had filed an "Unsuitability Petition" before the state government's Mining and Minerals Division, arguing that PNM subsidiary Sunbelt Mining Company should be barred from strip mining the 600-acre state coal lease lands immediately adjacent to the federal Bisti Wilderness Study Area. In August of that year, state officials rejected the petition and issued a mining permit for the Gateway Mine. Sierra Club appealed, but the State's Coal Surface Mining Commission rejected that as well, and strip mining in the Bisti effectively began in September 1982.

Absorbing that defeat, the environmentalists pressed on with their drive to have at least some of the public lands in the Bisti region designated as federally-protected Wilderness Areas.

Working with environmentalists, the two new Democratic congressmen began pushing for a wilderness bill that would preserve thousands of acres of Bisti region land forms in a natural state.

New Mexico Republican Congressman Manual Lujan, Jr. actually produced the first Bisti region wilderness bill, calling for protection of Bisti and De-na-zin Wilderness Study Areas, while dropping Ah-shi-sle-pah Wilderness Study Area.

Pushed by the newly-powerful environmentalists, Republican Senator Pete Domenici also submitted a Bisti wilderness bill, but it was clear that he and his staff were less than enthusiastic about encumbering coal development in any way. In any event, Domenici chose to enter a bill which would have preserved only the smallest of the three potential wilderness areas, Bisti, while turning down wilderness status for Ah-shi-sle-pah and deferring a decision on the larger De-na-zin. The pro-wilderness lobby scowled at Domenici's commitment, and pushed Bingaman and Richardson to produce a bill more to their liking.

They did so, and the New Mexico delegation was split for more than a year before a compromise was worked out. Finally, the San Juan Basin Wilderness Protection Act passed Congress in late 1984, in the final days of the 89th Congress. It designated the 3,968 acre Bisti WSA and the 23,872 acre De-na-zin WSA as federally protected wilderness, but held the Ah-shi-sle-pah area (6,563 acres) in WSA status, subject to the selection of major parts of it by the Navajo Tribe as part of its relocation lands authorized by the Navajo-Hopi Settlement Act. The bill also called for ten-year protection of the Fossil Forest to allow paleontological research.

Bingaman ventured even more boldly into the Chaco-Bisti controversy by hosting ongoing discussions aimed at reconciling the competing interests. Led into the squabble by his Santa Fe staffer, Ken Richards, the former state attorney general engaged in a series of conferences involving those individuals and groups which had been most involved in the San Juan coal wars over the years.

While these unofficial negotiations were going on, a new coal field was being opened which could, eventually, make the Bisti region coal deposits virtually irrelevant far into the future. A coal mining subsidiary of Santa Fe Industries (a railroad and natural resource corporation) was already hauling coal from its recently opened Lee Ranch Mine northeast of Grants. The mining company had contract commitments to ship coal from the new facility by October 30, 1984, and the deadline was met.

Under the direction of reasonable officials at Interior in Washington, BLM's professional land managers easily would have determined that the federal coal program in New Mexico should focus on leasing and mining in the Lee Ranch area, rather than in the heavily-conflicted lands in the Chaco-Bisti region. It could be shown irrefutably that all of the federal coal that was likely to be needed from the San Juan Basin well into the next century could be taken from this area, instead of the scenic, fossil-ladden, archeological lands inhabited by Navajos farther to the northwest. But reasonable minds were not prevailing at Interior under Watt, Carruthers, Clark, or his replacement, Hodel.

As the representative of the National Parks and Conservation Association argued before a congressional committee hearing, "At the very least, those coal areas near the (Chaco Culture National Historical) Park and other scenic and cultural sites should be established as the very lowest priority—the last to be phased into regional coal development, as determined by proven national need."

To the ideologues who still ran Interior, it was the principle that counted: environmental considerations should not deter the turning over of public resources to private corporations.

So BLM officials in New Mexico, under orders from Washington, continued with their re-write of the San Juan regional coal leasing environmental impact statement, hoping to make massive coal strip mining in the Chaco-Bisti region seem more palatable. Regardless of how much coal was needed, or how much could be provided at the less-damaging Lee Ranch Mine, BLM again set forth its plans to offer for lease 800 to 900 million tons, plus the billions expected to be approved under Preference Right Lease Applications.

After releasing two draft versions for public review, the final EIS was ready to go back to a critical public again by February 1984. But Assistant Secretary Carruthers instructed the Albuquerque BLM office to withhold the document temporarily so it would not seem to the public that production on the EIS had continued on schedule, unaffected by the much-publicized "reforms" in the federal coal program. Carruthers' concern was that if the San Juan coal leasing EIS appeared too soon after the Linowes Commission Report, and the department's response to it, the public would realize that the "thorough review" of the coal program was in fact a sham, that nothing had really changed. As the EIS coordinator explained, the impact statement was being withheld by Carruthers for political reasons, "to make it look right to the public". The document was not to be filed with the U.S. Environmental Protection Agency, or released to the public, until Carruthers gave the okay.

Carruthers' approval finally came on April 11, 1984. Even then, he insisted that, to the extent possible, the public at-large should be prevented from learning that the coal leasing document was released. On his instructions, there was to be no news release announcing the publishing of the final EIS. Less paranoid viewpoints later prevailed, and the BLM office in Santa Fe won Washington's approval to at least send out a "notice of availability" announcement, rather than a news release.

The 680-page final EIS was a major improvement over the earlier two versions, in that it finally acknowledged the monumental problems that still existed from inadequate cultural resource research work conducted on lands proposed for strip mining. After much internal bickering and negotiation, a preface to the EIS noted that seven proposed leasing tracts, mostly around Gallup, "lacked sufficient cultural inventory data to adequately analyze potential impacts. These tracts may not be recommended for further consideration for leasing by the RCT (Regional Coal Team) until identified problems are resolved."

The statement might well have applied to most of the 39 tracts, but that, of course, was not politically acceptable in Washington.

In the document's summary, BLM acknowledges that all of the alternative leasing proposals assessed by the EIS would aggravate "an already stressed situation". "The major environmental issues after extensive public review and comment are: 1) the availability of sufficient water for reclamation and mining; 2) the potential success of reclamation efforts; 3) the long-term scientific information losses to be incurred from destruction of cultural and paleontological resources, and if the information gained through excavation, extraction and study of these resources will be of greater value than the losses incurred, and; 4) the extent to which the proposed actions affect traditional lifestyles of nearly 22,000 Navajos living in the region. These major issues are very controversial and are not completely resolved. The need for coal leasing in a depressed market is also a major issue, but is not included in the analysis of this statement because it is beyond the scope of this EIS."

There, at last, was an honest, accurate assessment of the problem. It had taken four years and a congressional shutdown of the coal program to produce such a clear acknowledgment.

The impact statement notes that the federal government's preferred action is to offer for lease 916 million tons in areas with minimal surface owner conflicts (that is, in tracts that require no surface owner consent or for which consent has already been given), as well as the 2.3 billion tons covered by Preference Right Lease Applications. The summary portion of the document notes the impacts to be:

- Altering the topography of approximately 66,322 acres as a result of surface and subsurface mining;
- Destruction or disturbance of approximately 2,373 fossil localities;
- Consumption of approximately 18,950 acre-feet of water per year, and "a change in water quality";
- Vegetation would be removed on nearly 66,327 acres, resulting in a loss of support for an estimated 9,466 grazing animals per month until reclamation is completed;
- Mining would encounter 384 known cultural resource sites, and possibly as many as 2,200 sites, according to predictive computer modeling; and
- Approximately 62 Navajo families would have to be relocated off of land they now use. "Their lives could be substantially disrupted."

Although those impacts were to be expected from the "preferred action" of leasing the PRLAs and the "minimum surface owner conflict" tracts, the Secretary of the Interior could always decide to lease even more. The EIS examined the predictable impacts from a "high level" of leasing—up to 1.94 billion tons, plus the 2.3 billion tons within the PRLAs. The EIS notes that, with the high level alternative, 115,661 acres would be affected, including some 3,930 fossil sites, as many as 3,787 archeological sites, and would result in the relocation of 494 Navajo families "whose lives could be substantially disrupted". In addition to those who would have to be physically relocated, the mining would disrupt as many as 20,000 Navajo in the region.

The San Juan Basin coal leasing EIS was a perfect case-in-point for still another coal-related congressional report, issued in May 1984. The Office of Technology Assessment (OTA) produced a

154-page report entitled "Environmental Protection in the Federal Coal Leasing Program" which verified what critics of the Watt-Carruthers coal program had been saying for years—that the changes which Interior insisted upon had significantly jeopardized environmental protection.

The OTA authors noted: "We conclude that the recent policy changes very likely have raised the cost and difficulty of ensuring environmental compatibility, and have increased the risk of adverse environmental impacts should those [Watt-leased] tracts be developed." They go on to observe: "First, the high leasing rates—the large quantity of coal to be offered for lease combined with inflexible lease sale schedules—of the past three years taxed the resources of the Bureau of Land Management (BLM) beyond the point where they could adequately assess the acceptability of the tracts proposed to be offered. . . . Second, changes in program regulations in 1982 reduced the effectiveness of the environmental protection measures that contributed to the consensus of the 1979 Federal coal leasing program."

The OTA report found that "When BLM was not able to comply fully with regulatory requirements, the primary cause was time constraints resulting from high leasing rates—the combination of inflexible lease sale schedules and a substantial increase in the number of tracts to be evaluated for each sale. . . . It is OTA's judgment that, in many cases, BLM's pre-sale data and analyses have been inadequate to base a decision on whether recently leased tracts (and those proposed to be offered in future lease sales) can be developed in an environmentally compatible manner."

That finding, which certainly fits the conditions present as BLM prepared for leasing in the Chaco-Bisti region, would place the blame squarely on Carruthers, who elevated the San Juan River leasing targets from essentially zero tonnage needed to 1.5 billion, for purely political, ideological reasons.

According to OTA: "The primary cause of the inadequacy of data and analyses was high leasing rates—the ratio of leasing levels and lease sale schedules. . . . Even with perfect data and analyses, high leasing rates—in and of themselves—increase the probability that environmentally sensitive tracts will be leased because high leasing levels mean that a greater number of tracts must be offered for lease."

The OTA study also discussed the lack of attention given to reclamation potential as BLM went about its coal leasing decisions. "Considerable debate exists as to the need for an additional unsuitability criterion for reclaimability. Currently, reclamation potential is assessed by BLM during activity planning [following land use planning] and the results of that assessment considered by the RCT (Regional Coal Team) in tract ranking. However, there appears to be little relationship between such assessments of reclamation potential and overall tract rankings. [Some participants in the study] recommend that an unsuitability criterion relating to reclaimability should be applied in the leasing program. The National Resources Defense Council (NRDC) currently is suing BLM over the lack of an unsuitability criterion for reclaimability."

The OTA report lent support to assertions that the coal program changes set in motion by Watt needed to be evaluated through an entirely new environmental impact statement for the program as a whole; that is, a program-level EIS. Under attack across the West and in the Congress, Interior's top officials agreed to produce the new Coal Programmatic EIS "because many changes have occurred or are proposed in the coal program and because of changes in energy market conditions that formed the basis for the 1979 (programmatic) analysis."

Released for public review in February 1985, shortly after Interior Secretary Clark announced his resignation, the new programmatic EIS was first and foremost a public relations tool intended to make it seem as though the federal coal program was once again on the right track. However, the "new, reformed" program still did not repudiate the discredited "lease for coal company demand for reserves" policy which had been at the bottom of the massive overleasing, theft of revenues to the public and inadequate environmental protection. Throughout the new document, the authors take great pains to show the rosy, positive side of coal development, stressing jobs and payrolls, while downplaying, disguising, sidestepping or ignoring the negative aspects. Such deceits are most obvious in discussing impacts to Indians, cultural resources, fossils and reclamation.

In a portion dealing specifically with the San Juan region, for example, the new EIS noted, "Most of the region's soils have a fair to good reclamation potential and would provide adequate suitable plant growth materials for reclaiming surface mining disturbance. . . . The potential to reclaim and revegetate land is favorable with proper and timely use of effective reclamation, erosion control and revegetation measures."

Such an assertion is outrageous given the known, confirmed problems expected in strip mine reclamation in the Chaco-Bisti area. The statement is contradicted by BLM's own assessments, and especially by the scientific studies produced by the U.S. Geological Survey for the coal program in the San Juan Basin.

Similarly, the "reformed" coal program's EIS pretends that the people of New Mexico generally support additional federal coal leasing in the region. The authors assert blithely, "As in other western coal regions, current economic conditions have created some support for more coal development. Protection of the area's natural beauty, recreation opportunities, and air and water quality, however, remain important local concerns." There is no mention at all of the strong, persistent local opposition to the coal program, particularly from the Navajo residents in the coal area, and no acknowledgment of the fact that BLM's own public participation efforts confirmed an overwhelming opposition from the general public.

Even so, the biggest failing of Interior's new programmatic environmental impact statement was that it did not address the disrespect for law which characterized the actions and directives of top officials in the Interior Department. The period 1981-83 clearly demonstrated that high government officials intended to violate laws and intended to allow coal and utility interests to evade regulations. Yet nowhere, of course, were the enormous environmental impacts of that discussed.

The new Washington-level EIS was a grand pretense that the pertinent laws and regulations would be obeyed, when in fact, it was already proven that top Interior officials had no intention of requiring obedience and could be fully expected to encourage and abet violations.

CHAPTER 14

BATTLES STILL AHEAD

William Clark departed Interior less than 18 months after Watt was ousted. Garrey Carruthers went back to New Mexico as a gubernatorial candidate. David Russell (Carruthers' deputy) and Perry Pendley (acting director of Minerals Management Service) had been forced to resign. With Donald Hodel, Watt's former Number Two man at Interior, now running the show, many of the original ideologues controlling the federal coal program had been replaced. But those departures did not mean the public interest was now well-protected in the Chaco-Bisti region or in any other federal coal region.

In fact, most of the old, corrupted coal program remained in effect—without the combative personality of a James Watt to call attention to it. The public's lands and resources are still vulnerable to high Interior officials' natural resource giveaways, and to their commitment that mineral exploitation be given highest priority, regardless of the cost in human suffering, cultural survival or loss of other publicly-owned resources. If James Watt was determined that the public's mineral wealth should be handed over to industry with only token safeguards, at least the man-on-the-street knew that's what Watt would do if given the chance. But with Hodel, the public is less likely to pay any attention at all to the federal coal program, especially since Congress has already investigated it and has presumably corrected the abuses.

It should be pointed out, however, that Hodel was intimately involved in the old Watt coal program which led to the scandals. As Watt's Under Secretary of the Interior for two years, Hodel was involved in most of the controversial policies put forward by his boss. Indeed, Hodel repeatedly defended the corrupt coal program.

In its April 1983 investigation into the federal coal program, the U.S. House Appropriations Committee's Surveys and Investigations Staff found that Hodel played a critical role in the Powder River Coal lease scandal.

Hodel gave the formal approval for the last-minute change in federal coal leasing procedures which were responsible for the public's loss of $60-132 million on the 1982 Powder River coal lease sales.

The congressional committee report explains Hodel's involvement: "The Hodel memo of April 27, 1982, drafted by MMS/Reston [Minerals Management Service headquarters in Reston, Va.], nevertheless scrapped the pre-sale fair market value evaluation for a post-sale evaluation. In previous sales, Interior followed established competitive bidding procedures, with pre-sale determination of minimum acceptable bids based on a pre-sale estimate of fair market value, followed by a post-sale determination of bidder qualifications and the award of the lease to the high bidder at the sale.

"According to Interior sources, the published minimum acceptable bid in the sale notice was the same as the pre-sale fair market value estimate—the minimum price at which the Interior was prepared to sell the lease. All bidders would then be advised of Interior's estimate of fair market value and would be on a fairly equal footing as far as information on the tract. . . . In practice a bid at or above the minimum acceptable bid had guaranteed the lease sale."

The congressional report continued: "It is this internal determination of fair market value which MMS/Caspar [the Caspar, Wy., office of Minerals Management Service] stated was a 'farce'. The minimum acceptable bids were withdrawn by MMS/Reston, and the entry level bids, which the Investigative Staff was told represented 40 to 50 percent of the fair market value, were substituted in place of the minimum acceptable bids. According to MMS/Caspar, a review of the submitted bids for lease tracts at or above the entry level bid level during the post-sale analysis was controlled by the Hodel guidelines. These guidelines gave MMS/Caspar almost no discretion or latitude to effectively evaluate each bid as meeting the test of fair market value. The new procedures dictated by Hodel's guidelines suggest that the market will determine fair market value and not economic analysis.

"Hodel's guidelines ignored the procedures prescribed by the existing regulations. The only approved bidding system in use was fixed royalty and rental, variable bonus with possible deferred bonus payment. In announcing the Powder River Basin sale, without changing the regulations, Interior specified that (1) it was using an 'entry level bid' system which was not necessarily the minimum acceptable bid as determined by Interior and that (2) it would make the fair market value determination after the sale, taking into account the results of the sale, among other factors.

"Guidelines for evaluating the bids were approved [by Hodel] on April 27, 1982—the night before the sale—but the bidding system—fixed royalty, variable bonus—with sealed bids followed by oral auction was not in fact changed. What was altered was the Department's own procedures for its internal determination of fair market value and acceptance of bids (the regulation on fair market value determination and sale procedures do not acknowledge that other procedures can be used)."

The report further explains: "On the date of the Powder River Basin sale [April 28, 1982], the old regulations were still in effect. The Department [through Hodel's guidelines] nevertheless, modified the prescribed sales procedures. These changes may have violated existing laws and the 1979 regulations."

But Hodel was never confronted publicly for his involvement in the coal scandal. For one thing, Watt was such an easy target, and it was always Hodel's preference to keep a low profile. Besides, he was already gone from Interior by the time the public and Congress began to attack the federal coal program. President Reagan named Hodel as Secretary of Energy in November 1982. He headed that agency during 1983-84, and then came back to a presumably "cleaned up" Interior in 1985.

Thanks to interim-Secretary Clark and the Linowes Commission, the way is relatively clear now for Hodel to push the coal program in any direction he wants without the previous high level of public scrutiny.

If the public cannot count on James Watt shooting himself in the foot, what can it count on to safeguard the public interest? Very little, except for a handful of congressmen who are now briefed up on the coal issues, and public interest groups.

In the San Juan Basin, BLM officials expect the public to lose interest in the coal issue, leaving the program to continue down its old errant path of massive leasing and disregard for adverse impacts on Navajo families, wildlife, cultural resources, fossils, and federal wilderness areas.

Public vigilance is imperative. Despite the public relations assurances of the new programmatic EIS on the federal coal program, it is clear that the program is essentially unchanged from its earlier days under Watt and Carruthers. The underlying philosophy is to turn public mineral wealth over to the control of private industry as quickly and as cheaply as possible. For a pro-industry Interior Department, "quick" and "cheap" mean deliberate failure to uphold laws minimizing environmental damage, failure to protect the interests of local residents in the coal region, and failure to assure that the public is paid what its coal resource is really worth.

After all the congressional hoopla and the "reformed" Interior Department's posturing, the following prospects still remain for the Chaco-Bisti region and its inhabitants:

- Navajo families in the coal region face eviction from their ancestral homes with little or no possibilities of any economic benefit from the mining. Typically, they cannot count on the "surface owner consent" provisions of federal law which were intended by Congress to allow local residents a veto over strip mining of their land, or to demand a royalty in exchange for their consent.

- The legitimacy of the 26 Preference Right Lease Applications in the region remains unchallenged, which means the 2.3 billion tons of public coal there will not be offered for competitive bid, which could have resulted in bonus bid payments of many millions of dollars for the State Treasury and for mine-impacted communities.

- The newly-designated Bisti Wilderness Area may be in long-term jeopardy by Public Service Company of New Mexico's continuing plan to build a smoke-producing power plant nearby. Similarly, the precariously capped rock formations in the new wilderness area face the threat of dynamite and other vibration damage from any coal mining activity approved nearby.

- The fabulous ruins in Chaco Canyon are increasingly threatened by blasting, industrial vibrations, alteration of natural drainages from strip mining, and from atmospheric deposits of acid on the ancient masonry as a result of the proposed Bisti power plant.

- The Ah-shi-sle-pah Wilderness Study Area, recommended more than 70 years ago for inclusion in what became the Chaco National Monument (because its spectacular landforms are such a short distance from Chaco Canyon) is slated to be strip mined, either as a federal coal lease obtained through the PRLA process or as a Navajo Tribe-administered lease acquired as part of the Navajo-Hopi settlement.

- Indian sacred areas and other locations of special cultural significance remain unidentified throughout most of the coal lease tracts, and BLM continues to assert that it can "decommission" such religious sites by having coal companies hire a medicine man to conduct ceremonies there.

- Interior officials still have not agreed that any federal coal needed in the forseeable future from this region could be taken from the Lee Ranch area farther south, outside the heavily-conflicted Chaco-Bisti area. Instead Interior continues to favor leasing throughout the coal region to accommodate the wishes of Public Service Company of New Mexico and other companies with interests in the Bisti area.

- The public's world-class fossils will continue to be lost, crushed by strip mining claws, since they remain essentially unprotected. BLM intends voluntary compliance from the mining companies when they encounter the ancient bones in the earth strata over the coal.

- Strip mined land is unlikely to be rehabilitated due to harsh climatic conditions in the Chaco-Bisti area, and due to BLM's unwillingness to eliminate from strip mine lease consideration those lands where reclamation is improbable. Residents of the area, dependent on livestock grazing to maintain their culture, lifestyle and economic base, are unlikely to see their land productive again during their lifetimes. Several generations may pass before the land is usable, and the culturally significant land forms will never be restored.

- The massive leasing levels demanded by Assistant Secretary Garrey Carruthers (and then decreased at the insistence of New Mexico Governor Toney Anaya) could again be reinstated with Carruthers as governor. In the face of widespread criticism and congressional reports detailing the detriments of massive coal lease offerings, Carruthers has stubbornly defended the former ruinous policy, and could be expected to raise the leasing levels again through participation on the Regional Coal Team.

Current BLM plans call for issuance of leases on most of the easily strip mineable coal in the Chaco-Bisti region by 1987, through final determinations on the pending Preference Right Lease Applications.

And although BLM remained secretive about its plans for competitive coal lease sale schedules in the San Juan River Coal Region, the first of a series of such lease sales is expected during 1987.

Pragmatically, the first coal lease sale to grow out of the six-year preparation was expected to offer modest tonnages, in tracts expected to draw most bidding interest, or in tracts next to existing mining operations. As many as 12 of the 39 designated lease tracts might be offered the first time around.

Considered most likely to be offered first were a tract north of Farmington, near the La Plata Mine, another west of Gallup, near the Gamerco Mine, and another in the Hospah area. All of these are outside the heavily-conflicted Chaco-Bisti area, and could put more than 28 million tons out for bid.

At a later lease sale, possibly within a year of the first, several hundred million more tons might be offered. A likely tract for early lease is the 465 million tons in the Nageezi tract which would presumably be mined underground, rather than by strip mining. It would be the first major new coal lease in the Chaco area, and although it is generally assumed that coal companies are primarily interested in the cheaper, strip mine operations, the Nageezi tract has been actively sought by the Arizona-based Salt River Project for many years.

Other tracts were expected to be offered in the Chaco area, and in the Bisti area, as "bypass" offerings along side PRLA-initiated mines.

Perhaps offered later might be another 100 million tons in the Bisti region, adjacent to leases derived from the Bisti Coal Lease Exchange which removed leases from within the Bisti Wilderness Area, and another 200 million tons in the vicinity of the Lee Ranch Mine. Company interest in the latter lands would logically be high, since those tracts would be near the already-completed portion of the long-delayed Star Lake Railroad.

In all, more than one billion tons of publicly-owned coal are expected to be leased in the San Juan Basin by 1988, with minimal safeguards to impacted residents or to taxpayers whose commonly-owned property will be sold off at low prices. That "fire sale " of the public's coal will be in addition to the estimated 2.3 billion tons expected to be leased without competitive bidding, through the discredited PRLA process.

But those are not the only outrages against the public interest that can be expected. In the mid-1980s, coal and utility company lobbyists increased their pressure for additional changes in the federal coal program which would jack up their profits at the public's expense.

One of the first issues to surface was relaxation of the "diligent development" requirements for coal lease holders to mine the public coal, rather than simply hold onto it to control the market. Under current law, companies cannot obtain new public land mineral leases if they have held a federal coal lease for 10 years or more without producing commercial quantities of coal from it. The idea was to prevent speculation in federal leases. If a lease holder did not mine a significant amount from a federal lease within 10 years, the lease would revert back to the federal government. Several advantages to the public would occur if a company is required to turn back an unused lease: 1) the lease could be re-offered at competitive auction, thereby bringing additional bonus bid payments into the U.S. and state treasuries; 2) more permissive conditions written into older leases could be tightened up to comply with the environmental and public interest protections intended by legislation enacted in the 1970s; and 3) relinquished leases would be subjected to comprehensive land use planning, to determine afresh whether the proper use of a specific tract is strip mining or some other destiny.

The issue is whether companies should be required to turn back leases they never really needed in the first place, or whether the public lands, once leased, are to remain forever subject to the control of the coal and utility companies.

Another major area requiring citizen vigilance is Interior's permissiveness in setting lease stipulations for Preference Right Lease Applications. A large portion of the public's coal coming up for lease in the near future lies within areas that could be leased without attracting much attention. In the Chaco-Bisti region, the lease terms could provide the much-needed protection for area residents, for fossils, archeological site, and endangered species habitat. The companies acquiring the leases do not like restrictions, because they usually mean lost revenue. The Reagan Administration, under Watt, Clark and now Hodel, has made it clear that it steadfastly opposes "burdensome and unnecessary" restrictions on industry, so it is only reasonable to assume that strip mining lease stipulations between now and 1988 will be as lenient as the most pro-industry interpretation of the law will allow.

Even so, laws, regulations and court precedents will demand that certain protections be provided in lease stipulations. How protective they are will depend almost entirely on the public's demand for them. If the public and its watchdog organizations do not care enough to make demands during the stipulation-setting process, it is prudent to assume that the subsequent leaseholders will not be required to proceed as cautiously as they might.

For the Chaco-Bisti region, perhaps no issue is as important in the long term as post-mining reclamation. Until now, the Bureau of Land Management has done its best to ignore the probable outcome of strip mining in this region: a ravaged land incapable of returning to productive use for decades, perhaps generations.

This failure to give full consideration to reclamation potential in the San Juan Basin results partially from congressional neglect. The 1977 Surface Mining Control and Reclamation Act makes no clear provision for ruling out the leasing of coal lands for which reclamation prospects are poor or worse. In the absence of an "unsuitability criterion" for low reclamation potential, corporate lawyers and lobbyists have pressed forward with the assertions that all land can be reclaimed after strip mining.

The National Resources Defense Council, an environmental activist organization that regularly dogs the Department of the Interior, has sued BLM over the lack of an unsuitability criterion for reclaimability. In no other region of the country is the outcome of this suit more important.

If the coal lands of the San Juan Basin become a national sacrifice area, the coal mining companies want to be sure that it is the American taxpayer, and not they, who have the responsibility for it. If their reclamation efforts are eventually deemed failures, they intend that taxpayer money be used for salvaging operations, just as the mining industry has always done.

To help them escape responsibility for long-term reclamation, the coal and utility companies will continue to press for relaxation on federal requirements for reclamation bonds. Companies must post bonds that assure funds are available for needed reclamation work, but naturally they prefer to be released from this bond as quickly as possible. Under current rules, the bond would not be released until reclamation has been proven sustainable. In other coal regions where reclamation is more easily achieved, the bond may be released within five or ten years. However, in the Chaco-Bisti region, where federal officials admit it may take generations to reclaim the land, potential coal lease holders are determined to get out more quickly. Besides, while they steadfastly contend they will have no problems reclaiming the desert lands of the Chaco, they acknowledge that grazing by Navajo herders could tear up their fragile revegetation work in no time.

So the push is on to convince Interior that future strip miners need not continue their reclamation bond once the Navajo and their herds have been turned onto the presumably reclaimed land.

Another key element of the Reagan Administration strategy is budgetary cutbacks within Interior agencies deliberately intended to prevent effective enforcement of the laws and regulations. As a matter of policy, federal agencies such as the Bureau of Land Management, the Bureau of Indian Affairs, the Office of Surface Mining and the Environmental Protection Agency, are being rendered incapable of forcing coal and utility companies to comply with federal laws and regulations. The federal deficit is being used by ideologues within the Reagan Administration to justify agency budget cutbacks, the real purpose of which is to render those regulatory arms ineffective. While deliberately ignoring prospects for significant contributions to the federal treasury, the administration proceeds to dismantle the enforcement branches of government.

Government will no longer be on the backs of the strip miners, because government will not have the means to do so. Through disguised budget manipulations, the ideologues are making sure of that. The non-enforcement policy is tantamount to a breach of the U.S. Constitution. The president and his chief appointees are sworn to uphold the laws of the land, yet is has been clear since the earliest days of the Reagan Administration that the president and his lieutenants had no intention of doing so; that in fact, they intended to subvert the laws of the land, and render them ineffective.

The right-wing ideologues within Interior have implemented another strategy to assure that corporate interests, rather than the public interest is served in coming years. To a degree rarely, if ever, attempted, the federal civil service has been infiltrated by political appointees, in direct violation of its time-honored impartiality. A blatant example of this politicization of field levels of Interior agencies was the appointment of Lynn Engdahl as BLM Associate State Director in Nevada. Engdahl was the assistant to BLM Director Robert Burford who led the agency's public affairs conference in 1984 and tried to recruit the BLM's field level public affairs officers into helping Reagan win reelection. At that time, he stressed repeatedly that he was a "political type", rather than a career civil servant.

Never in the memory of veteran BLM personnel has the agency experienced such a deep penetration of political placements. Throughout most of BLM's history, the civil service positions of state director and below have been spared the litmus test of partisanship. No longer.

"They are trying to move a lot of political types into career jobs," warned a BLM veteran of more than 25 years. "And they are succeeding."

The results are a heavy infusion of ideologues at the field levels of government which previously were filled with career civil servants whose strong points were hands-on expertise and impartiality.

The traditional checks and balances of our form of government are meant to prevent the subversion of laws due to ideological commitments or de-funding of regulatory programs. The courts are to uphold the laws; over the years, Secretaries of the Interior have been sued repeated because citizens and their organizations believed those high officials, of both parties, were not acting in accordance with the law.

But it is in the judicial system that the ideologues have struck the most devastating blow of all. The courts, too, are being politicized. If the federal civil service can no longer be counted on to enforce the law, increasingly neither can the judges. Political appointees into the judiciary will make it harder for citizens to force the government to comply with laws passed by Congress. Ideologically-biased judges can thwart such suits and effectively eliminate this last recourse.

President Reagan is expected to appoint at least 286 judges to district and appeals courts, easily exceeding the number of appointments made by any previous president. There will be a long-term impact on federal judge appointments, according to *Congressional Quarterly.* By appointing people who are predisposed to favoring industry over individuals and environmental concerns, the Reagan Administration will have a major influence over what matters reach the U.S. Supreme Court. Appellate courts review the decisions of federal district judges. Anthony Podesta, president of People for the American Way, a group which lobbies for constitutional liberties, warned, "What is now being proposed is judges committed to undoing vast bodies of law, to throwing out legal precedent, to prejudging cases not on their merits—the traditional, time-honored way—but on ideological grounds."

Recovery from the decimation of federal enforcement agencies will take decades, even under a new administration, but a full return to an objective judiciary will take even longer.

Of course, presidents have historically taken advantage of their judgeship appointments to reinforce their stamp on the course of events after their term expires. Presidential appointments to the Supreme Court have often been important to consolidating programs initiated by an administration of whatever political stripe. The civil rights advances of the 1950s and 1960s, for example, were upheld by justices appointed by presidents who sought like-minded people to sit on the highest court in the land. But this time around, it is significantly different. Not just because the appointments to the judiciary are being made by a right-wing ideologue, but because closed-mindedness is part of the political litmus test. In the judiciary, just as in the civil service, the intrusion of ideology has reached new depths under the Reagan Administration. The appointees are people who, like James Watt, would equate liberalism with "un-Americanism" . . . people who would ban the Beach Boys because "they attracted the wrong crowd" for a Fourth of July Celebration.

By appointing judges who will be predisposed to allow Interior officials and corporations to break the environmental protection laws written by Congress, the ideologues may be able to eliminate the legal challenges which citizens have launched in the past. There is a second prong to this judicial strategy. The federally-funded legal aid services by which poor and powerless citizens can bring suit has long been a target of arch-conservatives, and now financial and other restrictions on the Legal Services Corporation are eating away at equal access to the courts for the poor.

Just as he appointed an "anti-public land" ideologue to head the Department of the Interior which oversees public lands, President Reagan's appointments to the Legal Services Corporation were people who opposed the very mission of that body. When confirmation of appointees Michael Wallace and LeaAnne Bernstein came before the U.S. Senate, New Mexico Senator Jeff Bingaman complained that the president had tapped those people precisely because they did not believe in the objectives of the Legal Services Corporation. Said Bingaman: "The 1974 Senate report on the Legal Services Act requires 'that the Board members understand and are fully committed to the role of legal assistance attorneys and support the underlying principle of this legislation that it is in the national interest that the poor have full access under law to comprehensive and effective legal services'. Mr. Wallace's past support of policies that discriminate against minorities and the poor render his appointment to the Legal Services Corporation board an affront to the constituency it serves."

Bingaman also noted: "New Mexico legal services directors indicate that the 1982 budget reductions resulted in a 45 percent decrease in staff. Prospective clients are therefore seen on a 'brief services' basis, which means limited representation or referral of their case. Further, outreach to more isolated rural communities has been greatly curtailed or even eliminated."

While the immediate prospects seem bleak for poor and powerless Navajo residents of the Chaco-Bisti region, and for citizens who stand opposed to reckless strip mining of the San Juan Basin, the longer perspective seems better.

With each passing year, it seems increasingly more likely that the Navajo will themselves determine what happens to their homelands. Remote Navajo ranchers who may not hold legal title to the lands they use (and thus are not qualified for "surface owner consent" rights under federal law) are increasingly more likely to receive just and fair treatment if the land is mined from under them. If a power plant is built in the Chaco-Bisti region, the Navajo Tribal government is likely to have a controlling interest in it. If coal strip mines do open up in the Indian areas, employment opportunities for Navajos will be much greater. Future strip miners in the region will have to operate under conditions set by the Navajo Tribe, whose lease stipulations are more likely to provide real protection for Indian sacred and sensitive areas. Navajo enforcement of mine reclamation may be less compromised than that administered by federal bureaucracies subject to ideology-blinded cabinet secretaries.

It may or may not be true that Indians are inherently better natural resource managers than other people. Certainly the depleted condition of much of the rangeland grazed by Navajo sheep and cattle in northwestern New Mexico does not speak well for their stewardship. (On the other hand, the inadequacy of the land base available to the Navajo has been recognized by the federal government for more than a hundred years.) Similarly, earlier coal strip mining on the Navajo Reservation, west of the Chaco-Bisti region, has not demonstrated a substantially better record for land use planning, cultural resource protection, or reclamation, although the tribal government has more voice in the administration of coal leases there.

In recent years, however, the Navajo Tribe has demonstrated far more sensitivity to local residents' concerns and to environmental protection than has the federal government. Granted that such a comparison is made between the Navajo administration of Peterson Zah, former director of the Navajo's legal aid service, and that of Watt-Clark-Hodel, the prospects for strict enforcement of laws and regulations are expected to improve steadily under Navajo administrations.

Several lawsuits were pending through the Navajo Department of Justice in 1986 which would turn control of Chaco-Bisti land and minerals over to the Tribe or to individual members. Suits such as the class action filed by Frank Etcitty, *et al*, which claims that ownership of the coal was unlawfully withheld from some Navajo individuals who did gain legal title to their land, would have the effect, if successful, of pulling affected lands out of public ownership and federal administration. Instead, the lands and the resources they contain—archeological ruins, sacred areas, forage, wildlife habitat, fossils, wilderness areas—would become Indian-owned, either as private property or as tribally-owned assets.

Similarly, public lands in the Chaco-Bisti area which the Tribe acquires through such congressional authorizations as the Navajo-Hopi Settlement Act would also remove these conflicted lands from federal ownership and control. The Navajo-Hopi Settlement Act allows the Tribe to select 35,000 acres of public land in northwest New Mexico onto which tribal members would be relocated from the long-contested Navajo-Hopi Joint Use Area in Arizona. The tribal government selected land in the Chaco-Bisti area, including the site sought by Public Service Company of New Mexico for its New Mexico Generating Station, the proposed company town site, and the Ah-shi-sle-pah Wilderness Study Area. The reason given for selecting Ah-shi-sle-pah was that it is among the best coal mining tracts. The Tribe has pressed to gain subsurface mineral rights as well as surface ownership through its selection.

There is every reason to believe that the Navajo Tribe will also promote coal strip mining in the Chaco-Bisti area, if the lands and resources are eventually turned over to them. The Navajo would also probably try to build an electrical generating plant in the Bisti vicinity to burn coal mined from their strip mines, since mine-mouth power plant are by far the most economic operations. In 1985, the Navajo Tribe announced its intention to proceed with the New Mexico Generating Station with PNM, Bechtel and General Electric as its partners.

So where's the difference then? If Watt and Public Service Company of New Mexico were planning to strip mine the area regardless of the environmental and lifestyle consequences, and were going to build a smoke-producing power plant in this sensitive location—but instead the Navajo Tribe does it, where's the gain?

The gain is in enforcement and who benefits. If the Navajo control the resource—instead of the utility and the coal companies—prospects are far greater for long-term commitment to restore the land's productive capacity after mining. It is, after all, the Navajo homeland, the land which they depend on to sustain them over generations. Navajos' stronger sense of responsibility to future generations will provide far superior guidance than mining executives' responsibilities to stockholders.

With Navajos controlling lease stipulations and selection of tracts to be offered for lease, local concerns over water, sacred areas, wildlife habitat, cultural resource sites and reclamation potential are more likely to receive effective protection in the face of mining activity. For civil servants in the political pressure-cooker agencies like BLM and the Office of Surface Mining, consideration of such issues is accomplished only grudgingly. Stipulations which might squeeze mining companies are put into leases only because they are required by federal law or regulation; the bureaucrats put in tougher-than-usual stipulations only at risk to their careers and paychecks.

If Navajos do proceed with mining coal in the Chaco-Bisti, and selling electricity generated from it, at least the tribal officials responsible for those decisions will be accountable to the local people affected, through elections. In the past, people like Watt, Carruthers, Clark and Hodel made the political decisions that had drastic implications for local residents' lives, yet the Navajo living over the land felt totally incapable of influencing those high officials in Washington.

And naturally the local people are more likely to share in the economic benefits of mining and marketing the coal. With the Tribe owning and administering the coal of the Chaco-Bisti area, the 12.5 percent royalty that would have gone to the U.S. Treasury would instead go to the Navajo treasury. Navajos living over the coal whose lives would be disrupted by strip mining would be expected to fare better in seeking remuneration from the Tribe than from the coal companies or the Department of the Interior. And tribal requirements for job hiring preferences for Navajos would spread revenues from the mineral extraction far better than would be the case with federal control of the leases.

Ultimately the improved protections for the people and their natural resources will result from better public participation in governmental decisionmaking. The people closest to the impacts will have a greater say in the decisions on mining and electrical production in the Chaco-Bisti region.

Through public involvement up to this point, coal companies have been prevented from gaining control of the resource. When James Watt took over at Interior in 1981, the 2.3 billion tons of coal in the Preference Right Lease Application areas were to have been handed over to corporations within months. Most of the remaining public coal in the San Juan Basin was to have been offered at competitive leases in June 1983. Those lands would have gone out of public control with minimal protective measures for the environment or for local residents' livelihood. Compliance with any mild stipulations that might have found their way into the leases would have been monitored and enforced by federal agencies under orders from above not to cause any grief for industry.

Instead, the public caused a shutdown of the federal coal program, and brought tight focus on the irregularities and illegalities that were occurring within Interior. It was as much a victory for the democratic process as any election ever was.

For many conservationists, that victory was sealed on January 22, 1986, when Sunbelt Mining Company signed an agreement with the Sierra Club, the State Land Commissioner and the N.M. Secretary for Energy and Minerals terminating the state coal lease at the Gateway Mine. The agreement called for an exchange of

Sunbelt's interest in coal at the Gateway Mine for coal under state lands elsewhere. The agreement was an out-of-court settlement of the Sierra Club's obstinate appeals on its 1981 Unsuitability Petition. Despite the highly visible strip mining effort, a relatively small portion of the 600-acre state lease had been disturbed; the most scenic parts remained intact, available for incorporation into BLM's new Bisti Wilderness Area.

New Mexico's Secretary for Energy and Minerals, Paul Biderman, evaluated the long, conflicted federal coal leasing program in the San Juan Basin, in an interview published in the August 1985 issue of *New Mexico Business Journal:* "There's been a lot put out that was just totally irresponsible, and yet, there are ways of doing it right. We've tried to work with the BLM to plan for gradual, orderly, responsible development. We think we've made considerable progress in that, although unfortunately it's been mostly by holding things off rather than getting the kinds of things we don't want to see.

"The attitude before had been, 'Well, the free market system says somebody wants this coal. It's right next to the wilderness area . . . there are Navajos there, but if that's what they want, we'll give it to 'em.'

"That's fine, but it means no effective planning and it simply puts all the burden on the courts. . . . What we're saying is we need a better planning process than that. Let's go to the coal that's the right coal, in the right areas; let's take care of these concerns over the Bisti (Wilderness Areas). Let's provide the transportation by making it accessible to transportation—why be in the heart of the basin when you can be right near existing railroads? That's the kind of planning we've been trying to do in the last couple of years. I think we're getting to it."

If the situation has improved significantly since the heydays of James Watt and Garry Carruthers, an essential element of that success was the public's access to information about the federal government's programs and procedures. The level of public input built into the 1979 federal coal program allowed the level of scrutiny and debate which eventually checked the over-zealous Secretary Watt.

But such access to information cannot be taken for granted. An unprecedented assault has been launched by the White House and department heads to curtail the ability of the public to hold high government officials accountable for their policies and actions. The Reagan Administration's campaign against the public's right to know began shortly after the president's first victory in 1980, and the measures being implemented to deny public scrutiny grew evermore subtle and diabolical. Paradoxically, Reagan's electoral successes were pegged to his dead-earnest commitment to diminish the power of the federal government, with an assumed corollary that the power of the general public would be enhanced thereby. But at no time in recent U.S. history has there been such an all-pervasive attempt to prevent the public from being able to hold the federal government accountable.

The Reagan ideologues' battering of the public's right to know has come from all sides, within practically every federal agency and within Congress. Since its inception, Reagan and his top officials have operated on the assumption that the public had no business spying on the affairs of government, and that the public should be allowed to know only that which the highest officials decided it should know. High-level paranoia over "leaks" of information reached new, surreal proportions. The problem with informing the public, as the Reaganites saw it, was that the public also included people who opposed them ideologically. The public included enemies, people (such as committed "environmentalists") who they regarded as un-American, Communist dupes, or traitors. Naturally, the people who supported the Reagan revolution didn't need to have access to information because they accepted on faith that the president and his team were working fervently for the good of America. It seemed that only those who wanted to see America fail pressed for public access to information. So strongly did the ideologues equate "America" with their own political objectives, that when members of the public questioned their motives and policies the enquirers were treated with contempt and deceit.

President Reagan himself addressed the dilemma his officials faced in dealing with the public's right to know what the government is doing. Said Reagan at an October 19, 1983 news conference: "You can't let your people know, without letting the wrong people know—those who are in opposition to what you're doing."

From the beginning of the president's first term, his ideological cadre attempted to curtail public scrutiny by eliminating the various requirements for public notice. Officials at Interior and other federal agencies time and again sought to repeal or substitute federal regulations without going through the established public process of promulgation. Under Watt, the federal government made numerous attempts to eliminate requirements for public meetings and public comment periods. In the federal coal program, Interior officials sought to undermine the effectiveness of the the Regional Coal Teams, which gave state governments an official forum for deliberating the pace, location and extent of federal coal leasing. Public information officers within the Bureau of Land Management were tormented with condemnation by the Washington-level political appointees when they persisted in informing the public about the coal program. Field level BLM officials were criticized by their superiors for being "too thorough" in their briefings for members of the public.

A contributing editor for *Harper's* magazine, Walter Karp, reported at length on the Reagan Administration's assault on the public's right to know in a November 1985 article entitled "Liberty Under Seige". After recounting year by year the administration's incursions against the concept of public information, Karp offered the following conclusion: "Imagine a venerable republic, the hope of the world, where the habits of freedom are besieged, where self-government is assailed, where the vigilant are blinded, the well informed gagged, the press hounded, the courts weakened, the government exalted, the electorate degraded, the Constitution mocked, the laws reduced to a sham so that, in the fullness of time, corporate enterprise may regain the paltry commercial freedom to endanger the well-being of the populace. Imagine a base-hearted political establishment "liberal" as well as "conservative", Democrat as well as Republican, watching with silent, protective approval this lunatic assault on popular government. Imagine a soft-spoken demagogue, faithful to nothing except his own faction, being given a free hand to turn Americans into the enemies of their own ancient liberties. Imagine this and it becomes apparent at last how a once-great republic can be despoiled in broad daylight before the unseeing eyes of its friends."

As the federal coal program proceeds in the Chaco-Bisti region and in other parts of the West, the public's access to information will be critical to responsible decisionmaking. But members of the public interested in the coal leasing process cannot expect to have information provided to them simply because it is necessary for informed participation. To the contrary, the information will be provided only grudgingly, and then only if specifically demanded.

Under conditions existing during the Reagan terms, the brightest prospects for public access to information lies in the consciences of federal civil servants, people with a sense of right and wrong who happen to be working within the executive branch of government. The federal bureaucrats are only human, after all, so some of them will react with sadness and dismay when Washington-level officials set them on a path of destruction and negligence. True, they have families to feed, college educations to finance and retirements to consider, but that doesn't mean all of them are willing to participate in the illegal and unethical schemes to defeat the public interest.

When federal civil servants took their positions they did not swear allegiance to Ronald Reagan. Instead, they took a solemn oath to serve the public interest. The federal civil service "Code of Ethics", established by Public Law 96-303, starts and ends with the following admonishments:

"Any person in Government Service should:

- *Put loyalty to the highest moral principles and to country above loyalty to persons, party or Government department.*

- *Uphold the Constitution, laws and regulations of the United States and all governments therein, and never be party to their evasion.*

- *Expose corruption wherever discovered.*

- *Uphold these principles, ever conscious that public office is a public trust."*